Africa Is Thunder and Wonder

Africa
Sleepy giant
You've been resting awhile
Now I see the thunder
and the lightning
In your smile
Now I see the storm clouds
In your waking eyes:
The thunder
The wonder
And the new surprise.
Your every step reveals
The new stride
In your thighs.

LANGSTON HUGHES

Priestess to Shango, Yoruba God of Thunder   ODITA

Africa Is Thunder and Wonder

CONTEMPORARY VOICES FROM AFRICAN LITERATURE

EDITED BY

BARBARA NOLEN

WITH AN INTRODUCTION BY
ABIOSEH NICOL
Former Ambassador to the United Nations
from Sierra Leone

ILLUSTRATED BY AFRICAN ARTISTS

CHARLES SCRIBNER'S SONS   NEW YORK

ACKNOWLEDGMENTS

Grateful acknowledgment is made to the following copyright holders for permission to reprint the poems and stories indicated below:

AFRICA by Langston Hughes   From *Selected Poems of Langston Hughes*. Alfred A. Knopf, Inc.

AFRICA'S PLEA by Roland Tombekai Dempster   From *Poems of Black Africa*, edited by Langston Hughes. Indiana University Press, Bloomington, 1969.

DRY YOUR TEARS, AFRICA by Bernard Dadié   From *West African Verse*, chosen and annotated by Donatus Ibe Nwoga. Longmans, Green & Co. Ltd., 1967; reprinted by permission of Editions Seghers, Paris.

AFRICA, MY AFRICA by David Diop   The poem *Afrique* ("Africa") appears in David Diop's *Coups de Pilon*, published by *Présence Africaine*, Paris, 1966.

PRAYER TO MASKS by Léopold Sédar Senghor   From *Selected Poems*, by Léopold Sédar Senghor, translated and introduced by John Reed and Clive Wake. Copyright © Oxford University Press, 1964; reprinted by permission of Atheneum Publishers, New York.

KENYA OUR MOTHERLAND by John Mbiti   From *Drum Beat*, chosen by Lennard Okola. East African Publishing House, Nairobi, 1967.

THE MEANING OF AFRICA by Abioseh Nicol   From *A Book of African Verse*, edited by John Reed and Clive Wake. Heinemann Educational Books Ltd., London, 1964.

MY MOTHER WAS A WITCH by D. O. Fagunwa   From *The Forest of a Thousand Daemons*, translated by Wole Soyinka. Thomas Nelson & Sons Ltd., London, 1968.

THE FETISH CHILD by Samuel Asare Konadu   From *A Woman in Her Prime*, by Samuel Asare Konadu. Heinemann Educational Books Ltd., London, 1967.

THE MAN WITH THE UGLY WIFE and THE SEVERED HEAD   From *A Selection of Hausa Stories*, compiled and translated by H. A. S. Johnston. Oxford at the Clarendon Press, London, 1966.

CHIEF SEKOTO HOLDS COURT by Bessie Head   From *When Rain Clouds Gather*, by Bessie Head. Copyright © 1968 by Simon & Schuster, Inc., New York.

HOW A DEVIL DANCED TO DEATH by A. Doris Banks Henries   From *Liberian Folklore*, by A. Doris Banks Henries. St. Martin's Press, Inc., New York, and Macmillan & Co. Ltd., London, Basingstoke, and Canada, 1966.

iv

ACKNOWLEDGMENTS

THE TELEVISION-HANDED GHOSTESS by Amos Tutuola From *My Life in the Bush of Ghosts*. Reprinted by permission of Faber and Faber Ltd., London, 1954, and Grove Press, Inc., New York; all rights reserved.

I SEE A LONELY DEAD by Prince Modupe From *I Was a Savage*, by Prince Modupe. Copyright © 1957 by Harcourt Brace Jovanovich, Inc., New York, and reprinted with their permission.

THE GOD OF WAR From *African Poetry*, edited by Ulli Beier. Cambridge University Press, London, 1966.

THE SORROW OF KODIO, translated by Miriam Koshland and recorded by Leon G. Damas. Copyright © 1959 by the Atlantic Monthly Company, Boston, Mass. Reprinted with permission.

DEATH From *African Poetry*, edited by Ulli Beier. Cambridge University Press, London, 1966; reprinted by permission of *Jeune Afrique*, Press Africaine Associée, Paris.

COMING OF AGE by John S. Kado From *When I Awoke*. East African Publishing House, Nairobi, 1966.

OUT OF DISASTER by R. Lucy Kuria From *When I Awoke*. East African Publishing House, Nairobi, 1966.

EXILE by Alhaji Sir Abubakar Tafawa Balewa From *Shaihu Umar*, by Alhaji Sir Abubakar Tafawa Balewa. Longmans, Green & Co. Ltd., London, 1967.

THE OLD MAN OF USUMBURA AND HIS MISERY by Taban Lo Liyong From *Fixions and Other Stories*, by Taban Lo Liyong. Heinemann Educational Books Ltd., London, 1969.

TEKAYO by Grace Ogot From *Land Without Thunder*, by Grace Ogot. East African Publishing House, Nairobi, 1968.

CHIEF PRIEST OF ULU by Chinua Achebe From *Arrow of God*, by Chinua Achebe. Copyright © 1964 by Chinua Achebe. Reprinted by permission of Harold Ober Associates, Inc., and the John Day Company, Inc., New York.

THE GEOGRAPHY LESSON by Mongo Beti From *Mission to Kala*, by Mongo Beti. Heinemann Educational Books Ltd., London, 1958; reprinted by permission of Rosica Colin Ltd.

MY HUSBAND'S TONGUE IS BITTER by Okot p'Bitek From *Song of Lawino*, by Okot p'Bitek. East African Publishing House, Nairobi, 1966.

THE UNTILLED FIELD by Joseph Waiguru From *Origin East Africa*, edited by David Cook. Heinemann Educational Books Ltd., London, 1965.

THE SWEETEST THING, THE MOON, and THE WELL From *Three Soussou Tales* (*Etudes Guineenes*), edited by Ezekiel Mphahlele and Ulli Beier. Longmans of Nigeria Ltd., 1947.

THE WINNER by Barbara Kimenye From *Kalasanda*, by Barbara Kimenye. Oxford University Press in Three Crowns Books, London, 1965.

THE EPIC OF LIYONGO by Muhammed Kijuma From *Swahili Poetry*, by Lyndon Harries. Oxford at the Clarendon Press, London, 1962.

IN THE STREETS OF ACCRA by Andrew Amankwa Opoku From *Voices of Ghana*. Ministry of Information and Broadcasting, Ghana, 1958.

THE CROOKS by Gabriel Okara From *Modern African Stories*, edited by Komey and Ezekiel Mphahlele. Faber and Faber Ltd., London, 1964; reprinted by permission of Gabriel Okara.

ACKNOWLEDGMENTS

A DAY OFF by Anthony M. Hokororo   From *Origin East Africa*, edited by David Cook. Heinemann Educational Books Ltd., London, 1965.

WITH STRINGS by Kuldip Sondhi   From *Ten One-Act Plays*, edited by Cosmo Pieterse. Heinemann Educational Books Ltd., London, 1968.

THE TRULY MARRIED WOMAN by Abioseh Nicol   From *The Truly Married Woman and Other Stories*, by Abioseh Nicol. Oxford University Press, London, 1965; reprinted by permission of David Higham Associates Ltd.

THE INVITATION by T. M. Aluko   From *Kinsman and Foreman*, by T. M. Aluko. Heinemann Educational Books Ltd., London, 1966.

THE SUITCASE by Ezekiel Mphahlele   From *Come Back, Africa*, edited by Herbert L. Shore and Mechelina Shore-Bos. Seven Seas Books, Berlin G.D.R., 1968; reprinted by permission of Curtis Brown Ltd.

COIN DIVER by Cyprian Ekwensi   From *Lokotown and Other Stories*, by Cyprian Ekwensi. Heinemann Educational Books Ltd., London, 1966; reprinted by permission of David Higham Associates Ltd. and Harold Ober Associates Incorporated.

THE APPRENTICES by Sembene Ousmane   From *God's Bits of Wood*, by Sembene Ousmane. Copyright © 1962 by Doubleday & Company, Inc., New York; Anchor edition 1970; reprinted by permission of the publisher.

GUEST OF CHIEF NANGA by Chinua Achebe   From *A Man of the People*, by Chinua Achebe. Copyright © 1966 by Chinua Achebe; reprinted by permission of the John Day Company, Inc., New York, 1966.

BUTCHERBOY by Alex La Guma   From *The Stone Country*, by Alex La Guma. Seven Seas Books, Berlin, G.D.R., 1967.

PARABLE OF THE EAGLE by James E. K. Aggrey   From *Aggrey of Africa*, by Edwin W. Smith. Doubleday, Doran, New York, 1929; reprinted by permission of the Phelps-Stokes Fund, New York.

THE AFRICAN ABROAD by William Conton   From *The African*, by William Conton. Copyright © 1960 by William Conton; reprinted by arrangement with The New American Library, Inc., New York.

SUNDIATA, HERO-KING OF OLD MALI by D. T. Niane   From *Sundiata: An Epic of Old Mali*, by D. T. Niane, translated by G. D. Pickett. Longmans, Green & Co. Ltd., London, 1969.

MASTER OF CEREMONIES by Camara Laye   From *The Radiance of the King*, by Camara Laye. Collins Publishers, London, 1956, reprinted by permission of Collier Books, New York. Copyright © 1971 by The Macmillan Company and reprinted with their permission.

THE MAN WHO SHARED HIS HUT by Jomo Kenyatta   From *Facing Mt. Kenya*. Martin Secker & Warburg Ltd., London; Random House, Inc., New York, 1962.

CALL TO THE PEOPLE by Peter Abrahams   From *A Wreath for Udomo*, by Peter Abrahams. Faber and Faber Ltd., London, 1956; reprinted by permission of Alfred A. Knopf, Inc.

Every effort has been made to locate all persons having any rights or interests in the material published here. If some acknowledgments have not been made, their omission is unintentional and is regretted.

Contents

CONTENTS

List of Illustrations

LIST OF ILLUSTRATIONS

Introduction

I have been called home to Africa on consultations, and thus have read this anthology in the air, on land, and on the beach. Perhaps it is fitting that I should write this introduction here in Africa, surrounded by the silent mountains, the blue sea, and the flaming hibiscus flowers.

The wonder and thunder of the African scene must be understood because of the increasingly important role that Africa is now playing in world affairs. A most useful introduction to the mind of the modern African can be found in his literature, which has been greatly stimulated by the surge of national independence sweeping over the continent. The great opportunities for self-government and self-expression have gone hand-in-hand and are amply reflected in the wide variety of imaginative and realistic writing included in this anthology.

Most African writers have a European language as their second language. There are a few exceptions, such as writers from some parts of Senegal, Gambia, Sierra Leone, Liberia, and South Africa. The majority of African writers from the former British colonial empire use English. Those in the former French and Belgian colonial territories, such as Senegal, Ivory Coast, and Congo-Kinshasa, have French as their second language. African writers from Angola, Mozambique, and Guinea-Bissau similarly use Portuguese.

Africa itself has many languages. In any one African country alone there may be many vernacular languages. Sierra Leone, for example, officially an English-speaking territory, has a population of three million, among whom there are fourteen languages, with Temne, Mende, and Limba being dominant. People from the different language communities speak or write to each other in the language of the European power of which they were once colonies. Thus the European language is not only a medium of expression to the outside world, as in this anthology, but it is also an internal unifying force for each nation. It may be argued that a second language learned at school cannot be used with sufficient conviction and skill. It should be remembered, however, that great writers of English prose like Arthur Koestler, and before him, Joseph Conrad, were not originally English-speaking. The mastery of European languages by Africans is another evidence of their adaptability to world currents of scholarship and literature.

Literature in African languages as such does exist and is found particularly with large language groups like North African Arabic, Swahili in East Africa, Hausa, Yoruba, and Twi in West Africa, and Zulu in South Africa. Some of it has been translated into English and French.

There is a great deal of imagination and style in African writing and this is displayed against the background of the experience of an individual, his community, his nation, and his race. These exotic qualities give African literature a flavor which is both attractive and educative.

Several arrangements are possible in the collection of any continent's literature. In African anthologies, classification has been often made into regions or by literary form in which the division is usually into poetry, articles, and novels. Barbara Nolen has chosen an unusual framework which hovers between the spirit world and the setting of urban modern Africa. Sometimes these two intermingle; at other times they separate; but throughout, the thunder and wonder remain evident.

Almost all the writers are established ones who have been writing for some years. The original publication may not be easily available, however, and it is very much to the credit of the anthologist that she has been able to bring them together in such a powerful form by grouping them under separate and significant umbrellas.

The first section, "Mother Africa," embraces all. It consists of poems which provide individual answers to the question of the famous black poet Countee Cullen, "What is Africa to me?"

Inevitably, in this section there is a confrontation between white and black in Africa. This confrontation originated long ago with exploration and continued with legitimate trade, and, later, the illicit slave trade, missionary endeavor, military conquest, subjugation, and finally, both colonialism and white and brown colonization. There was an implicit assumption that European civilization was

better for the black man than his own African variety. But even in
a country like Liberia, which has had over a century of contact and
some assimilation with Europe and the United States, the poet still
protested and insisted on his cultural identity. (I quote throughout
the introduction from poems reprinted in their entirety in the section "Mother Africa.")

> God made me *me*.
> He made you *you*.
> For God's sake
> Let me be *me*.
> —Dempster

　　The loss of liberty which colonialism brought to many Africans and all its griefs and humiliations are lightly passed over now
in the present era of independent Africa. But the grave acts of
racial injustice still remaining in South Africa, Rhodesia, and the
Portuguese territories are constant reminders of the past and are
like probes worrying a newly healed wound. The African has
learned to comfort himself.

> Dry your tears, Africa!
> We have drunk
> From all the springs
> of ill fortune
> and of glory . . .
> —Dadié

He has to comfort himself in order to free his mind and attention
for the greater task of nation-building.
　　For this, however, like all other nations and peoples, he needs
to draw strength from an heroic past, the existence of which has
always been denied him because others who had exploited him
wished to justify and ease their consciences by doing so. We know
from firm historical evidence that such an Africa existed.

> Africa of proud warriors in ancestral savannahs
> Africa of whom my grandmother sings
> On the banks of the distant river . . .
> —Diop

That Africa, which the poet Léopold Sédar Senghor, President of the Republic of Senegal, has seen in the silent masks distilling the "air of eternity" in which he breathed the air of his ancestors. . . .

The physical beauty of Africa shines through this anthology from the tree standing "in splendid loneliness amidst white and faded flowers" in the west of the continent to the snowcapped peaks of Mount Kenya and Mount Kilimanjaro in the east.

In a symbolic way the poets meet and join with Mother Africa, facing the future:

We are the men of the dance, whose feet draw
new strength pounding the hardened earth.
—Senghor

Sand dunes roll over eternal silence
Tomorrow's cure for strained nerves.
—Mbiti

The section on "Mother Africa" covers the scope of the anthology, outlining as it does the varied aspects of the world of spirits, the voices of the village, the people of the city, and the African personality.

More particularly, the section on "The World of Spirits" illustrates the mythology and religion of Africa, in a vivid way bringing to light the subjective emotions which are described in scientific detail in many works of social anthropology. This is a world peopled by demons and witches and images of death, made evident to human beings, and in some cases matched by man, especially when the latter is endowed with extra cunning or supernatural powers, as is the case with twins.

Yet even the supernatural must make some concessions to modernity. The suspected witch to be condemned to death is saved by a medical postmortem report; the ghostess has a magical television set in her hand. Another witch is unable to escape death from the bullets of a gun—although in death only her damaged skull changes back to human form, the remainder, even post-mortem, retaining the form of the antelope into which she usually changed for her predatory excursions. These are folktales half-believed and half in the form of the European Grimm-Andersen-Kafka tradition. They are most often told in villages in a small circle in the evening, under the starlit sky.

These villages in Africa and their busy, lively inhabitants crisscross in the third part of the anthology. Some are Moslem, some Christian, and some pagan. Some clearly are of the nineteenth century, as that written about in the excerpt from the book of the late Abubakar Tafawa Balewa, first Prime Minister of Nigeria. But, in others, the round mud hut has given way to the oblong house. Telegrams announcing the winning of football pools bring about the appearance of hordes of relations, and the reader finds himself firmly in the twentieth century even though he is still inside the African countryside.

The modern visitor to Africa, if he ventures outside the air-conditioned hotels and guided tours, will recognize immediately the characters of the "People of the City." Some of the excerpts in this section refer to the underprivileged, entangled like the poor everywhere in a web of frustration, unemployment, hunger, crime, squalor, and violence. It is important for the comfortable of the world—including both black and white in Africa—to know what happens after the paved highway and neon lights have petered out, and the dusty, rocky lanes, badly lit by flickering oil lamps and reminiscent of nineteenth-century Dickensian London, begin to lead out into the slums.

The African personality is many-sided, and this anthology shows the response of the African to the challenge of independence, to that of grappling successfully with a new world, and to that of fighting prejudices of race, sex, and color. No one can read the classic fable of Jomo Kenyatta, President of Kenya, about the occupation of Africa by foreign settlers, without being moved.

In African literature, the crackle of lightning of past memories gives a vivid flash of the African landscape before we hear the long roar of thunder; and then all is silence. But the wonder will always remain.

ABIOSEH NICOL

Africa, 1971

PART 1

MOTHER AFRICA

When water makes a great roar

there are rocks underneath it.

—KPELLE PROVERB

Africa's Plea

by ROLAND TOMBEKAI DEMPSTER

>--<

I am not you—
but you will not
give me a chance,
will not let me be *me*.

"If I were you"—
but you know
I am not you,
yet you will not
let me be *me*.

You meddle, interfere
in my affairs
as if they were yours
and you were me.

You are unfair, unwise,
foolish to think
that I can be you,
talk, act
and think like you.

God made me *me*.
He made you *you*.
For God's sake
Let me be *me*.

3

Dry Your Tears, Africa

by BERNARD DADIÉ

>--<

Dry your tears, Africa!
Your children come back to you
Out of the storm and squalls of fruitless journeys.

Through the crest of the wave and the babbling of the breeze
Over the gold of the east
and the purple of the setting sun,
the peaks of the proud mountains
and the grasslands drenched with light
They return to you
out of the storm and squalls of fruitless journeys.

Dry your tears, Africa!
We have drunk
From all the springs
     of ill fortune
     and of glory

And our senses are now opened
     to the splendour of your beauty
     to the smell of your forests
     to the charm of your waters
     to the clearness of your skies
     to the caress of your sun
And to the charm of your foliage pearled by the dew.

Dry your tears, Africa!
Your children come back to you

their hands full of playthings
and their hearts full of love.
They return to clothe you
in their dreams and their hopes.

Offering    ODITA

5

Africa, My Africa

by DAVID DIOP

>--<

Africa my Africa
Africa of proud warriors in ancestral savannahs
Africa of whom my grandmother sings
On the banks of the distant river
I have never known you
But your blood flows in my veins
Your beautiful black blood that irrigates the fields
The blood of your sweat
The sweat of your work
The work of your slavery
The slavery of your children

Africa tell me Africa
Is this you this back that is bent
This back that breaks under the weight of humiliation
This back trembling with red scars
And saying yes to the whip under the midday sun

But a grave voice answers me
Impetuous son that tree young and strong
That tree there
In splendid loneliness amidst white and faded flowers
That is Africa your Africa
That grows again patiently obstinately
And its fruit gradually acquire
The bitter taste of liberty.

Prayer to Masks

by LÉOPOLD SÉDAR SENGHOR

>--<

Masks! Masks!
Black mask red mask, you white-and-black masks
Masks of the four points from which the Spirit blows
In silence I salute you!
Nor you the least, Lion-headed Ancestor
You guard this place forbidden to all laughter of women, to all
    smiles that fade
You distil this air of eternity in which I breathe the air of my
    Fathers.
Masks of unmasked faces, stripped of the marks of illness and the
    lines of age
You who have fashioned this portrait, this my face bent over the
    altar of white paper
In your own image, hear me!
The Africa of the empires is dying, see, the agony of a pitiful
    princess
And Europe too where we joined by the navel.
Fix your unchanging eyes upon your children, who are given orders
Who give away their lives like the poor their last clothes.
Let us report present at the rebirth of the World
Like the yeast which white flour needs.
For who would teach rhythm to a dead world of machines and guns?
Who would give the cry of joy to wake the dead and the bereaved
    at dawn?
Say, who would give back the memory of life to the man whose
    hopes are smashed?
They call us men of coffee cotton oil
They call us men of death.
We are the men of the dance, whose feet draw new strength
    pounding the hardened earth.

Kenya Our Motherland

by JOHN MBITI

Beneath these mortal feet
Is motherland,
Our Kenya Motherland
Freed in tears and blood,
The hump of Africa
Soaring skyways amid the clouds,
Forever wearing the white cap
Like a covenant knot upon th' equator,
A sentry among the clouds
Forever pointing us to God,
For us soliciting rain
The blessed milk of African life.

Beneath thy heavenw'd heights
Tumble down the depths
That mark the Great Crack,
The scar of God's great axe
That split the rocks by force
Igniting fire beneath volcanic hills.

Oh Kenya Motherland,
Where flamingoes roost on sanctuary lakes,
And lions sunk in deep, deep slumber
Awake to the tune of hooting cars;
From whose eastern shores
Ever pounding waves scrub thy rocky ribs;
In whose northern desert land
Sand dunes roll over eternal silence
Tomorrow's cure for strained nerves.
Let God bless thee, our Motherland.

The Meaning of Africa

by ABIOSEH NICOL

Go up-country, so they said,
to see the real Africa.
For whomsoever you may be,
That is where you come from.
Go for bush, inside the bush,
You will find your hidden heart,
Your mute ancestral spirit.
And so I went, dancing on my way.

Now you lie before me passive
With your unanswering green challenge.
Is this all you are?
This long uneven red road, this occasional succession
of huddled heaps of four mud walls
And thatched, falling grass roofs
Sometimes ennobled by a thin layer
Of white plaster, and covered with thin
Slanting corrugated zinc.

These patient faces on weather-beaten bodies
Bowing under heavy market loads.
The peddling cyclist wavers by
On the wrong side of the road,
As if uncertain of his new emancipation.
The squawking chickens, the pregnant she-goats
Lumber awkwardly with fear across the road,
Across the windscreen view of my four-cylinder kit car.
An overladen lorry speeds madly towards me
Full of produce, passengers, with driver leaning
Out into the swirling dust to pilot his
Swinging obsessed vehicle along.

Beside him on the raised seat his first-class
Passenger, clutching and timid; but he drives on
At so, so many miles per hour, peering out with
Bloodshot eyes, unshaved face and dedicated look:
His motto painted on each side: Sunshine Transport,
We get you there quick, quick. The Lord is my Shepherd.
The red dust settles down on the green leaves.

We look across a vast continent
And blindly call it ours.
You are not a country, Africa,
You are a concept,
Fashioned in our minds, each to each,
To hide our separate fears,
To dream our separate dreams.

I know now that is what you are, Africa:
Happiness, contentment, and fulfillment,
And a small bird singing on a mango tree.

PART 2

THE WORLD OF SPIRITS

We do not really mean, we do not really mean,
that what we are going to say is true.

—ASHANTI STORYTELLER

My Mother Was A Witch

by D. O. FAGUNWA
and WOLE SOYINKA

Wole Soyinka is the translator and Chief D. O. Fagunwa is the author of this tale of the African world of spirits, in which it seems perfectly natural for a young man to say, "My mother was a witch." Both author and translator are Nigerians of the Yoruba tribe.

Wole Soyinka, born in Nigeria in 1935, is a poet, playwright, and novelist. He is best known as a playwright, however, and seven of his plays have been produced with distinction in England and Africa. No less gifted a writer could have translated the sound and action of Yoruba storytelling so sensitively into modern English.

The Forest of a Thousand Daemons, from which this selection is taken, is the first work of the late Chief Fagunwa to be translated into English. It is also his most famous novel. Four other novels in the Yoruba language have been published and distributed widely in Nigeria where they have been read and enjoyed by thousands. Their vivid language and vigorous action are typical of one aspect of Yoruba literature, and at the same time they are essentially African.

人 My name is Akara-ogun, Compound-of-Spells, one of the formidable hunters of a bygone age. My own father was a hunter, he was also a great one for medicines and spells. He had a thousand powder gourdlets, eight hundred *ato,* and his amulets numbered six hundred. Two hundred and sixty incubi lived in that house and the birds of divination were without number. It was the spirits who guarded the house when he was away, and no one dared enter that house when my father was absent—it was unthinkable. But deep as he was in the art of the supernatural, he was no match for my mother, for she was a deep-seasoned witch from the cauldrons of hell.

Once my father had nine children, of whom I was the eldest;

four wives and my mother was the most senior of them. She had four children, the wife who was next to her had three, the next two and the fourth had none at all. One day my mother and another of these wives had a quarrel and took the case to my father for settlement. He found my mother at fault and this so angered her that she resolved to take vengeance for the slight. She became so ruthless in her witching, that, before the year was out, eight of my father's children were dead and three of his wives had gone the same way. Thus was I left the only child and my mother the only wife.

Look on me, my friend, and if you are not yet married I implore you to consider the matter well before you do. True, your wife ought to be beautiful lest you tire of each other quickly; and a lack of brains is not to be recommended since you must needs hold converse with each other, but this is not the heart of the matter. The important requisite is that your wife should not be prone to evil, for it is your wife who gives you meat and gives you drink and is admitted most to your secrets. God has created them such close creatures that there hardly exists any manner in which they cannot come at a man; and when I tell you what my father suffered at the hands of this wife of his, you will be truly terrified.

It happened one day that my father prepared himself and set off to hunt. After he had hunted a long while, he felt somewhat tired and sat on a tree stump to rest. He was not long seated when, happening to look up, he saw the ground in front of him begin to split and smoke pour upwards from the rent. In a moment the smoke had filled the entire area where my father sat so thickly that he could not see a thing; all about him had turned impenetrably black. Even as he began to seek a way of escape he observed that the smoke had begun to fuse together in one spot and, before he could so much as blink, it fused completely and a stocky being emerged sword in hand and came towards my father. My father took to his heels instantly but the man called on him to stop and began to address him thus:

"Can you not see that I am not of the human race? I arrived even today from the vault of the heavens and it was on your account that I am come hither, my purpose being to kill you. Run where you will this day; kill you I most resolutely will."

When he had spoken thus, my father was truly afraid but even so he steeled his heart like a man and said, "Truly, as I observe you, I know you are not of this world, and I see also that the sword in your hand spells mortal danger for me. Nevertheless, I implore you, and I charge you in the name of the immortal God, do not fail to tell me the nature of my offence."

The man replied to him, saying, 'Do you not know that you have grievously offended your Maker? That you have ruined his handiwork even to this extent, that you sent eleven souls to heaven when it was not yet the hour allotted them by their God?"

These words of his were a great astonishment to my father, for while it was true that he well versed in magic and charms, he did no one any evil. So he replied to him, "If this is indeed your complaint then your mission is to a different man; it certainly is not I. Since the day I was born I have never harmed anyone: I do not see a man going about his business and take umbrage at his existence; I do not see a rich man and suffer thereby from envy. When I see a man at his dinner I continue on my own way. I have never inflicted wounds on any man, I have not shot a man down in my life, so how can you claim my life, and for a crime of which I am innocent!"

He waited for my father to finish his speech and then he replied, "True, you have not with your own hand killed anyone, but you have been responsible for the suffering of poor innocents. With your eyes wide open to what you did you married a deep-dyed witch for the mere beauty of her body—is that an act of goodness? Does the blood of your many wives not call out to you? Does the crime against your eight children not hang round your neck? And, despite all of this, do you have the gall to tell me that you have never been guilty of evil? Indeed there is no remedy; kill you I must."

Only then did my father call to mind the kind of woman he had taken to wife, and so he replied to him, "Truly I see now that I have sinned. I have a wife whom I cannot control, I strut like a husband merely in name. What I should have done I have left undone, the path I should have trodden I have neglected, the creature who deserved to die at my hand I have indulged with praises. Ah, stranger from the dome of heaven, forgive me."

When he heard this, the man forgave my father and desisted from killing him, but he warned him that he must, the moment he returned home, put my mother to death. So saying, he turned into the forest and continued his travels that way.

15

When he had gone my father took up his gun and returned home. And it so happened that the path he took led him past a field of okro on the way to the town. It was evening when he came there, the moon was already up, and, coming up to the field he looked over to the other side and observed someone approaching from that direction. Quickly he climbed up a tree, waiting to see what this person was about. The figure came on unswerving until it vanished into a large anthill. Shortly afterwards, an antelope emerged from this anthill, entered the field and began to feed on the okro. My father brought his gun to bear on the creature and drove furnaces into its skull. The gun had no sooner roared than there came from the antelope a human cry and the words, "Ah, woe is me!"

That night my father slept in a little hut by the field. When daylight broke he went to the spot where the antelope was shot, but he found nothing there, only blood. He began to follow the trail of blood, and it was with increasing astonishment that he found that the trail led homewards. He followed it until he arrived right home. But in midtown the trail vanished completely and he did not come upon it again until he was nearly at his own doorstep: then it led him straight into my mother's room.

I had not myself slept at home that night. Whenever my father was away I hated to spend the night at home because the spirits gave one no peace all through the night. Even my mother rarely slept at home and then only when my father gave his permission. I returned to the house just as my father was opening the door to my mother's room, and when he had opened the door and we entered, that moment when I caught sight of my mother, it was all I could do not to take flight. From her head down to her shoulders was human enough, but the rest of her was wholly antelope. She was all covered in blood and swarms of flies. My father touched her; she was dead and had begun to rot. Indeed she was the antelope stealing out at night to feast in the field of okro.

And so did my mother die, and hardly was a month over when my father also followed her. From that day was I orphaned, fatherless and motherless. And thus ends the story of my parents.

From The Forest of a Thousand Daemons, *by D. O. Fagunwa, translated by Wole Soyinka, Thomas Nelson & Sons Ltd., 1968.*

The Fetish Child

by SAMUEL ASARE KONADU

Samuel Asare Konadu is a member of the Ashanti tribe in central Ghana. Born in 1932, he was educated in local schools and served an apprenticeship in journalism and broadcasting in what was then the Gold Coast. He received a scholarship to study journalism in Europe and, on returning to Ghana, he began his writing career, basing his work on research into the traditional life of his people. Eight of his novels and a number of his short stories have been published, many of which deal with the African belief in the supernatural.

Pokuwaa, the heroine of his novel *A Woman in Her Prime*, from which the following selection is taken, is a mature, sensitive woman who has been married three times without bearing a child. In desperation and hope, she plans to sacrifice at the shrine of the great god Tano. If the god is pleased with her, she will bear a fetish child, as children in her village are called when they are born with the help of a god or goddess.

Today was Friday and the day of sacrifice for the great god Tano.

Pokuwaa returned home from her last trip to the river and went quickly into the kitchen to place the water there ready for use. Daybreak was near and her excitement was mounting. She ran through the compound to the bathroom outside her hut, bumping into the bamboo enclosure in her haste. She stripped off her clothes and scooped the water over her body. The water was a bit chilly in the morning air. She should have heated it, she thought, "but if it saves me a little bit of time . . ." Time at Brenhoma was counted by the sun and now although the sun was still behind the clouds, very soon it would break out and the shadows could lengthen. Speeding up, she slipped on the stone floor and had to step into the wooden water container to steady herself.

17

Very soon the house of Tano would begin to fill with people, and she had to hurry to get there in time for her turn at consultation and sacrifice. She could feel inside her the drums that would sound for the gathering for sacrifice in all the neighborhood. People would bring yams, sheep, goats, eggs, cowries. What a person had to sacrifice depended on her requirements. In some cases people were asked to bring cows.

Pokuwaa thought how lucky it was for her that it had to be simply a hen and eggs; though it had been difficult getting a hen that was black all over.

She dashed back to her room, rubbed her limbs with some shea cream; then she sprayed herself with smooth white clay powder. This was for purification and it was essential on this day of sacrifice. That done, she hurried out of her room with her calabash full of eggs.

Where was the black hen? Pokuwaa went to the post where the hen had been tied and at sight of the broken string, her mouth fell open. She began to tremble. Who could have given that string a twist and broken it? She rushed outside and began searching under the small bushes there.

"What evil spirit wants to spoil the day for me?" she moaned. "Help me, O Almighty. Help me."

She ran into her room to get some more grain. With this she started off to look for the hen in the village. If she could see it, she would spread the corn to lure it back to her.

For three days she had kept watch over the black hen and today, the day of the sacrifice, the hen was missing. It had been difficult to obtain such a hen in the vicinity of her own village, Brenhoma, and she had had to travel over six miles to buy one from the next village, Nsutem. The owner had insisted on taking two hundred cowries for it. Pokuwaa had tried to bargain for one hundred and sixty, and the owner, who knew the value of that black hen, had refused. These jet-black hens were always being sought after, and if this buyer didn't buy it, another was bound to come along some day. Someone else would be quite willing to pay two hundred cowries.

So Pokuwaa had paid and taken the hen to Brenhoma, put a single bead on its leg for identification and tied it up for safety. And now the hen was gone.

"But it was there this morning," she remembered. "I spread some corn for it." She looked round again.

" 'Eat well, this might be your last feed,' I said to the hen as I spread the corn. And it pecked eagerly and swallowed the lot before I could leave the house to collect another pot of water from the river. I went into the room with the water-pots, picked up the last pot and came out to find that it had already finished all the corn. I said, 'You need more. You must eat to keep alive. I need your blood.' I put down my pot, went back inside, scooped another handful of grain and spread it for the hen before I left the house."

Further than this she could not remember. Had the hen been there when she returned from the half-mile walk to the river? She couldn't remember. On her way down to the river she had been busy with her prayerful thoughts, beseeching her ancestors and the gods to bless her efforts to get a child. She had prayed to God:

"You are not an unforgiving God,
God of our forefathers.
Your assistance is not temporary.
You are almighty.
Let all evil men fall before you."

The importance of this Fofie, this festive Friday which came once every six weeks, had crowded her mind. This day, gods and goddesses moved among men to feast and grant people's requests. And they were powerful. They could answer her need for a child. The ancestors of her father and mother would surely help her. If she herself had wronged anyone or if the sins of her parents or ancestors were being avenged on her, the deities could be besought to spare her the pain of not having a child of her own. That was why she had been told to get the black hen. Jet black, that was it. Was the black hen not there when she returned from this last trip to the river?

What had happened in fact was quite simple: as soon as Pokuwaa had gone out of the house a cock had come along and joined in the feast. Then he had started making approaches to the hen. It was not easy in the game with a string round the hen's legs and so in the struggle that followed the string made of old raffia palm had snapped. The hen, now freed, had followed the cock out of the shed, and out of the yard. The hen had taken a dust bath, and then the two of them had ventured out into a narrow lane leading to the bush outside the village.

Pokuwaa rushed along at first, but, seeing no sign of the black hen, she slowed down to look more closely in nooks and corners among the crowding huts.

Soon she came upon some children playing in a lane. "Children," she pleaded, "have you seen a black hen here?" One of them started to run away. "Why," she called, "come back! I want you to help me find my black hen."

One of the children soon volunteered an explanation. "He is running away because he has been throwing stones at a black hen which passed . . ."

"What?" interrupted Pokuwaa eagerly.

". . . at a black hen which passed here a few minutes ago. That is why he is running away," he continued.

"Show me where you saw the hen," said Pokuwaa, controlling herself.

"There!" many eager mouths shouted; and many hands pointed towards the bush outside the village.

"Where? Come with me and show me." Pokuwaa now addressed herself to the little boy who was said to have been throwing stones at the hen. He looked younger than his seven years, and had bushy hair with cowries and shells tied in it.

Pokuwaa looked at this boy and felt immediate sympathy for him. She knew that such children should not be harshly treated, let alone beaten. For it was feared that if they were beaten the fetish would take them away. And so they were pampered and especially cared for.

"Take me where you threw stones at the hen," entreated Pokuwaa, reaching for the hand of the fetish child.

The other children trooped after them. Soon they reached a mango tree.

"That was where I first saw the hen. It was with a group of fowls, but it cackled the loudest, and I threw a branch. I just threw a branch," he rattled on. "And it went over there."

Pokuwaa was now getting impatient. She looked at the rising

sun in the crimson sky, and knew that if she was to get to Tano's home in time, she would have to hurry. It was with an effort that she reminded herself that she mustn't get cross with a fetish child. It was one such child that she herself was seeking—and if she was successful . . .

"Oh, God," she groaned, "who could have set that hen free? Who?"

They were almost at the bush outside the village, and there was nothing to do but to enter it and search there also. By now she was really worried.

Could this perhaps be the work of evil spirits who, knowing Tano's greatness, had spirited the hen away, to stop her from making her sacrifice? She knew, at least she had been told, of ghosts who walked the streets at night, of fiery witches who stayed on tree-tops doing all kinds of wickedness. They had power to turn things into small objects and, through incantations, spirit them away. She had been told of a child who had been turned into a chicken and slaughtered; of a man who had turned himself into a crocodile and devoured a young girl who had jilted him.

"But here I am," Pokuwaa thought aloud, "taking the words of Tano seriously. And now I can't find the black hen." It had been on a Friday six weeks ago that, in the unlit room of Tano's shrine, the oracles had told her to bring this black hen and eggs to be offered to the spirits so that they might bring her *madwowa* back to her. She had sacrificed four times before; white cloth, and cowries in tens, without any success; but this time the demand for sacrifice had come from Tano himself, and Tano was great.

"Great Tano," she cried, "assist me in my plight. You are powerful and nobody can thwart your will."

Would she find this hen in time, or was this day to be lost to her even if she did find it—if she found it too late?

"What a world. When you find the hoe you can't find the stick. When you find the stick you can't find the hoe. Oh, Adwoa Pokuwaa! I am in a tight lane." She was weeping now, seized with the fear that if she failed to make the sacrifice and lost this chance of bearing a child, her fate as a barren woman would be made certain. Then her old age would be doomed to loneliness; no child to care for her, no grandchildren to warm her compound and no issue of her

Mother and Child   WANGBOJE

blood at all to mourn at her death. She would be buried of course by the relatives and her brothers' children would be there, but there was nothing better than having your own children at your funeral.

The children with her had turned the search into a game of hide-and-seek. Some went behind bushes, throwing pebbles at each other and imitating bird and animal sounds. Others were giving chase. Only the fetish child continued to search with Pokuwaa.

They were getting into denser bush when her eyes fell on a shiny black back, through a tangle of thorny stems. Her heart leaped and she thrust her arm through the thorns without caution. Her hand was stabbed, but as she withdrew it what she noticed more than the pain was the blood that dripped on to the green leaves at her feet. She was fascinated by the red of her blood, and a thought ran through her that with this red fire in her, this fine blood, she was certainly young enough to have a child.

Why was the hen so still? Was it dead? The noise from the children should be enough to startle it if it was not dead. And yet dead hens always lay on their back or on their side, never on their belly. If this turned out to be a hen indeed, and alive, and with a single bead on its foot, then her day was saved.

She broke off a branch and began to push the thorns aside to make an opening, and before she knew it the fetish child had shot through to the other side and was making his way towards that black back in the bushes beyond. There could be no mistaking that cackling. It was a hen. But why was the fetish child pulling? They both saw at once. They saw the black snake that had been trying to swallow the hen.

Then everything happened at once. The fetish child shot back in fear; the children screamed and ran away; and Pokuwaa tore her way through the thorns towards the black hen and the black snake. She wasn't afraid of snakes. She had killed one at an early age and had lost her fear of them long since. Soon the black snake was flattened out on the ground and she was pinning it down with the sharp end of the branch in order to pull out the leg of the hen, which had been swallowed up to the thigh, while the hen flapped and cackled hysterically.

Pokuwaa was aware of a sense of triumph. If the black snake

was a bad spirit, or a man turned into a snake, it had been conquered.

The first round of her battle was over. A prayer was on her lips as she ran the whole way home:

> "Okatakyi Brempong,
>   Leader of men, linguist of all gods.
>   You know the deep and see what comes.
>   The rest of the fight is in your hand.
>   Okatakyi, my praises of you will never end."

When she arrived breathless in her compound, Kwadwo Fordwuo was standing there, waiting.

"Come," she panted, "I'll tell you about all this when we're on our way. We are lucky to be getting there at all. I'll fetch my eggs."

From A Woman in Her Prime, *by Samuel Asare Konadu, Heinemann Educational Books Ltd., 1967.*

HAUSA TALES
Translated by H. A. S. JOHNSTON

Tatsuniyoyi Na Hausa is the title of a large collection of Hausa tales, proverbs, and other traditional material. It is probably the largest repository of African folklore in any language. The original manuscripts were collected at the turn of the century by two British administrators in Africa, Frank Edgar and John Alder Burdon. These handwritten manuscripts filled three shelves, each five feet long. By this monumental labor of love and scholarship, a cultural treasure was preserved before it could be spoiled by Western influences.

H. A. S. Johnston has drawn on this source and other smaller collections, as well as some oral sources, for his own compilation and translation, *A Selection of Hausa Stories*, from which these two Hausa tales have been taken. "The Man with the Ugly Wife" has its counterparts in other folk literature, but "The Severed Head" appears only in Mr. Johnston's own collection. It is a good example of the Hausa's macabre sense of humor.

The Hausa people are the largest ethnic group in Northern Nigeria, and the second largest on the African continent. They are a trading and farming people whose language is used as the *lingua franca* in Nigeria and in many neighboring countries. The Hausa language, which combines simplicity and richness, is spoken by an estimated twenty million people. It is used not only by traders but by radio stations which reach into remote villages.

The Man with the Ugly Wife

There was once a man who was married to a very plain wife, in fact the ugliest woman in the town. They were so poor that the husband had no decent gown to wear, the wife had no wraps, and they never had more than a day's food in the house.

25

One day the husband set about building a hut apart from the rest of the house. When he had finished he said to his wife: "I'm going to go into this hut now and when I'm inside I want you to block up the entrance for me. I mean to live the life of a hermit for forty days and forty nights."

When the man had shut himself up in the hut his wife sealed up the door with clay. He then spent all his days and nights in prayer and fasting. On the very last night of his vigil, however, he went to sleep and had a dream. In his dream he learnt that he could pray for three things and that whatever he prayed for would be granted to him.

Early next morning, as his time was up, he called to his wife to open the door and let him out. So she took a mattock and hacked down the clay wall which she had built over the door and released him. "My prayers have been answered," he said. "For forty days and forty nights I prayed and fasted and on the last night of all I had a dream and in that dream it was revealed to me that I might pray for three things and that whatever I prayed for would be granted to me."

When his wife had time to think about what he had told her she went to him and said: "You know that I have no looks and am the ugliest woman in town and so I want you to pray for me to become beautiful."

At nightfall the husband began to pray that the wife might become beautiful and, lo and behold, in the morning she had changed. She was now of surpassing softness and beauty so that in all the town there was not a woman to match her.

This news was soon carried to the palace. "Indeed?" said the Chief when he heard of it. "Well bring her here then. What are you waiting for?" So the woman was seized by force and carried off to the palace.

When the husband first discovered that he had lost his wife to the Chief he was in despair. Later, however, he remembered that in all three prayers had been granted to him. He therefore prayed that his wife should be changed into a monkey.

Meanwhile in the palace the Chief was just preparing to go to his new bride when his people came running in to tell him to go and see what had happened to her. The Chief followed them to the woman's room and there instead of a bride he found a monkey sitting on the bed. He was very angry and ordered his slaves to take it away. They carried it to the husband's house and dumped it there.

When the husband found that his wife had indeed been changed into a monkey he prayed that she should be restored to her former self. His prayer was answered and she turned into the same ugly woman that she had been before.

Later the husband prayed for food and clothes and other things that he and his wife needed but his prayers were not answered because he had already used the three prayers which had been promised to him in his dream. "In this world," he said to himself "one thing is certain: any man who takes the advice of a woman will come to no good."

The Severed Head

A traveller was once making his way through the bush when he came upon a severed head standing on a tree stump beside the path. He was about to pass when the head said: "Whatever you do, learn to keep your mouth shut."

The traveller stopped in surprise and the head repeated: "That's what I said—learn to keep your mouth shut."

The traveller ran away in terror and when he reached the next town he went to the palace and asked to see the Chief.

"Why do you want to see the Chief?" asked the men at the gate.

"I have something very important to tell him," said the traveller.

After a time, therefore, the traveller was admitted to the audience chamber where the Chief was sitting on his throne surrounded by his courtiers.

"God give you long life," said the traveller, making his obeisance.

27

"Amen," said the Chief. "I hear that you have important news for me. Be sure that it is true, not false, or you will suffer for it."

"Oh, it's true enough," said the traveller and proceeded to tell the Chief of the severed head which he had seen on the road and of how it had opened its mouth and spoken to him.

"Have you any witnesses?" asked the Chief.

"God give you long life," said the traveller. "I was alone and have no witness but I left the head lying on a tree stump by the road and perhaps it will speak again."

"Very well," said the Chief, "let us test the truth of your story. If it proves to be true we will reward you but if it proves to be false you shall pay for the falsehood with your own head."

So saying the Chief ordered the executioner and some of his henchmen to go out with the traveller and find the head. "If the head speaks," he said, "bring it back here and I shall reward this man. But if it doesn't speak you are to execute him on the spot."

So the Chief's henchmen escorted the traveller back along the same road and when they reached the tree stump they found that the severed head was still there. They gathered round it and waited for it to speak but nothing happened.

"Well anyway," said the traveller, "it spoke to me before."

"That may be," said the executioner, "but you heard what our orders were."

They waited again but the head made no sound.

"For God's sake say something," cried the traveller.

Silence.

"Come on," said the executioner, "we're wasting our time."

"Just give me a bit longer," said the traveller, "and perhaps it will speak. It did before, I swear."

They waited again and again there was silence.

"That's enough now," said the executioner, "let's get it over."

So the traveller's hands were tied behind his back and he was made to kneel on the ground. The executioner then drew his sword and with one stroke cut his head off.

As the traveller's head rolled to the ground, the head on the tree stump at last spoke out.

"There you are," it said. "I told him before to keep his mouth shut."

Chief Sekoto Holds Court

by BESSIE HEAD

Bessie Head, born in South Africa in 1937, knows nothing about her parents. She was educated in a missionary orphanage in Durban and trained as an elementary school teacher. After several years as a teacher, she worked on the staff of *Drum*, an English-language magazine which became the proving ground for many African writers. When her life in South Africa became too frustrating, she emigrated to Botswana, the former Bechuanaland.

Of her adopted country she writes, "I really liked this country from the very day I came here. I have always been lonely and to me it was just like a fish finding a pond at last. A country like this forces you to find your underground spring in order to survive."

"Chief Sekoto Holds Court" is taken from Bessie Head's first novel, *When the Rain Clouds Gather,* an inspiring story of Botswana in transition from the old tribal ways and colonial domination to a new way of life.

⼈   Even those who did not like chiefs had to concede that Paramount Chief Sekoto was a very charming man. His charm lay not so much in his outer appearance as in his very cheerful outlook on life. In fact, so fond was he of the sunny side of life that he was inclined to regard any gloomy, pessimistic person as insane and make every effort to avoid his company. It was his belief that a witty answer turneth away wrath and that the oil of reason should always be poured on troubled waters.

Every weekday morning, Chief Sekoto listened to cases brought before his court, while the afternoons were spent at leisure unless there were people who had made appointments to interview him. This particular Monday morning a lively and rowdy case was in session when, out of the corner of his eye, Chief Sekoto saw his

29

brother Matenge drive up and park his car opposite the open clearing where court was held. Nothing upset Chief Sekoto more than
a visit from his brother, whom he had long classified as belonging
to the insane part of mankind. He determined to dally over the
proceedings for as long as possible in the hope that his brother
would become bored and leave. Therefore he turned his full attention on the case at hand.

The case had been brought in from one of the outlying villages, called Bodibeng, and the cause of its rowdiness was that the
whole village of Bodibeng had turned up to witness the trial. A
certain old woman of the village, named Mma-Baloi, was charged
with allegedly practicing witchcraft, and so certain were the villagers of her guilt that they frequently forgot themselves and burst
out into loud chatter and had to be brought to order by the president of the court with threats of fines.

Evidence was that Mma-Baloi had always lived a secret and
mysterious life apart from the other villagers. She was also in the
habit of receiving strangers from far-off places into her home who
would not state what dealings they had with Mma-Baloi. Now,
over a certain period, a number of the children of the village had
died sudden deaths, and each time a mother stood up to describe
these sudden deaths, the crowd roared in fury because the deaths
of the children and the evil practices of Mma-Baloi were one and
the same thing in their minds. The accused, Mma-Baloi, sat a little
apart from the villagers in a quaking, ashen, crumpled heap; and
each time the villagers roared, she seemed about to sink into the
earth. Noting this, Chief Sekoto's kindly heart was struck with pity.

Further evidence was that about a week ago a strange young
woman had turned up in the village of Bodibeng and made straight
for the hut of Mma-Baloi, where she had died a sudden death. This
had made Mma-Baloi run screaming from her hut, and it was only
the intervention of the police that had saved Mma-Baloi from being
torn to pieces by the villagers.

Chief Sekoto was silent for some time. The insanity of mankind never ceased to amaze him. At last he turned to the accused
and said gently, "Well, mother, what do you have to say in defense of yourself?"

"Sir, I am no witch," said the quavering old voice. "Even

30

though I am called the mother of the witches, I am no witch. Long ago I was taught by the people who live in the bush how to cure ailments with herbs and that is my business."

She pointed a shaking finger at a bag placed near her.

"I would like to see the contents of the bag," Chief Sekoto said with a great show of interest. The bag was brought to him and its contents tipped out on the ground. They were a various assortment of dried leaves, roots, and berries. He examined them leisurely, picking up a few items for closer inspection. This very deliberate gesture was meant to puncture a hole in the confidence of the crowd, who annoyed him. While he fiddled about he was aware of how silent and intent they had become, following his every movement with their eyes. Thus holding the stage, he turned to the old woman and said:

"Proceed with your defense, mother."

"About the deaths of the children of which I am accused, I know nothing, sir," she said. "About the young woman who died in my home last Saturday, I am also innocent. This young woman came to me on recommendation, being grievously ill. We were discussing the ailment when she fell dead at my feet. Never has such a thing occurred before, and this caused me to lose my mind and run out of the house."

"That is quite understandable, mother," Chief Sekoto said sympathetically. "Even I should have been grieved if some stranger was struck with death in my home."

He swept the crowd with a stern glance. "Who issues the certificates of death in Bodibeng?" he asked.

There was a short, bewildered silence. Then a car and a messenger had to be found to fetch the doctor of the Bodibeng hospital. There was a delay of two hours as the doctor was engaged in an operation. Throughout this long wait the court remained in session. At one stage Chief Sekoto received an impatient note: "Dear Brother," it said. "Please spare a few moments to discuss an urgent matter."

Chief Sekoto replied: "Is it life or death? I am at the moment faced with the life or death of an old woman. I cannot move."

It was near noon when the doctor arrived. His evidence was brief and to the point. Yes, it was true, he said. There had been a surprising number of child deaths in the village of Bodibeng, and death in each case had been due to pneumonia; and yes, he said, he had performed a postmortem on the body of a young woman last Saturday afternoon. The young woman had died of a septic womb due to having procured an abortion with a hooked and unsterilized instrument. He would say that the septic condition of the womb had been of three months' duration.

All that was left now was for Chief Sekoto to pass judgment on the case. This he did sternly, drawing himself up to his full height.

"People of Bodibeng," he said. "It seems to me you are all suffering from derangement of the brain."

He paused long enough to allow the villagers to look at each other uneasily.

"Your children die of pneumonia," he thundered, "and to shield yourselves from blame you accuse a poor old woman of having bewitched them into death. Not only that. You falsely accuse her of a most serious crime which carries the death sentence. How long have you planned the death of a poor old woman, deranged people of Bodibeng? How long have you caused her to live in utter misery, suspicion, and fear? I say: Can dogs bark forever? Oh no, people of Bodibeng, today you will make payment for the legs of the old mother who has fled before your barking. I say: The fault is all with you, and because of this I fine each household of Bodibeng one beast. From the money that arises out of the sale of these beasts, each household is to purchase warm clothing for the children so that they may no longer die of pneumonia."

He turned and looked at the old woman, changing his expression to one of kindness.

"As for you, mother," he said. "I cannot allow you to go and live once more among the people of Bodibeng. It is only hatred that the people of Bodibeng feel for you, and this has driven them out of their minds. As hatred never dies, who knows what evil they will not plot against you. I have a large house, and you are welcome to the protection it offers. Besides, I suffer from an ailment for which I am always given penicillin injections at the hospital. Now I am tired of the penicillin injections and perhaps your good herbs may serve to cure me of my troubles."

He stood up, signifying the end of the case. The people of Bodibeng fled in confusion from the courtyard, but the old woman sat for a long time on the ground, silent tears of gratitude dripping down into her lap.

From When Rain Clouds Gather, *by Bessie Head, Simon & Schuster, Inc., 1968.*

Upper Volta Tribesmen Wearing Demon-masks GUIRMA

How a Devil Danced to Death

by A. DORIS BANKS HENRIES

A. Doris Banks Henries was assisted by students at the University of Liberia and by tribal storytellers from the back country in writing down the ninety-nine stories which make up her collection of Liberian folklore.

Tribal literature in Liberia, as in other African countries, was passed by word of mouth until the twentieth century, and even now very little has been written down. For one thing, there are the different tribal languages: the Vai in the northwest, the Kru along the coast, the Golas in the west-central, and the Kpelle in the center and northwest. In addition, there are tales told by the Muslim traders and the Fanti fishermen from Ghana who travel back and forth.

So it is not surprising that the tales of many West African countries are similar. There are varying themes among the tales. Some are morality tales of trickery and foolishness. Many are animal stories, in which the animal characters vary, depending on the region. Where goats are common, the goat becomes a favorite character. Where insects are present in great numbers, the spider or the fly or the cockroach assumes human characteristics. And in most of the tales inhabitants of the spirit world—witches, ghosts, devils, and demons—play important roles.

人 A devil wandered through the forest until he came to a place where two big roads crossed. There he built himself a little house. This was a bad thing for the people who used these roads, for devils are wicked and devour human beings.

When anyone came to the cross-roads, the devil would jump out of his house on the corner, holding a drum under his arm. He would beat the drum and command the wayfarer to dance.

"Dance, O Man! Dance and I will play the drum for you. He who tires first must die!"

The unfortunate traveller, whether he was a man, woman or

child, would be obliged to dance a Dance of Death, for invariably the dancer tired first and was killed and eaten by the devil.

Men know that twins often have unusual powers. They make fine magicians and medicine men. They are wise in telling fortunes and know the use of herbs and poison. A pair of twins decided they would outwit and kill the devil who had killed many people from their town. They left their town one morning to see what they could do. One of them crept ahead very softly and hid behind an anthill close to the devil's house. Then his brother boldly approached singing a pleasant song.

The devil heard him coming and jumped from his house. "Ho!" he cried in great delight. He had not seen a man for days. "Ho, young man! Come and dance for me!" The devil began beating excitedly on his drum.

"Thank you, sir," said the lad. "It is a fine morning for a dance. Play on!"

The devil threw back his head and laughed at such insolence. "Do you know, youth, that the one of us who tires first must die?"

"Fine," said the twin. "That means the other one will live." He danced and danced to the devil's drumming or playing. When he was tired, he skipped behind the anthill and his brother skipped out in his place. In this fashion the twins danced for three whole days; whenever one was dancing, the other one was resting. The devil was astonished to see, as he thought, one person dance on and on, day and night and he himself grew tired. The twins continued to change places. The devil dropped, wilted and at last he fell exhausted on the ground.

The twins killed the devil by cutting his body into two parts. They impaled one half on a stake and carried it into town. There it stayed as a warning to all devils that twins lived in that place and would tolerate no wicked devil tricks.

The Television-handed Ghostess

by AMOS TUTUOLA

Amos Tutuola was born in 1920, a member of the Yoruba tribe in Nigeria. He was educated at a Christian missionary school and then became a coppersmith. He began to write in English, in an unspoiled, vigorous style, full of fantasy and imagination. He chose as his theme the African belief in ghosts and witchcraft, and has woven into his books much traditional mythology and supernatural imagery.

His first book, *The Palm-Wine Drinkard* (1952), established him as a master of storytelling in the oral tradition. Dylan Thomas called it "grisly and bewitching." There is both horror and comedy in his story of the drinker of palm wine who set out to explore the world of the dead. The same is true of his two later books, *My Life in the Bush of Ghosts* and *Simbi and the Satyr of the Dark Jungle*. Tutuola's use of English is often primitive and jarring, but his message comes through, loud and clear.

The following episode is taken from his second and probably most famous book, *My Life in the Bush of Ghosts*. The young hero, a boy of seven, flees from home to escape a slave raid and plunges into worse dangers in the ghost-ridden African bush. Tutuola's ghosts, like Fagunwa's, are not the ethereal ghosts of the western world, but evil demons— hideous, dirty, and smelly, and totally fearsome. The boy in the story is dragged fearfully through one ghost town after another for twenty-four years, until he meets the television-handed ghostess.

⅄   When it was about two o'clock P.M. I saw a ghostess who was crying bitterly and coming to me direct in a hut where I laid down enjoying myself. When she entered I noticed that she held a short mat which was woven with dried weeds. She was not more than three feet high. Immediately she entered she went direct to the fire, she spread the mat closely to the fire and then sat down on it without saluting or talking to me. So at this stage I noticed carefully that she was almost covered with sores, even there was no single hair on her head, except sores with uncountable maggots

36

which were dashing here and there on her body. Both her arms were not more than one and an half foot, it had uncountable short fingers. She was crying bitterly and repeatedly as if somebody was stabbing her with knives.

Of course, I did not talk to her, but I was looking at her with much astonishment until I saw the water of her eyes that it was near to quench the fire, then I got up with anger and told her to walk out of my hut, because if the water quenches the fire I should not be able to get another again, as there were not maches in the Bush of Ghosts. But instead of walking out as I said she started to cry louder than ever. When I could not bear her cry I asked her—"by the way what are you crying for?" She replied—"I am crying because of you." Then I asked again—"because of me?" She said—"yes" and I said—"What for?" Then she started to relate her story thus—

"I was born over two hundred years ago with sores on my head and all over my body. Since the day that I was born I have no other work more than to find out the doctor who could heal it for me and several of them had tried all their best but failed. Instead of healing or curing it would be spreading wider and then giving me more pains. I have been to many sorcerers to know whether the sore would be healed, but every one of them was telling me that there is an earthly person who had been lost in this Bush of Ghosts, so that if I can be wandering about I might see you one day, and the sorcerers said that if you will be licking the sore every day with your tongue for ten years it would be healed.

So that I am very lucky and very glad that I meet you here today and I shall also be exceedingly glad if you will be licking the sore with your tongue every day until the ten years that it will be healed as the sorcerers had told me. And I am also crying bitterly in respect of you because I believe that no doubt you have been struggling for many years in this Bush of Ghosts for the right way to your home town, but you are seeing the way every day and you do not know it, because every earthly person gets eyes but cannot see. Even it is on the right way to your home town that you found this hut and sleep or sit in it every day and night. Although I believe that you will not refuse to lick the sore until it is healed."

Having related her story and said that if I am licking the sore it would be healed as the sorcerers said, so I replied—"I want you

to go back to your sorcerers and tell them I refuse to lick the sore."
After I told her like this she said again—"It is not a matter of going
back to the sorcerers, but if you can do it look at my palm or hand."
But when she told me to look at her palm and opened it nearly to
touch my face, it was exactly as a television, I saw my town, mother,
brother and all my playmates, then she was asking me frequently
—"do you agree to be licking the sore with your tongue, tell me,
now, yes or no?"

Because when I thought over how the sore was dirty and
smelling badly, especially those maggots which were dashing here
and there all over the sore, so it was hard for me to say "yes." But
as I was seeing my town with all my people, it was also hard for
me to say "No." But as I was hearing on this television when my
mother was discussing about me with one of her friends with a
sorrowful voice at that time that—"She was told by a fortune teller
that I am still alive in a bush." So as I was enjoying these discussions the television-handed ghostess took away the hand from my
face and I saw nothing again except the hand.

After that she asked again whether I would do her request,
of course, I was unable to answer at that moment, but only thinking about my people whom I saw on the television and also thinking
how to reach the town as quickly as possible. But as it was just a
dream for me, I told her again to let me look at them once more
before I would answer her request. Immediately she showed it to
me my people appeared again at the same time and as I was looking at them and also hearing what they were talking about me
which I ought to answer if I was with them, luckily, a woman
brought her baby who had a sore on its foot to my mother at that
time to tell her the kind of leaf which could heal the sore. But as
my mother knows many kinds of leaves which can heal any sore,
so she told this woman to follow her. Having reached a small bush
which is near the town, then she cut many leaves on a kind of plant
and gave them to this woman, after that she told her that she must
warm the leaves in hot water before using it for the sore. But as I
was looking at them on the television I knew the kind of leaf and
also heard the direction how to use it.

After a while this "Television-handed ghostess" took her hand away from my face and I saw nothing again. Then she asked again whether I would do her request, so I said—"Yes, but not with my tongue would I heal the sore." After I said "yes" I got out of the hut and I went round near the hut. God is so good, this kind of leaf or plant were full up there. Then I cut some and came back to the hut, after that I was using it for the sore according to the direction that my mother told the woman who brought her baby to her. It was so I was using these leaves for the sore every day and to my surprise, this sore had been healed within a week. But when this "Television-handed ghostess" saw that she had no more sores again she was exceedingly glad.

Having eaten and drunk to my satisfaction I told her to tell me the right way to my home town as she had promised me before I healed her sore. She agreed, but warned me seriously that I must not attempt to enter into the Bush of Ghosts forever, because ninety percent of ghosts hate any of the earthly persons to enter this bush, as I myself am aware of it since I have been struggling to find the right way back to my town, but none of the merciless ghosts would show me the way. After the above warning she said further—"Do not tell anybody that I am the 'Television-handed ghostess' who shows you the right way whenever you reach your town." Then she opened her palm as usual, she told me to look at it, but to my surprise, I simply found myself under the fruit tree which is near my home town (the Future-Sign). It was under this fruit tree my brother left me on the road when he was running away from the enemies' guns which were driving me farther and farther until I entered into the Bush of Ghosts, and it was the fruit of this tree I ate first immediately I entered the Bush of Ghosts. This is how I ot out of the Bush of Ghosts, which I entered when I was seven years old.

From My Life in the Bush of Ghosts, *by Amos Tutuola, Faber and Faber Ltd., London, 1954, and Grove Press, Inc., 1970.*

Mystical Awakening   RAKGOATHE

I See a Lonely Dead

by PRINCE MODUPE

Prince Modupe was born on the Guinea Coast, a member of the Susu (or So-So) tribe. At an early age, young Modupe left his native village in search of education and studied at a missionary school in Freetown. By the time he grew up, he had become interested in seeing the world outside of Africa. In 1922 he traveled to the United States and studied at Hampton Institute in Virginia. Later he married an American and settled in California. He became a filmwriter, actor, and lecturer on African subjects.

When his American-born children were small, he told them stories of his childhood. He showed them scars on his body which were the marks of initiation into the Leopard Society. When they begged for these stories over and over, he wrote some of them down in a book called *I Was a Savage*, recently reissued under the title *A Royal Prince*. More than fifty years have passed, some names have been changed, and perhaps not all of the incidents are strictly autobiographical. But this story of "a lonely dead" could very well be true.

When my father returned from his long overland trading trips, his clothing was always stained with the dust of the journey. There was in the cloth the smells of the cargo he carried—hides, ground nuts (peanuts), cola. I knew these things came from places which were only names to me—Bomako, Kauroussa, Kankan. They seemed as remote as the moon, and this made the odors seem exotic. The smell of leather was the smell of travel. I inhaled it as I walked one morning beside him, his country-cloth robe fluttering in the breeze, flapping against my face. He was taking me to call on my grandfather.

We were in the prayer room when a messenger arrived from the Bambara tribe. I retreated with my father to a far corner of the room while my grandfather granted audience. Before my eyes, I saw the familiar, kindly old grandfather become the stern, majestic chief attending to important affairs.

Africans are a ceremonious people. There were long polite inquiries. The health of everybody? I could see that the messenger was fairly bristling with excitement under the calm surface of politeness. I hoped Grandfather would forget my presence in the room. I wanted to know what this was about!

They finally got around to the point and exciting enough it was! A *lappa* had been stolen from the house of a Bambara woman. A So-So warrior had been seen running from the village with something in his hand which resembled a *lappa*.

Theft was almost unknown among our people. It was punishable by death. If the Bambara were mistaken, if the accusation were false, tribal war would follow. If they were correct, if one of our people had stolen, the guilty So-So would have to be discovered and punished.

Grandfather's voice was terrible to hear. It was sort of a growl with a crack in it. Was the name of the So-So youth known to the Bambaras?

The witch doctor had called the name, a youth known as Santigi.

I felt my father stiffen. I no longer wanted to be in that room but I dared not move. Santigi!

Santigi was betrothed to my sister N'gadi. The marriage had been arranged except for one detail—Santigi had not accumulated all of the necessary dowry. The part he lacked was a bright new *lappa*, the wrap-around skirt which tribal women wear.

Tribesmen do not "buy" their brides. The dowry is a sort of marriage insurance. It means that the man appreciates the value of the girl and he wants to make a token of this appreciation to the girl's parents. It is the tangible way to show his respect for the girl and her family.

Santigi was not rich, even by bush standards, but he was strong and hard-working, and fearless, a well-liked fellow. My sister N'gadi loved him and he was acceptable to our family. N'gadi was studying to be a medicine woman and already had her own house away from ours.

Grandfather dispatched a messenger to fetch Santigi to the

prayer room where we waited. The silence in the room seemed jungle heavy. Neither my grandfather nor the Bambara spoke.

When Santigi came in, after what seemed a long time, he stood straight and proud. He seemed to fill the doorway as he came through it. The questioning began. Had Santigi been to the Bambara town?

Santigi nodded, easily enough. He had gone to the Bambara market.

Why had he gone to a Bambara market? Was not every needful thing to be had in our own market?

He had gone to look for a fine bright new *lappa*! He got over the word *lappa* without a pause.

He brought a *lappa* back with him? He shook his whole body with his head. No *lappa*!

There was nothing for it now but trial by ordeal. That was the tribal way of establishing innocence. One's innocence was one's protection. If after drinking the judgment poison, a brew called *wobia,* Santigi was able to keep his feet under him, war would follow. The Bambara's witch doctor's word would have been challenged. The Bambara were a powerful tribe.

There was a great commotion among our people when the word got around. Some of the more excitable thought the warriors might as well get their weapons ready. It seemed unlikely that Santigi would steal, even more unlikely that he would be able to steal and then lie about it without a quiver of guilt showing in his face.

Excitement kept sleep away from me that night. I thought about N'gadi, the way she would feel if Santigi did not survive the judgment poison. N'gadi was thin as early-morning shadow and not robust in any part except her spirit which was staunch. She was probably sobbing alone in her medicine hut, forgotten in the turmoil by everyone except myself.

I thought about war, how exciting that would be, how disgusting that I was less than warrior age. How unspeakable to be left at home with women and children, probably hiding out in the forest in case our town should be taken.

I thought about Santigi. Would he be alive or dead after another sundown? If the poison caught him, and he were buried face down as criminals are, N'gadi would have to watch this disgrace. I wondered how it would feel to be dead, a dead criminal, unable to join the spirits of the reverenced dead, how lonely. How would a lonely dead feel when the feast was made to the spirits of deceased elders and he could not join the festival. I knew that a man who lives the laws of his tribe is never alone, living or dead. Surely Santigi had not risked becoming a lonely dead, not even for love of N'gadi!

Death was interesting to think about. I tried to imagine that the dark hut was a grave, that the *canda* mat beneath me was a burial mat. People would sing praise-songs over me, recounting deeds of great valor . . . N'gadi in mournful sing-song telling how I had saved her from a terror of a Bambara warrior . . .

N'gadi! Everything I thought about led my mind to my sister. I had given myself the shivers thinking about death. I wanted to feel the comfort of my sister's arms around me. I would run to N'gadi. Night is the roaming time of spirits and it would be terrifying to go out alone at night. I was so frightened by the thoughts I had been thinking that I had to leave them behind in this hut, so I would make a dash for it. In no time at all I would be with N'gadi and we could sob together.

No one stirred as I slipped out the door. Moonlight flooded the village but I stayed clear of it by moving between huts until my sister's house and the medicine man's behind it were the only ones to be seen in front of me.

I was gathering up my courage for the final spurt of distance when I saw a figure moving stealthily as a leopard toward the medicine man's hut. The figure was a woman and she carried a gourd carefully so as not to spill the contents. The figure was slim like N'gadi. In fact, it almost certainly was N'gadi! Was it her spirit walking? The figure disappeared behind the medicine hut for only as long as it takes an elephant to trumpet. When she reappeared there was still a gourd in her hands.

I slipped back to my *canda* as quickly as I could get there. I had seen something which no one should have looked upon because it should not have happened. I did not understand it but I knew it was evil. Curled up into a small ball of frightened humanity, I finally fell asleep.

The drums began talking early the next morning. As soon as

44

Moon-bride I RAKGOATHE

the Bambara arrived, the people gathered for the trial. Santigi was at the center of a great circle, surrounded by elders and warriors and the witch doctor. My sister was there but I was afraid to meet her eyes. She had strange powers which I feared.

The witch doctor poured the *wobia* from a gourd into a larger pot over the fire. He talked to the steaming juice. The drums beat loud and fast, then ceased. All sound and motion ceased with the drums. In the silence, the witch doctor reached out a calabash full of the hot liquid to Santigi. I could not tell whether Santigi's hand shook or whether it only seemed to because of the heat waves above the poison pot. He planted his legs far apart as though to brace himself upright. He watched N'gadi as he drained the calabash. N'gadi looked at the ground. Everyone else seemed intent on Santigi. He seemed to sway once but quickly recovered himself. It was finally apparent to everyone that the poison was not going to topple him.

My grandfather stood up. The Bambara stood up. My grandfather spoke in a harsh voice. The warrior had proven his innocence. If war had to come, we were ready.

Santigi's friends swarmed around him, whooping their joy— all but N'gadi. She walked home with the rest of my family and was strangely quiet.

It was after the midday resting time when some exciting news went around the town. Matara, my mother, had dozed and dreamed that *uba*, the vulture, had perched in her house. There is no omen more terrible than this. Calamity of the worst sort is sure to follow. What had it to do with the strange thing I had seen in the moonlight? I must speak.

I found my father alone. His face became grim when I told him what I had to say. His first thought was to ask N'gadi whether she had substituted some innocent brew for the powerful *wobia*. Talking to himself rather than to me, he changed his mind. He would ask Santigi. He would tell Santigi of the ruin that was sure to fall on all of the people, even on N'gadi, if he had done an evil he would not confess.

We heard the message drums that evening: Santigi guilty . . . Santigi to die . . . Santigi guilty . . . Santigi to die . . . We have lappa . . . Santigi to die.

46

People gathered quickly in the central compound, Santigi in the center of the throng, his head bowed. The witch doctor held up a bright new *lappa* so that all could see it before Grandfather dispatched a runner to carry it to the Bambara town.

The witch doctor explained that the power of the *wobia* had been crossed. Santigi had confessed to this as well as to the stealing and lying—all terrible crimes. N'gadi's lips were parted. I was afraid she was going to declare herself. I saw that Santigi was looking at N'gadi too. Ever so slightly, he shook his head at her. There was great pride in both of them as they stared at one another across the space which separated them.

Santigi was to die three sundowns hence. From the time Grandfather announced the execution until it was carried out, the *taboole*, the sacred drums of sorrow, never ceased throbbing. They spoke slowly at first, gathering pace gradually as the death hour approached. Their voice seemed like great sobs, yet they were more sorrowful than anything that could come from a human throat. The vibrations shuddered the earth beneath our feet and I thought that the earth itself joined in the crushing lament.

By the third day no one found it possible to do any work. The call to sorrow and shame was too urgent. The adults went about with set, sad faces. For the first time in my childhood the days seemed long, endless. The death chant was taken up all through the town. A great many friends and relatives of Santigi's overflowed his home. As many as could find seating room on the floor wailed there and threw ashes over their heads. I looked for N'gadi but she was nowhere about. My mother stayed in her house grieving over the sin of the youth who was to die because he loved her daughter above the laws of the tribe.

As the execution time neared, all women and children were shooed toward their homes. The women would continue their lament behind closed doors. What was to be done was not a thing for children to see.

I hid behind the trunk of a tree. In my overexcited imagination I had already witnessed the execution a hundred times over. I felt strangely a part of what was going on. If I had not told my father what I had seen in the moonlight, the warriors might at that moment have been going to war instead of to the sacrifice rock. I was horribly fascinated by this affair I had stumbled into and I wanted to stay with it to the end.

It was easy during the confusion to maneuver my way from tree to tree until I neared the great rock. The sacrifice altar was screened by trees. I scrambled up one of them and fastened myself tight against a horizontal limb.

The fire in the center of the clearing was burning brightly when I attained my lookout perch, but the death procession had not reached the place.

Boom . . . Boom, boom, boom . . . My tree trembled with the thuds. War drums joined in with the drums of sorrow.

Warriors of his own age group escorted Santigi to a spot in front of the sacred rock. They were dressed in full regalia, hide shields, spears, plumed headgear. The dancing firelight glinted on the edges of the spears. The warriors formed a circle, leaving an opening for the entry of the older men, the tribal elders, the witch doctor, the executioner. These two came in last, wearing masks. The executioner carried a long, broad knife, curved on the end. It is called a sacrifice knife because this really was a sacrifice that was about to be made—the sacrifice of a life to the sacred principles of tribal law. The masks embodied the spirit of that law as it had come down to us from the ancient ones who had died, yet who live forever through the laws and the customs.

Santigi's expression was resigned as the warriors bound him. He must have thought that the best he could do was to die like a true tribesman, he who had not been able to live as one. Perhaps by this last bit of brave living he would be allowed to sit on the far edge of the conclave of tribal dead.

The warriors danced, spears in hand. At the edge of the circle was a large calabash filled with palm wine to which herbs of strange powers had been added. This was taken in great gulps by the dancers as the tempo of the drumming and dancing increased. The longer they danced, the higher they leaped, the faster they whirled. The light and heavy drums, combined with the thud of feet and the chorus of chant, shook the tree where I perched. I dug my hands into the bark of the branch. If I fell like a ripe fruit, the executioner might have double duty that night!

Sweat gleamed on the bodies of the frenzied dancers, their

eyes rolled, some of them were overcome with paroxysmal spasms and fell at the edge of the circle with foam on their lips.

The executioner did not dance. He stood with folded arms looking down at Santigi. When the big drum stopped, every sound and movement stopped with it. The executioner grasped the end of the knife with both hands, raised it high and swung. After that single sweeping motion, Santigi's head rolled sideways. A gush of blood rose out of his neck. The sacred rock was red.

The drums came to life again. The booming was no longer frenzied, but sad, so sad. I wanted to sob. Santigi who had always seemed to me to be so much of one piece, his whole body springing forward to run, to leap, to wrestle, to dance, Santigi was severed. Boy that I was, I understood that even as his head was separated from his body, his soul was separated from the body of his tribe. That, not his death, was the real horror of what I had seen.

From I Was a Savage, *by Prince Modupe, Harcourt Brace Jovano-vich, Inc., 1957.*

IMAGES OF DEATH

In tribal Africa, death is neither the end of life nor the gateway to immortality. It is rather a stepping stone between generations, a link with one's ancestors and one's descendants.

Ulli Beier, founder and editor of the magazine *Black Orpheus*, in commenting on the theme of the ancestors in African poetry, writes: "The living and the dead are in continuous contact and a large part of the religious life of the African is devoted to establishing a harmonious contact with the dead."

In the three poems which follow, anonymous poets from the Yoruba, the Baulé, and the Kuba tribes record their feelings and attitudes toward death.

The God of War

He kills on the right and destroys on the left.
He kills on the left and destroys on the right.
He kills suddenly in the house and suddenly in the field.
He kills the child with the iron with which it plays.
He kills in silence.
He kills the thief and the owner of the stolen goods.
He kills the owner of the slave—and the slave runs away.
He kills the owner of the house—and paints the hearth with his blood.
He is the needle that pricks at both ends.
He has water but he washes with blood.

YORUBA TRIBE

The Sorrow of Kodio

We were three women
Three men
 And myself, Kodio Ango.
We were on our way to work in the city
And I lost my wife Nanama on the way.
I alone have lost my wife
To me alone such misery has happened,
To me alone, Kodio, the most handsome of the three men,
Such misery has happened.
In vain I call for my wife,
She died on the way like a chicken running.
How shall I tell her mother?
How shall I tell it to her, I Kodio,
When it is so hard to hold back my own pain.

BAULÉ TRIBE

Death

There is no needle without piercing point.
There is no razor without trenchant blade.
Death comes to us in many forms.

With our feet we walk the goat's earth.
With our hands we touch God's sky.
Some future day in the heat of noon,
I shall be carried shoulder high
through the village of the dead.
When I die, don't bury me under forest trees,
I fear their thorns.
When I die, don't bury me under forest trees.
I fear the dripping water.
Bury me under the great shade trees in the market,
I want to hear the drums beating
I want to feel the dancers' feet.

KUBA TRIBE

PART 3

VILLAGE VOICES

If relatives help each other,
what evil can hurt them?

—ETHIOPIAN PROVERB

SONS OF AFRICA

John S. Kado and R. Lucy Kuria are two of the twenty secondary school students whose writings were selected for publication in a competition held in Kenya in 1966. Each student was asked to write about an experience that began with the words, "When I awoke . . ." The Honorable James S. Gichuru, in his foreword to the book, says, "These young writers exhibit an astonishing facility and command of the English language which my older generation cannot but envy."

Coming of Age

by JOHN S. KADO

⅄ When I awoke, there was an unusual silence in the air and I found myself listening for something—the sound of a warning horn. As it sounded I slipped on a skin cloak and rushed from my hut. This was an important day. A day when a group of brave youths was going to be tested and enlisted in my tribe's defence force as men. On such occasions quietness was, without reason, maintained and the early morning cry of birds rare.

"If I succeed, I will be able to act and think in love, fame and glory as men of my tribe do," I told myself as I hurried to offer sacrifice to my dead ancestors.

"Quee! Quee! Quee!!" cried the hen as I cruelly butchered it with a blunt ancestral knife. But I cared not for the cry. I was only after success. The cruel deed done, I gave the sun my back and threw the dying hen towards it—to the sun-rays. For that is where my dead ancestors lived.

55

Shortly I was on my way to the "Oak of the ancestors" where the test was to be.

"Be grateful to those who brought you up by hand, my son. Remember, it will be a mere beating of your back till blood appears," were my father's only words of encouragement.

When I arrived, there was a big crowd waiting anxiously to see this cruel test.

Suddenly the sweet pomp of the African drums was on the beat. This evoked in me the pride of being a true son of Africa. We were summoned to stand on a line in front of the elders of our tribe. The test was about to begin. Our backs were to be beaten with whips till blood appeared. The drum-beats were to regulate the speed of beating. To show one's manliness one was not allowed to shake or cry. It was cruel.

The first boy passed well. But the second, alas, the womb that carried him! After a beating he burst out with a loud cry releasing and urinating as if his guts had no way to control the swallowed food. His father was greatly ashamed. Then came my turn. The first beating made my blood run madly around my body. I felt the pain on top of my forehead. The whole of my back was paralyzed instantly. As the beating went on I felt no further pain. Then I knew that the ghosts of my dead ancestors had clustered on my back to receive the beatings. The sacrifice was good—a fat, clean hen.

"Blood!" the crowd shouted. I had passed the test. As my father and relatives rushed to hail me, I felt some deadly pain. I nearly cried but the test was over. I was a man!

I was carried home amid cheers as the test was continued on the others. My wounded back was nursed first. Then I was given the best of food—fried mutton. Meanwhile gifts poured in from my relatives, which put together made me a man of meagre wealth— enough to start life with.

After eating I went to sleep to avoid pain. I was proud to be a son of Africa. Africa the land of black proud warriors like myself in the ancestral savannah. I took opium to make me fall asleep quickly.

Out of Disaster

by R. LUCY KURIA

⅄   When I awoke, there was an unusual silence in the air and I found myself listening for something I used to hear whenever I awoke in the hot afternoons.

I then remembered how, two days before, I had been looking after my master's cattle and how two Masai warriors had come and had taken the cattle. They had beaten me savagely. They did not, however, leave me lying on the ground, half dead. Instead they managed to get me into their land somehow. I was a strong boy of twenty and I should guess that was the reason why they took me along with them. After they had beaten me, I was unconscious and did not come back to myself until the second day.

My friends and I had often fallen asleep in the hottest times of the day and when I awoke, I always heard the same sounds in the air. I always heard the sound made by flying grasshoppers ka-rrrrrrr-ah, the sound of men chopping wood with their axes in the forest near by, kong-kong-kong. The sun was always so hot that one would say it shone loudly! Its heat seemed to have a sound to me. These sounds were familiar. They were the sounds I was expecting to hear when I awoke that morning.

The two men had put me in a mud hut with no windows. The door was very small and low and the inside of the hut was very dark. I recalled what had happened and then sat in the darkness staring at nothing. Presently the door opened and three men came in followed by a beautiful girl, who had hardly anything on her body. She was carrying a gourd which she offered to me. I took it and drank it, not caring what was inside. After that the men took me outside and treated my wounds. They were kind and I liked them.

I could recognise the hills on which we were. They were the hills one saw far in the distance when at home. I hoped that when I got better, I would run away. Knowing how hard my master was at home, I could not go back to him. I would seek happiness among some other tribes.

The Masai family looked after me very well. Meat was our food. The girl I had first seen brought me milk and meat daily. We grew to like each other very much. She taught me the Masai language and I learned very quickly. After some weeks I got better, but I did not want to run away. I stayed with the family and proved to be a trustworthy man. I became one of the members of the family and took part in every event.

I remember once the two men, Muriu and Karau, who had taken the cattle, and me, went out to steal more cows. We were caught in the act by the owners. We all fought against them but I fought so bravely that afterwards when we got home, I was rewarded by the two men. They gave Ngini to me as my wife. She was the girl I had liked very much and who had made me love Masailand so much; we loved one another. I did not ever again think of leaving Masailand. I grew old and my sons carried on the work of stealing cattle. Every morning when I awoke I remembered the morning when I awoke and found myself listening for something; but the familiar sounds were lost for ever.

Exile

by ALHAJI SIR ABUBAKAR TAFAWA BALEWA

Sir Abubakar Tafawa Balewa was the first Prime Minister of independent Nigeria in 1960. Educated in Nigeria and at London University, he belonged to the Hausa, an important ethnic group already introduced in this anthology (page 25). Today Hausas are devout Moslems, and Balewa was no exception. He had made the pilgrimage to Mecca and was entitled to use the title Alhaji. As a political leader, he was respected for his honesty, his tolerance, and his vision of a united Nigeria. He was accidentally killed during the military coup of January 1966.

Few people outside Nigeria know that he was a novelist as well as a political leader. He had tremendous pride in Hausa tradition and in the Islamic way of life, which he portrays in his novel *Shaihu Umar*. The story is set at the end of the nineteenth century when Arab slave caravans still ran regularly from Kano across the Sahara to Egypt. It was the custom for the Muslims to raid the neighboring pagan tribes for slaves and cattle. They were a very pious people who believed that their activities were blessed by Allah, the god of the Muslims.

The hero is a young Hausa boy who was kidnapped and sold into slavery. Unlike the majority, he was given an education and became an Islamic *malam*, or teacher. One day, just before evening prayer, a student asked him to tell about the country from which he came, and why he had left home. It was a long story which caused pity and wonder in all who heard it. The first episode follows.

⅄   Away back (began Shaihu Umar) I was a native of this country, but even so, I did not grow up and pass my boyhood here. It was far away in the country of the Arabs that I grew up. Long long ago I was a native of a certain country near Bida, and the name of our town was Kagara. My father was a tall light-skinned man whose craft was leather-working. My mother was a native of Fatika. Now when my mother was carrying me, my father died and left me an inheritance of six cows, three sheep, and his riding mare. At this time the mare was in foal. All these things were handed over to my mother, who was told to keep them until in God's good time she should give birth, for they were the property of her son, since this husband of hers had no other relatives to claim the inheritance.

So things went on until one day I was born, and I turned out to be a boy. Now when the naming day came round, my mother had one of my rams caught and slaughtered, and the name of "Umar" was whispered in my ear. Time passed until, when I was two years old (that is, the time for weaning), my grandmother on my father's side took me to wean me. I lived with her until the time came when my mother wanted to marry again.

Then my mother said to my grandmother, "You know that apart from you, I have no relations in this town besides this boy, and now I want to marry. What is more, many suitors have come forward to press their suit, saying that I must marry the one that I like best. I have come to you for advice. So-and-so and so-and-so seek my hand, but up to now I have not made up my mind which one I like best. I want first to hear what you have to say. Among them is a certain courtier, especially close to the Chief, called Makau."

When my grandmother heard the name of Makau among the suitors, she said, "My daughter, indeed God has brought you great good fortune! When there is one with good eyesight, would you marry a blind man? If you ask my advice, you should marry none save Makau. I know that he is a modest man, who is in no way mean-minded, and certainly if you marry him your home will be a happy one."

My mother accepted this advice. The next day the marriage ceremony was performed, and a day was appointed upon which she was to move into her husband's compound. When the time came my mother went to live in her own hut, and I remained with my grandmother. I lived happily with my grandmother, and then one day a fatal illness came upon her. When she realised that she was not to recover, she sent for my mother to warn her, saying: "See now, I do not think that I shall rise again from this illness, so I want you to take this boy home with you, because I do not want to see him cry even a single tear. It would make me very unhappy to see that." My mother replied, "Very well."

Shortly after we had left, my grandmother died. Many people assembled, prayers were said over her, and she was laid in her grave.

When this was all over, I was living comfortably with my mother in Makau's compound, when one day the Chief had all his courtiers summoned. When they had assembled he said to them, "The reason I have summoned you is this. I want you to make ready, and set out on a raid on my behalf to Gwari country. I am in dire need, and therefore I want you to make haste to set out, in the hope that you will return quickly."

When the courtiers heard what the Chief had to say, they all went mad with joy. They were delighted, saying, "Just give us half a chance, and we'll be off!" The reason for their delight was because, as you know, on a raid they would gain many cattle, and slaves as well. And then when they returned, the Chief would give them a part of everything which they had won. Thus if a man were to capture three slaves, the Chief would take two of them, and he would be allowed to keep one.

The reason for this raid that the Chief was planning, was that he wanted to obtain some slaves. Some he would put with his own, and send to Kano so that clothes and saddlery might be bought and sent back to him, while others he would send to Bida in order to procure muskets.

Among the horsemen whom the Chief had appointed as raiders was Makau. When the time came for their departure, after the Chief had sought an auspicious hour from a certain malam, Makau came into his compound and gathered his family together. He said to them, "Now you know that I am going on a raid to Gwari country, and I do not know when I shall return. Whether I shall be killed there, God knows best. For this reason I want to bid you all farewell, and I want you to forgive me for all that I have done to you, for any man in this world, if you live with him, some day you are bound to cause him unhappiness."

His family all spoke up together. "By God, you have never done anything to make us unhappy. We wish you a safe journey, and a safe return." Thereupon all of us burst out crying, so that none of us could hear the other!

The raiders all began to make ready, and in the early dawn they set out and made for the interior of Gwari country. They continued until they reached a small pagan village on a rocky strong-hold in the forest. On their arrival in this place, they all dismounted from their horses, and lay down at the foot of some thick shady trees, where no-one could see them. At this season the rains had begun to set in, and all the farmers were about to clear their farms. Now there was no way that these pagans could sow a crop sufficient to feed them for a whole year, so they had to come out of their towns and come down to the low ground to lay out their farms in the plain. Despite this however, they were not able to tend their farms properly, for fear of raiders.

When the raiders reached the village they hid on the edge of the farms. Early in the morning, just before the time of prayer, the pagans began to come out from their villages, making for their farms. The raiders crouched silently, watching everything that they were doing. They held back until all the people had come out. Then, after they had settled down to work, thinking that nothing would happen to them, the raiders fell upon them all at once, and seized men and women, and even small children. Before the pagans had realised what was happening, the raiders had already done the damage. At once other pagans began to sally forth, preparing to fight to wrest back their brothers who had been captured. Af! Before they were ready, the raiders were far away. They started to follow them, but they had no chance of catching them. Those in front got clean away, leaving their pursuers far behind.

When the raiders saw that they had escaped, they took to the high road, for, as you know, they would not have followed the high road in the first place, lest the pagans should catch up with them. Then, when they got onto the high road they made haste, each saying to his companion, "Come on, come on." They kept on going until, by God's grace, they reached home safely. When they entered the town, each one made straight for the palace, bringing with him his booty from the raid. All of them had at least two slaves, and there were some with three slaves, and even some with four. Each of them presented before the Chief that which he had obtained. Except for Makau. On his return, he had not gone by way of the palace, but had gone straight to his own compound. But this was not with any deceitful intent.

When everybody was present, each one handed over what he

62

had brought. Then the Chief said, "Where is Makau? Was he perhaps killed out there, and you are hiding it from me?"

The whole company answered together, "Oh no, God save your Majesty, but you know what men are like. As for us, we kept quiet right from the start, when we saw he was your favorite, so as to see how it would all turn out between you. For we well know that anyone who is trusted, and betrays the trust, God will punish him, let alone in a case such as that of you and Makau, to whom you have entrusted everything that you possessed. Let us now skin the monkey for you, right down to its tail! In this whole town you will never find one who betrays your trust like this Makau. Why, it's Makau who shames you by revealing all your secrets to the common people, who you see, are giving themselves airs now. Why, there is never a secret that you tell him that some of them don't hear about. You know, from the time that we set out on this raid until we returned, this fellow never ceased to abuse you, to such an extent that Sarkin Zagi became angry and drew his sword, intending to strike off his head, until the Barde had to bid him hold his hand. The reason that you do not see him here now is that he gone by way of his own compound, in order to hide some of the slaves which he has acquired, for he capturned four, two young girls, and two boys, but one of them is almost grown up. But of course, we don't know, let's just wait and see what he is going to bring."

When the Chief heard their words he said, "So that's it, Makau has done well!"

After a little while Makau approached with the two young slaves whom he had captured, entirely unaware of what his fellow courtiers were plotting against him. Now these two slaves which he had brought were all that he had ever obtained, and the story that he had captured four slaves was a fabrication of his enemies. As Makau approached the gate of the palace, he saw from a distance the Chief seated outside, holding court. When the courtiers saw him they began to say, "Aha, there's Makau coming with only two slaves, so he's hidden the other two, has he?" When Makau reached the Chief he prostrated himself in greeting, but the Chief did not reply. In the whole company there was not one who said as much as a single word to him. Each one just kept staring at him, and his rivals were overjoyed, as though they had been given hump to roast!

After a little while the Chief said, "Makau, is it only now

that you have arrived?" He replied, "No, God save your Majesty, I went by way of my compound, so as to tether my horse and change my clothes, before coming to your presence."

The Chief said, "I see, and how many slaves did you get?" Makau said, "Two."

The Chief said, "Right. Are you sure you only got two? Do you agree that if I investigate and find that it was not two that you got, I should do to you whatever I like?"

Makau said, "Most certainly, I agree."

When they had finished this exchange, the Chief called the Sarkin Zagi and asked him, "How many slaves is it that Makau brought back from the raid?"

Now all along the Sarkin Zagi had been waiting eagerly for this to happen, and he said, "Four slaves, but he only entered the city with two, because he sold the other two on the road to a caravan of Kano people who were going to fetch locust-bean cake for Bauci."

The Chief said, "So, do you hear that, Makau?"

Makau replied, "God save your Majesty, I have nothing more to say, for these people have already told so many lies that there is nothing more that I can tell you that you will believe."

Then the Chief became enraged, and sent the courtiers off and gave them permission to go and ransack Makau's compound, ordering them not to leave him a single thing, even if only a sleeping mat. The courtiers went and stripped his compound to the ground, even the grass with which the roofs of the huts were thatched, all was stripped. He had some cattle in a little village near the town, and there and then someone was sent to fetch them. Now when they went to bring back these cattle of Makau's, they included mine, which my father had left me as an inheritance, and also my sheep, and my mare, and her foal. After they had completely finished this pillage they gathered up the property and took it to the Chief.

When it was brought Makau rose and said to the Chief, "God save your Majesty, I beg you, among this property there are some things which do not belong to me, such as this mare and her foal, the sheep, and some cattle. These things belong to a certain boy, an orphan, whose mother I married. I beg you, take out this orphan's property and restore it to him."

64

On hearing this the courtiers all spoke at once, "Aha, you hear, there he goes with those lies of his again! How do you come to be making out that you've got an orphan's property in your keeping? May God save your Majesty, he's lying. This property of the orphan that he's talking about, it's not in his keeping at all, it's in the keeping of the boy's mother and she knows what she has done with it." (At this time I was a small boy, hardly able to talk properly, much less could I understand what was happening. When they ransacked the compound, all I knew was that my parents were weeping.)

Then and there, without making any inquiries at all, the Chief accepted what the courtiers told him. After it was finished, he said to Makau, "So, you see, this is the reward which you get from God for having betrayed my trust, after I had trusted you. Now I have nothing more to say to you; what has been done to you is suffi-cient. After this, as long as I am Chief in this town, I will not permit you to remain in it. And so I shall banish you to somewhere far away, not under my jurisdiction. However, I will not forbid you to take your family with you. Any one of your wives, if she loves you, let her follow you, and you can go together. But if she does not love you, then you must leave her behind."

Makau said, "God save your Majesty. I hear and I obey. But I beg you, in the majesty of your kingship, allow me a few days here to obtain certain provision to eat on the road, for as you know, I am now going to an unfamiliar place."

The Chief raised his head for a time. Then he answered Makau, saying that he agreed, but that he would give him four days only, to make ready for his exile.

Makau thanked him, got up, came back to his compound, and gathered all his family together, old and young, male and female, and said to us, "Well now, you have seen how God has decreed that this thing should happen to me. The Chief has said that I must leave his country, but he will allow me to take with me any wife who wishes to follow me, and in addition he has said that I must leave this town within four days. Now what I want to say is this, if any woman among you is sure in her heart that she can bear to follow me, well and good, let her come."

His whole family burst into tears together, saying, "By God,

65

we swear that even if it be no other country on earth that you are bound for, even if it be the next world, if it is possible to accompany you there, we shall accompany you."

Makau asked us thrice, according to the Law, but not one of us changed his mind.

From Shaihu Umar, *by Alhaji Sir Abubakar Balewa, Longmans, Green and Co. Ltd., 1967.*

Luo Craftsman OWITI

The Old Man of Usumbura and His Misery

by TABAN LO LIYONG

Taban Lo Liyong was born in Uganda about 1939. He left home to study writing at the Writer's Workshop of the University of Iowa, where he was the first African to receive a Master of Fine Arts degree. On his return to Africa, he began writing short stories that combined the elements of the traditional storytelling style of the Luo and Masai tribes with a keen sense of humor and tragedy. In addition to short stories and poems, he has written essays concerning the role of the creative artist in Africa.

His work has been collected in two anthologies, *Fixions and Other Stories* and *Eating Chiefs*. In *The Old Man of Usumbura and His Misery* he has created an African myth based on the hidden evil in mankind and the perils of curiosity.

人   There was an old man of Usumbura who was very rich. This old man of Usumbura. He was so rich he had eight thousand cows. This rich old man of Usumbura. With these cows he married for himself sixty-five wives. The old man of Usumbura. He was so healthy that he had three hundred children from these wives. Our healthy man of Usumbura. He was so happy and successful that with industry his wealth increased manifoldly. This happy successful and industrious man of Usumbura. He and all the members of his family were so lucky none of them ever felt sick. These lucky people of Usumbura. All his life he had never known the pangs of sorrow or grief. This lucky Usumburan.

There was another old man of Kigali who was very poor. This old man of Kigali. He was thoroughly sunk in misery. This miserable man of Kigali. His eyes were always red with weeping.

67

The eyes of the man of Kigali. He was rich once. This previously rich man of Kigali. But he had lost all his worldly goods to the last bit. This erstwhile rich man of Kigali. He had not even a wife left him now. This old man of Kigali. Not even a child was left to console him in his old age and poverty. This bereft man of Kigali. All day long he mourned for his lost cows. This old man of Kigali. He also wept for his dead wives. This single man of Kigali. He wept all night for his dead children. This mourning old man of Kigali. He always cried, "Oh, my misery! Oh, my misery!" This miserable old man.

The rich, happy old man of Usumbura and the poor, miserable old man of Kigali were friends. These old men of Usumbura and Kigali.

One day the rich old man of Usumbura went on a journey. This rich old man of Usumbura. He went to Kigali. This rich man of Usumbura. He went to visit his poor friend. This rich man of Usumbura. When he arrived at Kigali he was struck by his friend's cry of "Oh, my misery" and became sympathetic. This happy man of Usumbura. He asked to be shown the nature of misery. This healthy man of Usumbura. The miserable man of Kigali tried to discourage him. This adventurous old man of Usumbura. But he would hear none of that. This happy healthy rich old man of Usumbura. He seemed to have been so bored with his constantly happy life that he needed a change. This lucky man of Usumbura. Any kind of a change would be better than that drab happy life. That life of this unmiserable man of Usumbura. At last the miserable old man of Kigali consented to give a slice of misery to his happy friend from Usumbura. These old friends of Kigali and Usumbura.

They appointed a date when misery would be conveyed from Kigali to Usumbura. These old men of Kigali and Usumbura. The rich man's sons were to come and convey misery from Kigali to Usumbura. These lucky sons of Usumbura. They were to transport misery from the poor man's home to their rich father's home. These happy obedient sons of Usumbura.

On the day appointed all the one hundred and fifty-one sons started off early for Kigali. These fat children of Usumbura. They ran part of the way. These expectant sons of Usumbura. Instead of taking two days to reach Kigali they did it in one day. These impatient and obedient sons of Usumbura. It was evening when they reached Kigali. These heirs of Usumbura. They rested a while but ate nothing in Kigali. These worthy agents of fate. In the evening they insisted they be given misery straightaway to take home to Usumbura. These playful sons of Usumbura. The old man of Kigali suggested they wait till the following morning. This unknown old man of Kigali. But as would be expected these hot-headed sons of Usumbura would not like a delay. These children full of great expectations. The old man of Kigali thought the time had come to give them misery. And he was right, this old man of Kigali.

The old man of Kigali gave them a very large straw bundle. This large straw bundle. This bundle was tightly tied with ropes. The tightly tied bundle. It contained the very misery so greatly desired by the old rich Usumbura man. This loved misery. It contained the misery so desired by the hundred and fifty-one children. This loved misery.

The old man of Kigali gave the sons of Usumbura a few orders. This knowing man of Kigali. The children were never to tamper with the luggage. They were to carry it right before their father. These inquisitive children. The children shouted for joy. These live children of Usumbura. They managed in their own way to convey this heavy burden a few steps at a time. Nothing was heavier to each of them than this pregnant egg. The incurious Usumburans.

When the bundle had left Kigali the old man started to smile. This prescient man of Kigali.

Midway between Kigali and Usumbura these boys stopped. These obedient children of Usumbura. Some of them said they were tired. These lively children of Usumbura. Others thought they needed to enjoy a bit of the sunset. These observant children of Usumbura. A few thought a little rest was in order. These restless children of Usumbura. One admitted he really needed a relaxation. These playful children of Usumbura. One said the rope looked green. These children who can see green at night. One thought the rope had surely loosened since they had left Kigali. One wagered he would loosen one, just one of the knots. These indefatigable children of Usumbura. One said he was tickled by misery on the side next to him. These sensible children of Usumbura. One boy exhibited with triumph a rope unloosened. These active children of

Usumbura. The elder ordered there be no tampering with misery. This orderly elder son. But another thought only blind people carry what they cannot see. These seeing children of Usumbura. So an argument grew up between the children who wanted to see misery before it reached their father and those who wanted their father to see misery first. These factious children. While the argument was in progress some children stayed unconcerned. These apathetic and reflective children. But a few boys were busy with their nimble hands. These constant active few.

The bundle became smaller and smaller as the argument became louder and louder. This bundle and strife. Nothing substantial could be seen yet from the bundle although brother was already abusing brother. This cause of strife. Blows started to rain on brothers' heads. These headbreaking blows. At last a handful of the luggage remained. That fatal unknown. Curiosity brought brothers together to see this famed thing. The curiosity that killed the cat. They squeezed together, they held their breaths, they were ready to see, they were all attention. These humans.

When the bundle was opened, nothing was seen. The cheated sights. Only a little whirring sound was heard. The noise that has no path. It sounded like a mosquito. This child of the egg.

Now that there was no more misery to carry home, what were these boys to carry home to their father? These obedient boys of Usumbura. One brother's hands were already striking another for having opened the bundle. These useful hands we have. Another hit another on the head, another smote another, another slew another, another clubbed another, another speared another, another strangled another, another castrated another, another drank another's blood. These killers of their own brothers. Now only fifty brothers remained in the internecine war. These brother-killing brothers. Three minutes later we see only three blood-intoxicated brothers. These committed brothers. Two brothers have ganged up on a brother. The unhappy company. The last round ends with brother killing brother. Oh, the fatal end. Death, you have reaped a rich harvest. Death that levels all. Alas, who will inform the rich man of Usumbura? That rich, happy, wealthy, unmiserable old man of Usumbura.

But one boy remained alive. This unlucky boy of Usumbura.

70

He had always been a coward. This life-preserving son of his mother. He had hidden away during the life-destroying brotherly exercises. That fatal exercise. He became the messenger of misery to his father. Oh, the fatal messenger that should never arrive. Out of breath with sorrow and running, he approached his expectant father with the news. This sorrow-filled son of his beaming father. The father anticipated an advance information on the approaching misery. This happy father of Usumbura. He asked how near misery was. This impatient father of Usumbura. He repeated the question with anger. This father who can't even wait for his son to regain his breath. He struck the son once for the delay. This father who had never known how to strike a blow. But only good news comes out pat. This bad news which demands a cautious framing. The son started to sob, more from internal blows. This vessel of deaths. At last he said misery had escaped. The misery that travels in the air. The old man of Usumbura was so mad he struck his son dead instantly. This happy, rich, healthy, misery-less old father of Usumbura.

The rich, happy, healthy, worry-less old man of Usumbura has now killed his son. This father who does not know misery. The wife whose son was struck dead started to mourn. In this home that has never known mourning. Other wives realized that she had deserved such a treatment for a long time past. Oh, human wisdom that always condemns those who are afflicted. This mother's wrong deeds consist of insolence. Oh, the home that never knew insolence. And her son was said to have been disrespectful to their worthy husband. Oh, the love that is intensified by the degradation of others. He was the only black sheep in this snow white home. Give a dog a name and you hang him. His mother left the home of the rich old man that very night. The darkest of nights. She did not carry her son's corpse with her. The lifeless luggage. It was her share of misery she took along with her. Oh, misery that curiosity brings.

The old man of Usumbura set out that very night to find his other hundred and forty-nine sons. These all-virtuous sons. He took along with him his fifty-five wives. The wives that love their husband and never do wrong. Husband and wives went to find sons and misery. Oh, obsessions that are so dear to the hearts.

On the way the smell of new blood tickled their noses. Smell that travels in the wind. They became wild. These good people. Soon they stepped on cadaver instead of earth. Oh, organic flesh and earth. They kissed their lifeless sons because there was nothing else to do. These virtuous sons and wives. They had no more stomach for misery. These misery-filled parents.

They abandoned their happy husband to his fate and went off to their several parents' homes. These good wives of Usumbura. They took with them all their daughters and shares of wealth. These unlike-the-other-wife wives.

At last the old man was left to bear his misery alone. The old man who had wanted so much to see misery. He sang a song called "Oh, my misery! Oh, my misery!" This rich, healthy, happy, misery-less old man of Usumbura.

Tekayo

by GRACE OGOT

Grace Ogot is one of the most sensitive woman writers in Africa. Born in Nyanza province, Kenya, in 1930, she trained as a general nurse and midwife in Uganda and England. She helped to set up students' health services at Makerere University College and worked as a community development officer in Nyanza. Her talent for writing led her to a job as scriptwriter for the British Broadcasting Company and subsequently as public relations officer for an international airline.

Mrs. Ogot has had many short stories published, and one novel, *The Promised Land.* Her stories reflect her rich experiences with many different kinds of people, and the conflicts which naturally arise between the generations and between superstition and modern scientific knowledge.

⋏ The period of short rains was just starting in a semi-arid part of the Sudan. The early morning mist had cleared, and faint blue smoke rose from the ground as the hot sun touched the surface of the wet earth.

> "People in the underworld are cooking.
> People in the underworld are cooking!"

The children shouted, as they pelted one another with wet sand.

"Come on, Opija," Tekayo shouted to his son. "Give me a hand, I must get the cows to the river before it is too hot."

Opija hit his younger brother with his last handful of sand, and then ran to help his father. The cows were soon out of the village and Tekayo picked up the leather pouch containing his lunch and followed them.

They had not gone far from home when Tekayo saw an eagle

73

flying above his head with a large piece of meat in its claws. The eagle was flying low searching for a suitable spot to have its meal. Tekayo promptly threw his stick at the bird. He hit the meat and it dropped to the ground. It was a large piece of liver, and fresh blood was still oozing from it. Tekayo nearly threw the meat away, but he changed his mind. What was the use of robbing the eagle of its food only to throw it away? The meat looked good: it would supplement his vegetable lunch wonderfully. He wrapped the meat in a leaf and pushed it into his pouch.

They reached a place where there was plenty of grass. Tekayo allowed the cows to graze while he sat under an *ober* tree watching the sky. It was not yet lunch time, but Tekayo could not wait. The desire to taste that meat was burning within him. He took out the meat and roasted it on a log fire under the *ober* tree. When the meat was cooked he ate it greedily with millet bread which his wife had made the previous night.

"My! What delicious meat," Tekayo exclaimed. He licked the fat juice that stained his fingers, and longed for a little more. He threw away the bitter herbs that were the rest of his lunch. The meat was so good, and the herbs would merely spoil its taste.

The sun was getting very hot, but the cows showed no desire to go to the river to drink. One by one they lay down in the shade, chewing the cud. Tekayo also became overpowered by the afternoon heat. He rested against the trunk and slept.

While asleep, Tekayo had a dream. He was sitting before a log fire roasting a large piece of liver like the one he had eaten earlier. His mouth watered as he watched rich fat from the roasting meat dropping into the fire. He could not wait, and although the meat was not completely done, he removed it from the fire and cut it up with his hunting knife. But just as he was about to take the first bite, he woke up.

Tekayo looked around him, wondering what had happened to the meat! Could it be that he was dreaming? "No, no, no," he cried. "It was too vivid to be a dream!" He sat upright and had another look around, as if by some miracle he might see a piece of liver roasting on the log fire beside him. But there was nothing. All he saw were large roots of the old tree protruding above the earth's surface like sweet potatoes in the sandy soil.

The cattle had wandered a long way off. Tekayo got up and followed them. They reached the river bank, and the thirsty cows ran to the river. While the cows drank, Tekayo sat on a white stone cooling his feet and gazing lazily at the swollen river as it flowed mightily towards the plain.

Beyond the river stood the great "Ghost Jungle." A strong desire for the rich meat came back to Tekayo, and he whispered, "The animal with that delicious liver must surely be in that jungle." He sat there for a while, thinking. The temptation to start hunting for the animal nagged him. But he managed to suppress it. The afternoon was far spent and they were a long way from home.

The next morning Tekayo left home earlier than usual. When his wife begged him to wait for his lunch, he refused. He hurried from home, taking his hunting spears with him.

Tekayo made it impossible for the cows to graze. He rushed them along, lashing at any cow that lingered in one spot for long. They reached the edge of the "Ghost Jungle" and there he left the cows grazing unattended.

Tekayo could not see any path or track leading into the "Ghost Jungle." The whole place was a mass of thick bush and long grass covered with the morning dew. And except for the sounds of mating birds, there was a weird silence in the jungle that frightened him. But the vehement desire within him blindly drove him on, through the thick wet grass.

After walking for some time, he stood and listened. Something was racing towards him. He turned round to look, and sure enough a big impala was running frantically towards him. Warm blood rushed through Tekayo's body, and he raised his spear to kill the animal. But the spear never landed. He came face to face with a big leopardess that was chasing the impala. The leopardess roared at Tekayo several times challenging him, as it were, to a duel. But Tekayo looked away, clutching the spear in his trembling hand. There was no one to fight and the beast went away after her prey.

"What a bad start," Tekayo said slowly and quietly when his heart beat normally again. "That wild cat will not leave me alone now."

He started to walk back towards the plain, following the

track he had made. The roaring leopardess had taken the life out of him.

He saw another track that cut across the forest. He hesitated a little, and then decided to follow it, leaving his own. The track got bigger and bigger, and without any warning Tekayo suddenly came upon a baby wildebeeste which was following a large flock grazing at the foot of a hill. He killed it without any difficulty. He skinned the animal and extracted its liver, leaving the rest of the carcass there.

Tekayo returned to the herd, and he sat down to roast the meat on a log fire. When the meat was cooked he took a bite and chewed it hurriedly. But he did not swallow it: he spat it all out! The liver was as bitter as the strong green herbs given to constipated children. The back of his tongue was stinging as if it had been burned. Tekayo threw the rest of the meat away and took his cows home.

He arrived home tired and disappointed; and when his young wife set food before him, he refused to eat. He pretended that he had a stomach-ache and did not feel like eating. That night Tekayo was depressed and in low spirits. He did not even desire his young wife who slept by his side. At dawn the young wife returned to her hut disappointed, wondering why the old man had not desired her.

The doors of all the huts were still closed when Tekayo looked out through his door. A cold east wind hit his face, and he quickly shut himself in again.

It was getting rather late and the calves were calling. But it was pouring with rain so much that he could not start milking. He sat on the hard bed looking at the dead ashes in the fire-place. He longed to get out to start hunting.

When the rain stopped, Tekayo milked the cows in a great hurry. Then he picked up the lunch that had been left near his hut for him, and left the village. His disappointed wife of the previous night watched him till he disappeared at the gate.

When he reached the "Ghost Jungle," it was drizzling again. The forest looked so lonely and wet. He left the cows grazing as usual, and entered the bush, stealing his way through the dripping leaves. He turned to the left to avoid the thick part of the jungle.

Luck was with him. He spotted a family of antelope grazing not far from him. He crawled on his knees till he was quite close to them, and then threw his spear killing one animal instantly. After skinning it, he extracted its liver, and also took some delicate parts for the family.

When he sat down under the tree to roast the meat, Tekayo was quite sure that he had been successful. But when he tasted the meat, he shook his head. The meat was tender, but it was not what he was looking for.

They reached the river bank. The cows continued to graze after drinking, and Tekayo, without realising it, wandered a long way from his herd, still determined to discover the owner of that wonderful liver. When he suddenly looked round, the herd was nowhere to be seen. The sun was sinking behind Mount Pajulu, and Tekayo started to run, looking for his cows.

The cows, heavy with milk, had gone home without Tekayo. For one day when Tekayo's children got lost in the forest, the cows had gone home without them, following the old track they knew well. On that day the whole village came out in search of the children in fear that the wild animals might harm them.

It was getting dark when Tekayo arrived home. They started to milk and Odipo remarked, "Why, Father, you are late coming home today."

"It is true," replied Tekayo thoughtfully. "See that black bull there? He went to another herd across the river. I didn't miss him until it was time to come home. One of these days, we shall have to castrate him—he is such a nuisance."

They milked in silence until one of the little girls came to fetch some milk for preparing vegetables.

At supper time the male members of the family sat around the log fire waiting and talking. One by one, baskets of millet meal and earthen dishes of meat and vegetables arrived from different huts. There was fish, dried meat, fried white ants, and herbs. A little food was thrown to the ground, to the ancestors, and then they started eating. They compared and contrasted the deliciousness of the various dishes they were having. But Tekayo kept quiet. All the food he tasted that evening was bitter as bile.

When the meal was over, the adults told stories of war and

77

the clans to the children, who listened attentively. But Tekayo was not with them: he was not listening. He watched the smoky clouds as they raced across the sky.

"Behind those clouds, behind those clouds, rests Okenyu, my great-grandfather. Please! Please!" Tekayo beseeched him. "Please, father, take this longing away from me. Give me back my manhood that I may desire my wives. For what is a man without this desire!"

A large cloud covered the moon giving the earth temporary darkness. Tears stung Tekayo's eyes, and he dismissed the family to sleep. As he entered his own hut, a woman was throwing small logs on the fire.

He offered many secret prayers to the departed spirits, but the craving for the mysterious liver never left him. Day after day he left home in the morning, taking his cows with him. And on reaching the jungle, he left them unattended while he hunted. The rough and disappointed life that he led soon became apparent to the family. He suddenly became old and disinterested in life. He had nothing to tell his sons around the evening fire, and he did not desire his wives. The sons of Tekayo went to Lakech and told her, "Mother, speak to father—he is sick. He does not talk to us, and he does not eat. We don't know how to approach him."

Though Lakech had passed the age of child-bearing and no longer went to Tekayo's hut at night, she was his first wife, and he loved her. She therefore went and asked him, "Man, what ails you?" Tekayo looked at Lakech, but he could not look into her eyes. He looked at her long neck, and instead of answering her question he asked her, "Would you like to get free from those heavy brass rings around your neck?"

"Why?" Lakech replied, surprised.

"Because they look so tight."

"But they are not tight," Lakech said softly. "I would feel naked without them."

And Tekayo looked away from his wife. He was longing to tell Lakech everything, and to share with her this maddening craving that was tearing his body to pieces. But he checked himself. Lakech must not know: she would not understand. Then he lied to her.

"It is my old indigestion. I have had it for weeks now. It will soon pass."

A mocking smile played on Lakech's lips, and Tekayo knew that she was not convinced. Some visitors arrived, and Lakech left her husband.

Tekayo hunted for many months, but he did not succeed in finding the animal with the delicious liver.

One night, as he lay awake, he asked himself where else he could hunt. And what animal would he be looking for? He had killed all the different animals in the "Ghost Jungle." He had risked his life when he killed and ate the liver of a lion, a leopard and a hyena, all of which were tabooed by his clan.

A little sleep came to Tekayo's heavy eyes and he was grateful. But then Apii stood beside his bed calling:: "Grandpa, Grandpa, it is me." Tekayo sat up, but the little girl was not there. He went back to sleep again. And Apii was there calling him: "Can't you hear me, Grandpa?"

Tekayo woke up a second time, but nobody was there. He lay down without closing his eyes. Again the child's fingers touched his drooping hand, and the playful voice of a child tickled the skin of the old man. Tekayo sat up a third time, and looked round the room. But he was alone. The cock crew a third time, and it was morning.

And Lakech died without knowing her husband's secret, and was buried in the middle of the village, being the first wife. Tekayo sat at his wife's grave morning and evening for a long time, and his grief for her appeased his hunger for the unknown animal's liver. He wept, but peacefully, as if his craving for the liver was buried with his wife.

It was during this time of grief that Tekayo decided never to go hunting again. He sat at home and looked after his many grandchildren, while the younger members of the family went out to work daily in the fields.

And then one day as Tekayo sat warming himself in the early morning sun near the granary, he felt slightly sick from the smell of grain sprouting inside the dark store. The shouting and singing of his grandchildren attracted his attention. As he watched them playing, the craving for the liver of the unknown animal returned powerfully to him.

Now among the children playing was a pretty little girl called Apii, the daughter of Tekayo's eldest son. Tekayo sent the other

Baganda Women with Children MSANGI

children away to play, and as they were going, he called Apii and told her, "Come my little one, run to your mother's hut and bring me a calabash of water."

Apii ran to her mother's hut to get water for her grandfather. And while she was fumbling in a dark corner of the house looking for a clean calabash, strong hands gripped her neck and strangled her. She gave a weak cry as she struggled for the breath of life. But it was too much for her. Her eyes closed in everlasting sleep, never to see the beauty of the shining moon again.

The limp body of the child slipped from Tekayo's hands and fell on the floor with a thud. He looked at the body at his feet and felt sick and faint. His ears were buzzing. He picked up the body, and as he staggered out with it, the air seemed black, and the birds of the air screamed ominously at him. But Tekayo had to eat his meal. He buried the body of Apii in a nearby anthill in a shallow grave.

The other children were still playing in the field when Tekayo returned with the liver in his bag. He roasted it in his hut hastily and ate it greedily. And alas! It was what he had been looking for for many years. He sat lazily resting his back on the granary, belching and picking his teeth. The hungry children, back from their play in the fields, sat in the shade eating sweet potatoes and drinking sour milk.

The older people came back in the evening, and the children ran to meet their parents. But Apii was not amongst them. In great desperation they asked the grandfather about the child. But Tekayo replied, "Ask the children—they should know where Apii is. They were playing together in the fields."

It was already pitch dark. Apii's younger brothers and sisters sat in front of the fire weeping with their mother. It was then that they remembered their grandfather sending Apii to fetch water for him. The desperate parents repeated this information to the old man, asking him if Apii had brought water for him that morning.

"She did," Tekayo replied, "and then ran away after the others. I watched her go with my own eyes. When they came back, I was asleep."

The grief-stricken family sat near the fire-place, their heads in their hands. They neither ate nor drank. Outside the little crickets sang in chorus as if they had a secret to tell.

For many days Apii's parents looked for their child, searching every corner and every nook. But there was no trace of her. Apii was gone. Months went by, and people talked no more about the disappearance of Apii. Only her mother thought of her. She did not lose hope of finding her child alive one day.

Tekayo forgot his deed. And when he killed a second child in the same way to satisfy his savage appetite, he was not even conscious of what he was doing. And when the worried parents asked the old man about the child, Tekayo wept saying, "How could I know? The children play out in the fields—I stay here at home."

It was after this that Tekayo's sons said among themselves, "Who steals our children? Which animal can it be? Could it be a hyena? Or a leopard? But these animals only hunt at night. Could it be an eagle, because it hunts during the day? But no! Father would have seen the eagle—he would have heard the child screaming." After some thought, Aganda told his brother, "Perhaps it is a malicious animal brought upon us by the evil spirits."

"Then my father is too old to watch the children," put in Osogo. "Yes, Father is too old, he is in danger," the rest agreed.

And from that time onwards the sons kept watch secretly on the father and the children. They watched for many months, but nothing threatened the man and the children.

The sons were almost giving up the watch. But one day when it was the turn of Apii's father to keep watch, he saw Tekayo sending away the children to play in the field—all except one. He sent this child to fetch him a pipe from his hut. As the child ran to the hut, Tekayo followed him. He clasped the frightened child and dragged him towards the fire-place. As Tekayo was struggling with the child, a heavy blow landed on his old back. He turned round sharply, his hands still holding the child's neck. He was facing Aganda, his eldest son. The child broke loose from the limp hands of Tekayo and grabbed Aganda's knees as if he had just escaped from the teeth of a crocodile. "Father!" Aganda shouted.

Seeing that the child was not hurt, Aganda pushed him aside saying, "Go to your mother's hut and lie down."

He then got hold of the old man and dragged him towards the little windowless hut built for goats and sheep. As he was being dragged away, the old man kept on crying, *"Atimo ang'o? Atimo ang'o?"* (What have I done? What have I done?)

Anganda pushed the old man into the little hut and barred the door behind him, as you would to the animals. He went to the child, who was still sobbing.

The rest of the family returned from the fields, and when Apii's father broke the news to them, they were appalled. The family wore mourning garments and went without food.

"Tho! Tho!" they spat towards the sun which, although setting on them, was rising on the ancestors.

"Great-grandfathers, cleanse us," they all cried.

And they lit the biggest fire that had ever been lit in that village. Tekayo's eldest son took the old greasy drum hanging above the fire-place in his father's hut and beat it. The drum throbbed out sorrowful tunes to warn the clan that there was sad news in Tekayo's home. The people who heard the drum left whatever they were doing and ran to Tekayo's village following the sound of the drum. Within a short time the village was teeming with anxious-looking relatives.

"What news? What news?" they asked in trembling voices.

"And where is Tekayo?" another old man asked.

"Is he in good health?" asked another.

There was confusion and panic.

"Death of death, who will give us medicine for death? Death knocks at your door, and before you can tell him to come in, he is in the house with you."

"Listen!" Someone touched the old woman who was mourning about death. Aganda spoke to the people.

"Men of my clan. We have not called you here for nothing. Listen to me and let our sorrow be yours. Weep with us! For several months we have been losing our children when we go to work on the fields. Apii, my own child, was the first one to disappear." Sobbing broke out among the women at the mention of the children's names.

"My people," Aganda continued, "the children in this clan get sick and die. But ours disappear unburied. It was our idea to keep watch over our children that we may catch whoever steals them. For months we have been watching secretly. We were almost giving up because we thought it was probably the wrath of our ancestors that was upon us. But today I caught him."

"What man? What man?" the people demanded angrily.

"And from what clan is he?" others asked.

"We must declare war on his clan, we must we must!"

Aganda stopped for a while, and told them in a quavering voice, "The man is in that little hut. The man is no one else but my father."

"*Mayo!*" the women shouted. There was a scuffle and the women and children screamed as if Tekayo was around the fire, and they were afraid of him. But the men kept quiet.

When the commotion died down, an old man asked, "Do you speak the truth, man?"

The son nodded. Men and women now shouted, "Where is the man? Kill him! He is not one of us. He is not one of us. He is an animal!"

There was nothing said outside that Tekayo did not hear. And there in the hut the children he had killed haunted him. He laid his head on the rough wall of the hut and wept.

Outside the hut the angry villagers continued with their demand, shouting, "Stone him now! Stone him now! Let his blood be upon his own head!"

But one of the old men got up and calmed the people.

"We cannot stone him now. It is the custom of the clan that a wicked man should be stoned in broad daylight, outside the village. We cannot depart from this custom."

"Stone me now, stone me now," Tekayo whispered. "Take me quickly from this torture and shame. Let me die and be finished with."

Tekayo knew by the angry shouting of the men and the shrill cries of frightened women and children that he was banished from society, nay, from life itself. He fumbled in his leather bag suspended around his waist to find his hunting knife, but it was not there. It had been taken away from him.

The muttering and shouting continued outside. There was weeping too. But Tekayo was now hearing them from afar as if a powerful wave were carrying him further and further away from his people.

At dawn the villagers got up from the fireplace to gather stones from nearby fields. The sun was not up yet, but it was just light enough to see. Everyone in the clan must throw a stone at the murderer. It was bad not to throw a stone, for it was claimed that the murderer's wicked spirit would rest upon the man who did not help to drive him away.

When the first rays of the sun appeared, the villagers had gathered enough stones to cover several bodies. They returned to the village to fetch Tekayo from the hut, and to lead him to his own garden outside the village. They surrounded the hut and stood in silence, waiting to jeer and spit at him when he came out.

Aganda and three old men tore the papyrus door open and called Tekayo to come out. But there was no reply. They rushed into the hut to drag him out to the people who were now demanding, "Come out, come out!"

At first it was too dark to see. But soon their eyes got used to the darkness. Then they saw the body of Tekayo, hanged on a short rope that he had unwound from the thatched roof.

The men came out shaking their heads. The crowd peered into the hut in turn until all of them had seen the dangling body of Tekayo—the man they were preparing to stone. No one spoke. Such a man, they knew, would have to be buried outside the village. They knew too that no new-born child would ever be named after him.

Chief Priest of Ulu

by CHINUA ACHEBE

Chinua Achebe, born in 1930 in Eastern Nigeria, is the author of several novels about traditional Ibo society, spanning several generations and going back to the days of his grandfather. Although he includes the white man in his novels, the viewpoint is primarily African, and the characters in his books speak with the authentic voice of their African heritage.

One of his most memorable characters is the Chief Priest of Ulu in *Arrow of God*, a novel of Ibo life set in the thirties, well before independence. This story of the impact of colonialism on traditional African society won the British New Statesman novel award in 1965. Throughout the book, in scene after scene, the author builds a picture of Ibo society as the chief priest sees it.

Arrow of God is richly told, in the language of symbolism, full of proverbs, tribal wisdom, and humor. In one scene, the priest Ezeulu says, "The white man is like hot soup, and we must take him slowly, slowly, from the edges of the bowl." Even his caution is not enough to avoid the confrontation between old and new ways in the following episode involving his son Oduche and the sacred python.

人   The place where the Christians built their place of worship was not far from Ezeulu's compound. As he sat in his *obi* thinking of the Festival of the Pumpkin Leaves, he heard their bell: GOME, GOME, GOME, GOME, GOME. His mind turned from the festival to the new religion. He was not sure what to make of it. At first he had thought that since the white man had come with great power and conquest it was necessary that some people should learn the ways of his own deity. That was why he had agreed to send his son, Oduche, to learn the new ritual. He also wanted him to learn the white man's wisdom, for Ezeulu knew from what he saw of Wintabota and the stories he heard about his people that the white man was very wise.

But now Ezeulu was becoming afraid that the new religion was like a leper. Allow him a handshake and he wants an embrace. Ezeulu had already spoken strongly to his son who was becoming more strange every day. Perhaps the time had come to bring him out again. But what would happen if, as many oracles prophesied, the white man had come to take over the land and rule? In such a case it would be wise to have a man of your family in his band. As he thought about these things Oduche came out from the inner compound wearing a white singlet and a towel which they had given him in the school. Nwafo came out with him, admiring his singlet. Oduche saluted his father and set out for the mission because it was Sunday morning. The bell continued ringing in its sad monotone.

Nwafo came back to the *obi* and asked his father whether he knew what the bell was saying. Ezeulu shook his head.

"It is saying: Leave your yam, leave your cocoyam and come to church. That is what Oduche says."

"Yes," said Ezeulu thoughtfully. "It tells them to leave their yam and their cocoyam, does it? Then it is singing the song of extermination."

They were interrupted by loud and confused talking inside the compound, and Nwafo ran out to see what it was. The voices were getting louder and Ezeulu who normally took no interest in women's shouting began to strain his ear. But Nwafo soon rushed back.

"Oduche's box is moving," he said, out of breath with excitement. The tumult in the compound grew louder. As usual the voice of Ezeulu's daughter, Akueke, stood out above all others.

"What is called 'Oduche's box is moving'?" he asked, rising with deliberate slowness to belie his curiosity.

"It is moving about the floor."

"There is nothing that a man will not hear nowadays." He went into his inner compound through the door at the back of his *obi*. Nwafo ran past him to the group of excited women outside his mother's hut. Akueke and Matefi did most of the talking. Nwafo's mother, Ugoye, was speechless. Now and again she rubbed her palms together and showed them to the sky.

Akueke turned to Ezeulu as soon as she saw him. "Father, come and see what we are seeing. This new religion . . ."

Preparing Fufu in Ghana ASIHENE

"Shut your mouth," said Ezeulu, who did not want anybody, least of all his own daughter, to question his wisdom in sending one of his sons to join the new religion.

The wooden box had been brought from the room where Oduche and Nwafo slept and placed in the central room of their mother's hut where people sat during the day and food was cooked.

The box, which was the only one of its kind in Ezeulu's compound, had a lock. Only people of the church had such boxes made for them by the mission carpenter and they were highly valued in Umuaro. Oduche's box was not actually moving; but it seemed to have something inside it struggling to be free. Ezeulu stood before it wondering what to do. Whatever was inside the box became more violent and actually moved the box around. Ezeulu waited for it to calm down a little, bent down and carried the box outside. The women and children scattered in all directions.

"Whether it be bad medicine or good one, I shall see it today," he said as he carried the box at arm's length like a potent sacrifice. He did not pass through his *obi*, but took the door in the red-earth wall of his compound. His second son, Obika, who had just come in, followed him. Nwafo came closely behind Obika, and the women and children followed fearfully at a good distance. Ezeulu looked back and asked Obika to bring him a matchet. He took the box right outside his compound and finally put it down by the side of the common footpath. He looked back and saw Nwafo and the women and children.

"Every one of you go back to the house. The inquisitive monkey gets a bullet in the face."

They moved back not into the compound but in front of the *obi*. Obika took a matchet to his father who thought for a little while and put the matchet aside and sent him for the spear used in digging up yams. The struggling inside the box was as fierce as ever. For a brief moment Ezeulu wondered whether the wisest thing was not to leave the box there until its owner returned. But what would it mean? That he, Ezeulu, was afraid of whatever power his son had imprisoned in a box. Such a story must never be told of the priest of Ulu.

He took the spear from Obika and wedged its thin end between the box and its lid. Obika tried to take the spear from him, but he would not hear it.

"Stand aside," he told him. "What do you think is fighting inside? Two cocks?" He clenched his teeth in an effort to lever the top open. It was not easy and the old priest was covered in sweat by the time he succeeded in forcing the box. What they saw was enough to blind a man. Ezeulu stood speechless. The women and the children who had watched from afar came running down. Ezeulu's neighbor, Anosi, who was passing by, branched in, and soon a big crowd had gathered. In the broken box lay an exhausted royal python.

"May the Great Deity forbid," said Anosi.

"An abomination has happened," said Akueke.

Matefi said: "If this is medicine, may it lose its potency."

Ezeulu let the spear fall from his hand. "Where is Oduche?" he asked. No one answered. "I said where is Oduche?" His voice was terrible.

Nwafo said he had gone to church. The sacred python now raised its head above the edge of the box and began to move in its dignified and unhurried way.

"Today I shall kill the boy with my own hands," said Ezeulu as he picked up the matchet which Obika had brought at first.

"May the Great Deity forbid such a thing," said Anosi.

"I have said it."

Oduche's mother began to cry, and the other women joined her. Ezeulu walked slowly back to his *obi* with the matchet. The royal python slid away into the bush.

"What is the profit of crying?" Anosi asked Ugoye. "Won't you find where your son is and tell him not to return home today?"

"He has spoken the truth, Ugoye," said Matefi. "Send him away to your kinsmen. We are fortunate the python is not dead."

From Arrow of God, *by Chinua Achebe, The John Day Company, Inc., 1964.*

The Geography Lesson

by MONGO BETI

Mongo Beti was born in the former French Cameroons in 1932. Rebelling against the Catholic mission where he started his schooling, he finished his education in France. He married a French girl and settled down to live and teach in Paris. There he became the center of a lively circle, both radical and literary.

Mongo Beti's third novel, *Mission to Kala*, was published both in French and English (1958). His gift for dialogue is especially evident in this story of a student who returns to his native village after failing his Lycée examinations. To the student's surprise he is treated by his relatives and friends as a prodigy of learning. They defer to him as a "scholar."

His uncle persuades him to undertake a difficult mission to a small bush town to bring back a runaway wife, saying, "*You* are that formidable man, *you* speak with the voice of thunder, and have never suspected your own powers. Shall I tell you what your special thunder is? Your certificates, your learning, your knowledge of white men's secrets."

When he arrives in Kala, Metza is invited to dinner with his cousin Zambo and his uncle, and finds himself the target of a barrage of questions about the world outside their personal experience.

人 "Are there many White children at your school?" my hostess inquired.

I said yes, there were a lot.

"More White than Colored?"

"No; not nearly so many."

"What are they like, these White children? Tell us what they're like," she persisted.

"Heavens—just like children anywhere, the world over—"

"Really? Just like ordinary children?"

"Exactly," I said. "They have rows, and fights, and are insubordinate—there's no difference at all."

91

A man's voice broke in. "And in class," he said, loudly. "Are they cleverer than you in class?"

"No. They aren't either more clever or more stupid than we are. They're just the same as—us—a mixed bunch."

"Will the learned gentleman please explain, then," the same voice went on, in astonished tones, "how it is that their minds work faster than ours?"

"They don't. They grasp a point no faster and no slower than we do."

"Well, well. That's really surprising. They ought to be quicker in the uptake, though, oughtn't they?"

"Why should they?" another man's voice broke in. "Why are you so determined that they should be quicker than our children? We don't breed young animals, do we? What are you thinking of?"

"How can you ask such a question?" the first man replied. "It's perfectly reasonable to suppose that White children should learn faster than Black. What are they being taught? Their ancestral wisdom, not ours, isn't that so? Who invented airplanes and trains and cars and steamships? The Whites. Very well, then. Now if it was our ancestral wisdom that was taught in this school, it would be normal to expect Colored children to learn faster than Whites, wouldn't it?"

The company were divided over this question, which provoked several fine displays of rhetoric, not least from the women. The argument went on till the man who had opposed this ingenious theory—having, to judge by the peremptory fashion in which he called the room to silence, thought up a superb and irrefutable gambit—now declared brusquely: "Listen to me, all of you. Here's my personal opinion, for what it's worth. It's by no means certain that it was the Whites who invented cars and airplanes and all that. When you talk about Colored folk, you mean us, don't you? All right, we're nobodies. But what about all the other Colored peoples, all over the world? How can you be sure that they don't make planes and trains and cars?"

To judge by the approving murmur which greeted it, this argument was a popular one. Finally the first man admitted that its proposer was probably right, yes, he might very well be right.

Scarcely was dinner over when my hostess began to fire a whole fusillade of questions at me. She sat next to me and went on absolutely ruthlessly, dragging detailed explanations out of me, and going back over muddled points with a needle-sharp clarity. She obviously was aware of all my weaknesses and shortcomings; she was equipped to give me the most humiliating oral I had ever been through in my life.

Then they all got down to it, and interrogated me non-stop. As there was a great number of them, they were often all asking me questions at once. This embarrassed me horribly, because I didn't know which ones to answer first: They varied in subject, but were all of equal interest. I was utterly disconcerted, and one thing embarrassed me in particular: the attitude of the women and young girls. They absolutely devoured me with their eyes, and the expressions they wore were so unequivocal that I could not help recognizing them for what they were at once, despite my natural modesty. It was like reading a young peasant girl's passionate love-letter.

Sometimes I glanced at Zambo, who squatted in a corner miserably, indifferent to the atmosphere of enthusiasm permeating the room, perhaps even hating it, but in any case the disregarded odd man out. Occasionally I caught my uncle's eye, too; he looked strangely complacent, rather like an old French peasant who has just married off his daughter to the richest, best-looking young man in the district. He was gay and pleased, and obviously willing me to make a success of the occasion.

Soon Zambo got up and left, abandoning me to my unhappy dilemma, rather as though I were a drowning man being sucked under by the current, and beyond any hope of rescue. I was the most unlucky man in the world, I thought.

Apart from anything else, I was stifling. The room was far too hot and very small; the air was thick with smoke, and smelt of palm-wine, tobacco, and chewing-gum. I made a tremendous effort, which pushed me sluggishly, like a sack of coconuts, on to the platform of benevolent resignation and cordiality reserved for scapegoats such as myself. I no longer felt any desire to discourage the attentions of my audience; I abandoned my useless and egotistic attempts at revolt. I began to chew the local gum myself, and certainly nothing I could have done would have pleased them more.

"Look at him!" they exclaimed, audibly. "Look, he's not snobbish, for all his learning. He's chewing gum just like us."

At such moments, conscious of all those staring eyes converging on me like so many rays, I got the feeling that the atmospheric gravity had at least doubled its pressure. There was a hurricane-lamp burning on the table, its glass bulging and rounded like an old man's belly. The light it gave out was in fact not very strong, but to me it seemed as blinding as a searchlight set up at the same distance—at point-blank range, in fact. As a result they all saw me very clearly, and I could hardly make them out at all.

I sat there wondering to what extremes of idiocy the whole business could go. Lucky for me, I thought, that my friends couldn't see me pontificating in this half-witted fashion—and, anyway, what did it matter? I realized that my affection for these people outweighed any resentment I felt at my own ridiculous position. It was certainly a serious occasion as far as they were concerned.

"And what do the Whites teach you?" my hostess was still inquiring mercilessly.

"Oh—heaps of things—"

"Come on, then: tell us them."

"Would you understand if I did?" I snapped. The remark was greeted with a murmur of disappointment. God, what a clanger, I thought. If I'm going to stay—and I must—I've got to behave myself.

"Listen to me, my boy," said an old man, getting to his feet and interspersing his remarks with placatory gestures, as though he were soothing a baby. "Listen: it doesn't matter if we don't understand. Tell us all the same. For you the Whites are the real people, the people who matter, because you know their language. But we can't speak French, and we never went to school. For us you are the White man—you are the only person who can explain these mysteries to us. If you care for us at all, my son, do this thing for us. If you refuse, we've probably lost our only chance of ever being able to learn the White man's wisdom. Tell us, my son."

He has a point there, I thought. These people were all so damnably persuasive.

"All right, then," I said. "They teach us—let's see—well, geography—"

"Geography?" exclaimed someone, fumbling over the unfamiliar syllables. "What's that?"

I gave them what must have been the most feeble, certainly

the most arguable definition of geography ever presented to any audience. I had never tried to formulate such a definition in my native tongue before, and now the thing had to be done for an audience who hung on my every word. Then, to make my ideas more intelligible, I decided to illustrate them with an example. I found myself (somewhat to my surprise) telling these simple people about New York—an inconceivable city to them, with its seven million inhabitants and skyscrapers of anything up to seventy-five floors, soaring up for a thousand feet. It was child's play to describe New York, probably because my only knowledge of it derived from the cinema. There was no longer any question of my drying up. I warmed to the theme, losing myself in an intoxicated sea of details. I imagined that my audience would be galvanized by the picture I conjured up; but, in fact, I went to all this trouble for nothing. The really astonishing thing, which still bothers me in retrospect, was that America left these simple-minded people stone-cold indifferent.

I quickly changed the subject, just as the other evening the young guitarist had switched his rhythms; and without exactly knowing why, I played a Russian chord, to which they at once responded. I probably acted on instinct; since I could spot at once what touched them or stirred them to enthusiasm. I must have been closer to them psychologically than I dreamed at the time.

"Russia?" they asked. "Where's that?"

"In the east, where the sun rises," I said. "The inhabitants are called Russians."

I carefully avoided mentioning the more complicated aspects of Soviet farming and spread myself as fully as possible on the kolkhoz system. A kolkhoz, I declared, with an absolutely straight face, was a kind of field held in common, where every person worked for several days a week, spending the rest of his time on his own private allotment. After the harvest, the produce from the kolkhoz was distributed to each family according to their needs. At this point in my exposition the whole room exploded like a Brock's Benefit.

"Those sound like sensible people," said one man, and another exclaimed how fond of one another they must be. "A very pleasant country to live in," observed a third, and others echoed him. I was

95

astounded at the effect I was having. Full marks for this one, boy, I thought.

I decided to work this miraculous vein till it ran out. I waxed lyrical over tractors, and State farms, and the superb administration of rural communities. I pointed out what the system had achieved—production increased tenfold since the old days of individual, private cultivation. My audience positively panted with excitement. At one point I stopped to get my breath back—I had talked myself to a standstill: lecturing is by no means a sinecure—and a youngish man took advantage of my silence to comment on my previous remarks.

"These people are very like us at bottom," he declared. "They've got a sense of solidarity. They stand by one another, just as we do. Look at the way our women get through their work at ploughing-time—they all spend a day in one family's fields, and the next in another's, and so on. These people, what d'you call them, boy, eh?—oh yes, Russians—well, these Russians are extraordinarily like us. If only someone would give us some tractors—one to each tribe would do—we'd do just as good work, and perhaps produce ten times the amount we do now, as well. Only one tractor per tribe! But then who on earth would ever give us a tractor?"

Another man broke in, asking me if it was true that the men drove these tractors in the fields? He sounded a little worried. I told him yes, normally it was the men who did this type of work.

"What do the women do with their time, then?"

"They stay at home," I said briskly. "They stay at home to look after the children and manage the household generally. They do sometimes go out in the fields, but only to do light work. In Russia," I added, seeing that the man was by no means resigned to this new scheme of existence, "they consider that, since men are stronger than women, they ought to do the heavy labor; and personally I agree with them. Besides, Russian women are very pretty—they keep their looks right into middle age because they don't have to work so hard."

I knew perfectly well that as my knowledge of real Russian life was very vague and sketchy, my only chance of coming through this ordeal unscathed was to invent my own version. The illusory nature of college learning could hardly have been better illustrated, as I learnt for myself that night. I was not without a certain pride in all I had learnt during the past academic year; yet at the first real test of my knowledge—a test imposed by genuine circumstance, not under the artificial conditions of an examination-room—I had already discovered vast gaps in the frontiers of my tiny kingdom. Now I was desperately trying to plug these gaps, and straining my imagination to the uttermost in the process.

Everything finally has to come to an end, and at last the party broke up. My hostess thanked me for the evening's entertainment, and her husband promised to deliver a little present for me the following morning at my uncle's home.

As we walked back by ourselves my uncle said: "They'll talk about you here for ages, boy."

From Mission to Kala, *by Mongo Beti, Heinemann Educational Books Ltd., 1958.*

My Husband's Tongue Is Bitter

by OKOT P'BITEK

Okot p'Bitek is a young philosopher and poet who was born in 1931 of the Acholi tribe in Northern Uganda. Educated both in Africa and England, he has studied education, law, and anthropology. Football and the theater are among his other interests. He has had one novel published in the Luo language, and two long poems in English, *Song of Lawino* (1966) and *Song of Ocol* (1970). He served as Director of the National Cultural Center in Uganda and founded the Gulu Festival.

The selection which follows is from *Song of Lawino*. It is a wife's lament which can be heard all over Africa. She voices the sorrows of a woman brought up in traditional tribal society who is married to a man educated in the ways of the white man.

My clansmen, I cry
Listen to my voice:
The insults of my man
Are painful beyond bearing.

My husband abuses me together with my parents;
He says terrible things about my mother
And I am so ashamed!

He abuses me in English
And he is so arrogant.

My husband pours scorn
On Black People,
He behaves like a hen
That eats its own eggs
A hen that should be imprisoned
Under a basket.

98

His eyes grow large
Deep black eyes
Ocol's eyes resemble those of the Nile Perch!
He becomes fierce
Like a lioness with cubs,
He begins to behave like a mad hyena.

He says Black People are primitive
And their ways are utterly harmful,
Their dances are mortal sins
They are ignorant, poor and diseased!

Ocol says he is a modern man,
A progressive and civilized man,
He says he has read extensively and widely
And he can no longer live with a thing like me
Who cannot distinguish between good and bad,
He says I am just a village woman,
I am of the old type,
And no longer attractive.

Ocol is no longer in love with the old type.
He is in love with a modern girl;
The name of the beautiful one
Is Clementine.

Brother, when you see Clementine!
The beautiful one aspires
To look like a white woman;
Her lips are red-hot
Like glowing charcoal,
She resembles the wild cat
That has dipped its mouth in blood,
Her mouth is like raw yaws
It looks like an open ulcer,
Like the mouth of a fiend!
Tina dusts powder on her face
And it looks so pale;
She resembles the wizard
Getting ready for the midnight dance;

And she believes
That this is beautiful
Because it resembles the face of a white woman!
Her body resembles
The ugly coat of the hyena;
Her neck and arms
Have real human skins!
She looks as if she has been struck
By lightning;
Or burnt like the *kongoni*
In a fire hunt.

I am not unfair to my husband,
I do not complain
Because he wants another woman
Whether she is young or aged!
Who has ever prevented men
From wanting women?

The competition for a man's love
Is fought at the cooking place
When he returns from the field
Or from the hunt.

You win him with a hot bath
and sour porridge.
The wife who brings her meal first
Whose food is good to eat,
Whose dish is hot
Whose face is bright
And whose heart is clean
And whose eyes are not dark
Like the shadows:

The wife who jokes freely
Who eats in the open
Not in the bed room,
One who is not dull
Like stale beer,

Such is the woman who becomes
The head-dress keeper.

I do not block my husband's path
From his new wife.
If he likes, let him build for her
An iron roofed house on the hill!
I do not complain,
My grass thatched house is enough for me.

I am not angry
With the woman with whom
I share my husband,
I do not fear to compete with her.

Listen Ocol, my old friend,
The ways of your ancestors
Are good,
Their customs are solid
And not hollow
They are not thin, not easily breakable
They cannot be blown away
By the winds
Because their roots reach deep into the soil.

I do not understand
The way of foreigners
But I do not despise their customs.
Why should you despise yours?

Listen, my husband,
You are the son of a Chief.
The pumpkin in the old homestead
Must not be uprooted!

From Song of Lawino, *by Okot p'Bitek, East African Publishing House, 1966.*

The Untilled Field

by JOSEPH WAIGURU

Joseph Waiguru was born in Nyeri, Kenya, in 1939. He was a student at Makerere University College, Kampala, from 1959 to 1964, during the first years of Independence. He studied English, Economics, and Political Science. His work in English under David Cook encouraged him to combine criticism with creative writing. His stories and poems have been broadcast by the British Broadcasting Company African Service and by Radio Uganda, and are now published for the first time in David Cook's anthology, *Origin East Africa*.

人   Mwangi thought of nobody else but his wife Wanjiku. She was lazy; always going to work late in the day when everybody else had already done half their digging. By the time she reached the field, it was already so hot that to lift a hoe was almost a torture. The heat of the sun disturbed the flies from their rest so that they buzzed around her as she slowly lifted her tool. She had to drop it again to strike the biting fly. There was no point in continuing to labor. After all she would come here tomorrow and the day after. Even the day after that she would be here.

She sat down in the cool shade of a *muthaithi* tree and soon fell asleep. Mwangi watched her from afar, where he was herding his cattle. By now it was his field alone which lay untilled, and the rains were near. An hour went by, two hours, three hours and Wanjiku still slept. Was she dead? Could a snake have bitten her? He would have heard cries. Mwangi decided to find out.

He left his cattle and slowly approached the spot where his wife lay. He looked back to see whether the cattle would stray far before he returned to them. Satisfied that they would not, he moved on. He quickened his step, hoping that she would wake up before he reached her. He did not want to show her that he had all along been watching her. But he would never be satisfied until he knew whether or not his wife's expression betrayed any guilty conscience for the neglect of her duties. He changed his pace. Quietly he stalked her as a lion stealthily hunts a deer, or like a cobra just about to strike. He feared to make a rustle.

Mwangi remembered the cows and goats he had paid her father as a dowry. The marriage feast surpassed any he had ever seen, or even heard of. Is this the wife he had married, the woman he had so dearly paid for? Was she created only for child-bearing? What was she for? He would soon learn from the appearance of her face when asleep. He reached her.

There she was, sleeping like a log, except that a log does not breathe. The sight shocked him. Where he had expected to find at least a slight element of guilt, he found only a pure, peaceful, calm face—only blissful happiness. Wanjiku was content to lie idle, a basket, a hoe and a *panga* by her-side.

He stood there, not knowing what to do next. His mind was as blank as a white sheet. At last, his lips set as if to smile and then changed into a grin which looked sinister. His jaw dropped, showing milky-white teeth. He thought of beating her with the thick walking-stick he was carrying and then that evening sending her packing to her father's. No, he would gain nothing by such an action.

After all, women were just little, defenseless creatures. He was annoyed when he realized he could not beat her. Oh, but she was beautiful too! He knelt down and touched her lips with the back of his right hand, moving the fingers along them. She stirred and turned face downwards, but did not open her eyes. Mwangi was furious with himself and with her. He turned to see what work she had done—there was no sign of freshly dug ground. She should have finished this field since she informed him that she had started on it, but at this rate she would not have completed even half of it before the rains poured madly down. Would she ever wake? After deciding not to disturb her, he quickly went back to his cattle.

Mwangi thought for a moment. Then he rounded up his animals and drove them home at the greatest speed the beasts could manage. He shut them in a shed, though it was only two o'clock, and hurriedly took a hoe from his hut. There was no time to lose, and within fifteen minutes he was back in the field. Wanjiku was still

Making a Pot   MSANGI

sleeping. He would not wake her up: that he had resolved the moment he decided to take his cattle home.

Mwangi planted his feet firmly on the ground and lifted the hoe high over his head. He struck the first blow on the too, too soft earth. He struck another and yet another. Thud, thud, thud went the hoe, on and on. He labored and was never tired. Drops of sweat flowed down his face and their sour taste only added more energy to his stout arms.

Lumps of earth were following him as he proceeded farther and farther away from where he started. He neither looked back nor forwards, lest the length of the field he had to dig should discourage him. All he saw was the place where he had to push in his hoe. He labored on.

He was twenty yards away when Wanjiku woke up and saw him. What was it? She looked up at the sun in the sky and knew it was half past three; the time she started collecting firewood. Was she always sleeping like this? She watched mesmerized as he dug and dug.

Mwangi stopped for breath without looking back. The sweat was too much. His shirt and trousers were glued to his body. He dropped the hoe, took off his clothes and then cut a banana leaf which he tied round his waist. He then picked up the hoe, lifted it and once again resumed his work.

As Wanjiku watched, he moved farther and farther away from her. He furiously attacked the ground which was becoming as stubborn as a mule. His black frame dripped wet and as drops of sweat flowed down his whole body, they cut lines in the red dust which had stuck to his skin. The more he turned the ground, the madder he grew.

Suddenly, Wanjiku stood up and picked up her hoe. She rushed to his side and wanted to stop him. He barked at her and she gave up. Within a few minutes, he was ahead of her by six feet. He would not rest until the work was over. Was he her husband any more? Certainly.

With a force she had never felt before, she went to his right-hand side and started digging. She would dig as long as he dug, and stop when he stopped. If they were to die, they would die together. She soon caught up and fell into step with him. The earth was softer than she had ever known it to be. They dug and never stopped to see what work they had done.

Neither was thinking of the other but only of their field. The sun was, however, faster than they were and the last flickers of light would soon disappear. They went on and on, and neither dared to speak.

It was cool now, and a soft breeze blew over them but was not enough to dry away the sweat. In unison, they attacked the enemy who had brought them together. It grew dark but they never thought of going home. They saw the edge of the field and stopped petrified. Only two feet away! They looked at one another and then at the edge. They turned back and could not see where they had started. With smiles they embraced and fell down. There they lay till the following morning when they woke up as if from a dream, completely satisfied of their future life together.

The Sweetest Thing

There is in this world something
That surpasses all other things
in sweetness
It is sweeter than honey
It is sweeter than salt
It is sweeter than sugar
It is sweeter than all
existing things.
This thing is sleep.
When you are conquered by sleep
Nothing can ever prevent you
Nothing can stop you from sleeping.
When you are conquered by sleep
And numerous millions arrive
Millions arrive to disturb you
But millions will find you asleep.

The Moon

The moon lights the earth
It lights the earth but still
The night must remain the night.
The night cannot be like the day.
The moon cannot dry our washing
Just like a woman cannot be a man
Just like a black can never be white.

The Well

There is a well
That has five kinds of water.
There is sugared water
and salty water
There is tasteless water
and bitter water
The fifth water is red
red like blood.
This well is the head.

108

The Winner

by BARBARA KIMENYE

Barbara Kimenye is a Ugandan journalist, author of two collections of short stories, *Kalasanda* and *Kalasanda Revisited*, both published in 1965. In these stories, she recreates the ups and downs of everyday life in rural Uganda. The time is now. Modern inventions such as automobiles, radios, and telegrams exist side by side with the traditional way of life.

The people in *The Winner* live in mud and wattle huts behind which each householder owns a small bit of land, his *shamba*. Here he grows most of his own food—bananas and coffee, sweet potatoes, beans, and cabbages—with perhaps a small surplus to give away or sell. The old men have their cronies and the women their ambitions and their jealousies.

When Pius Ndawula won the football pools, overnight he seemed to become the most popular man in Buganda. Hosts of relatives converged upon him from the four corners of the kingdom: cousins and nephews, nieces and uncles, of whose existence he had never before been aware, turned up in Kalasanda by the busload, together with crowds of individuals who, despite their downtrodden appearance, assured Pius that they and they alone were capable of seeing that his money was properly invested—preferably in their own particular businesses!

Also lurking around Pius's unpretentious mud hut were newspaper reporters, slick young men weighed down with cameras and sporting loud checked caps or trilbies set at conspicuously jaunty angles, and serious young men from Radio Uganda who were anxious to record Pius's delight at his astonishing luck for the edification of the Uganda listening public.

The rest of Kalasanda were so taken by surprise that they could only call and briefly congratulate Pius before being elbowed out of the way by his more garrulous relations. All, that is to say,

109

except Pius's greatest friend Salongo, the custodian of the Ssaba-langira's tomb. He came and planted himself firmly in the house, and nobody attempted to move him. Almost blind, and very lame, he tottered out with the aid of a stout stick. Just to see him arrive had caused a minor sensation in the village, for he hadn't left the tomb for years. But recognizing at last a chance to house Ssabalan-gira's remains in a state befitting his former glory, made the slow tortuous journey worthwhile to Salongo.

Nantondo hung about long enough to have her picture taken with Pius. Or rather, she managed to slip beside him just as the cameras clicked, and so it was that every Uganda newspaper, on the following day, carried a front-page photograph of "Mr. Pius Ndawula and his happy wife," a caption that caused Pius to shake with rage and threaten legal proceedings, but over which Nantondo gloated as she proudly showed it to everybody who visited.

"Tell us, Mr. Ndawula, what do you intend to do with all the money you have won . . .?"

"Tell us, Mr. Ndawula, how often have you completed pools coupons . . .?"

"Tell us . . . Tell us . . . Tell us . . ."

Pius's head was reeling under this bombardment of questions, and he was even more confused by Salongo's constant nudging and muttered advice to "Say nothing!" Nor did the relatives make things easier. Their persistent clamoring for his attention, and the way they kept shoving their children under his nose, made it impossible for him to think, let alone talk.

It isn't at all easy, when you have lived for sixty-five years in complete obscurity, to adjust yourself in a matter of hours to the role of a celebrity, and the strain was beginning to tell.

Behind the hut—Pius had no proper kitchen—gallons of tea were being boiled, whilst several of the female cousins were employed in ruthlessly hacking down the bunches of *matoke* from his meagre plantains, to cook food for everybody. One woman—she had introduced herself as Cousin Sarah—discovered Pius's hidden store of banana beer, and dished it out to all and sundry as though it were her own. Pius had become very wary of Cousin Sarah. He didn't like the way in which she kept loudly remarking that he needed a woman about the place, and he was even more seriously alarmed when suddenly Salongo gave him a painful dig in the ribs and muttered, "You'll have to watch that one—she's a sticker!"

Everybody who came wanted to see the telegram that announced Pius's win. When it had arrived at the Ggombolola Headquarters—the postal address of everyone living within a radius of fifteen miles—Musisi had brought it out personally, delighted to be the bearer of such good tidings. At Pius's request he had gone straight away to tell Salongo, and then back to his office to send an acknowledgment on behalf of Pius to the pools firm, leaving the old man to dream rosy dreams.

An extension of his small coffee *shamba*, a new roof on his house—or maybe an entirely new house—concrete blocks this time, with a verandah perhaps. Then there were hens. Salongo and he had always said there was money in hens these days, now that the women ate eggs and chicken; not that either of them agreed with the practice. Say what you liked, women who ate chicken and eggs were fairly asking to be infertile! That woman Welfare officer who came around snooping occasionally, tried to say it was all nonsense, that chicken meat and eggs made bigger and better babies. Well, they might look bigger and better, but nobody could deny that they were fewer! Which only goes to show.

But news spreads fast in Africa—perhaps the newspapers have contacts in the pools offices. Anyway, before the telegram had even reached Pius, announcements were appearing in the local newspapers, and Pius was still quietly lost in his private dreams when the first batch of visitors arrived. At first, he was at a loss to understand what was happening. People he hadn't seen for years and only recognized with difficulty fell upon him with cries of joy.

"Cousin Pius, the family are delighted!"

"Cousin Pius, why have you not visited us all this time?"

Pius was pleased to see his nearest and dearest gathered around him. It warmed his old heart once more to find himself in the bosom of his family, and he welcomed them effusively. The second crowd to arrive were no less well received, but there was a marked coolness on the part of their forerunners.

However, as time had gone by and the flood of strange faces had gained momentum, Pius's *shamba* had come to resemble a political meeting. All to be seen from the door of the house was a turbulent sea of white *kanzus* and brilliant *busutis*, and the house itself was full of people and tobacco smoke.

The precious telegram was passed from hand to hand until it was reduced to a limp fragment of paper with the lettering partly obliterated: not that it mattered very much, for only a few members of the company could read English.

"Now, Mr. Ndawula, we are ready to take the recording." The speaker was a slight young man wearing a checked shirt. "I shall ask you a few questions, and you simply answer me in your normal voice." Pius looked at the leather box with its two revolving spools, and licked his lips.

"Say nothing!" came a hoarse whisper from Salongo.

The young man steadfastly ignored him, and went ahead in his best BBC manner. "Well, first of all, Mr. Ndawula, let me congratulate you on your winning the pools. Would you like to tell our listeners what it feels like suddenly to find yourself rich?" There was an uncomfortable pause, during which Pius stared mesmerized at the racing spools and the young man tried frantically to span the gap by asking, "I mean, have you any plans for the future?"

Pius swallowed audibly, and opened his mouth to say something, but shut it again when Salongo growled, "Tell him nothing!"

The young man snapped off the machine, shaking his head in exasperation. "Look here, sir, all I want you to do is to say something—I'm not asking you to make a speech. Now, I'll tell you what. I shall ask you again what it feels like suddenly to come into money, and you say something like 'It was a wonderful surprise, and naturally I feel very pleased'—and will you ask your friend not to interrupt! Got it? Okay, off we go!"

The machine was again switched on, and the man brightly put the question, "Now, Mr. Ndawula, what does it feel like to win the pools?"

Pius swallowed, then quickly chanted in a voice all off key, "It was a wonderful surprise and naturally I feel very happy and will you ask your friend not to interrupt!" The young man nearly wept. This happened to be his first assignment as a radio interviewer, and it looked like being his last. He switched off the machine and mourned his lusterless future, groaning.

At that moment Cousin Sarah caught his eye. "Perhaps I can help you," she said. "I am Mr. Ndawula's cousin." She made this pronouncement in a manner that suggested Pius had no others. The young man brightened considerably. "Well, madam, if you could tell me something about Mr. Ndawula's plans, I would be most grateful."

Cousin Sarah folded her arms across her imposing bosom, and when the machine again started up, she was off. Yes, Mr. Ndawula was very happy about the money. No, she didn't think he had any definite plans on how to spend it—with all these people about he didn't have time to think. Yes, Mr. Ndawula lived completely alone, but she was prepared to stay and look after him for as long as he needed her. Here a significant glance passed between the other women in the room, who clicked their teeth and let out long "Eeeeeehs!" of incredulity. Yes, she believed she was Mr. Ndawula's nearest living relative by marriage . . .

Pius listened to her confident aplomb with growing horror, whilst Salongo frantically nudged him and whispered, "There! What did I tell you? That woman's a sticker."

Around three in the afternoon, *matoke* and tea were served— the *matoke* on wide fresh plantain leaves, since Pius owned only three plates, and the tea in anything handy—tin cans, old jars, etc.— because he was short of cups, too.

Pius ate very little, but he was glad of the tea. He had shaken hands with so many people that his arms ached, and he was tired of the chatter and the comings and goings in his house of all these strangers. Most of all he was tired of Cousin Sarah, who insisted on treating him like an idiot invalid. She kept everybody else at bay, as far as she possibly could, and when one woman plonked a sticky fat baby on his lap, Cousin Sarah dragged the child away as though it were infectious. Naturally, a few cross words were exchanged between Sarah and the fond mother, but by this time Pius was past caring.

Yosefu Mukasa and Kibuka called in the early evening, when some of the relatives were departing with effusive promises to come again tomorrow. They were both alarmed at the weariness they saw on Pius's face. The old man looked utterly worn out, his skin grey and sickly. Also, they were a bit taken aback by the presence of Cousin Sarah, who pressed them to take tea and behaved in every respect as though she was mistress of the house.

"I believe my late husband knew you very well, sir," she

113

told Yosefu. "He used to be a Miruka chief in Buyaga County. His name was Kivumbi."

"Ah, yes," Yosefu replied. "I remember Kivumbi very well indeed. We often hunted together. I was sorry to hear of his death. He was a good man."

Cousin Sarah shrugged her shoulders. "Yes, he was a good man. But what the Lord giveth, He also taketh away." Thus was the late Kivumbi dismissed from the conversation.

Hearing all this enabled Pius to define the exact relationship between himself and Cousin Sarah, and even by Kiganda standards it was virtually nonexistent, for the late Kivumbi had been the stepson of one of Pius's cousins.

"Your stroke of luck seems to have exhausted you, Pius," Kibuka remarked, when he and Yosefu were seated on the rough wooden chairs brought forth by Cousin Sarah.

Salongo glared at the world in general and snarled, "Of course he is exhausted. Who wouldn't be with all these scavengers collected to pick his bones?" Pius hushed him as one would a child. "No, no, Salongo. It is quite natural that my family should gather round me at a time like this. Only I fear I am perhaps a little too old for all this excitement."

Salongo spat expertly through the open doorway, narrowly missing a group of guests who were preparing to bed down, and said, "That woman doesn't think he is too old. She's out to catch him. I've seen her type elsewhere."

Yosefu's mouth quirked with amusement at the thought that "elsewhere" could only mean the Ssabalangira's tomb, which Salongo had guarded for the better part of his adult life. "Well, she's a fine woman," he remarked. "But see here, Pius," he went on, "don't be offended by my proposal, but wouldn't it be better if you came and stayed with us at Mutunda for tonight? Miriamu would love to have you, and you look as though you need a good night's rest, which you wouldn't get here—those relatives of yours outside are preparing a fire and are ready to dance the night away!"

"I think that's a wonderful idea!" said Cousin Sarah, bouncing in to remove the tea cups. "You go with Mr. Mukasa, Cousin Pius. The change will do you as much good as the rest. And don't worry about your home—I shall stay here and look after things."

Pius hesitated. "Well, I think I shall be all right here—I don't like to give Miriamu any extra work . . ."

Salongo muttered, "Go to Yosefu's. You don't want to be left alone in the house with that woman—there's no knowing what she might get up to . . ."

"I'll pack a few things for you, Pius," announced Cousin Sarah and bustled off before anything more could be said, pausing only long enough to give Salongo a look that was meant to wither him on the spot.

So Pius found himself being driven away to Mutunda in Yosefu's car, enjoying the pleasant sensation of not having to bother about a thing. Salongo too had been given a lift to as near the tomb as the car could travel, and his wizened old face was contorted into an irregular smile, for Pius had promised to help him build a new house for the Ssabalangira. For him the day had been well spent, despite Cousin Sarah.

Pius spent an enjoyable evening with the Mukasas. They had a well-cooked supper, followed by a glass of cool beer as they sat back and listened to the local news on the radio. Pius had so far relaxed as to tell the Mukasas modestly that he had been interviewed by Radio Uganda that morning, and when Radio Newsreel was announced they waited breathlessly to hear his voice. But instead of Pius, Cousin Sarah came booming over the air. Until that moment, the old man had completely forgotten the incident of the tape-recording. In fact, he had almost forgotten Cousin Sarah. Now it all came back to him with a shiver of apprehension. Salongo was right. That woman did mean business! It was a chilling thought. However, it didn't cause him to lose any sleep. He slept like a cherub, as if he didn't have a care in the world.

Because he looked so refreshed in the morning, Miriamu insisted on keeping him at Mutunda for another day. "I know you feel better, but after seeing you yesterday, I think a little holiday with us will do you good. Go home tomorrow, when the excitement has died down a bit," she advised.

Soon after lunch, as Pius was taking a nap in a chair on the verandah, Musisi drove up in the landrover, with Cousin Sarah by his side. Miriamu came out to greet them, barely disguising her curiosity about the formidable woman about whom she had heard

115

so much. The two women sized each other up and decided to be friends.

Meanwhile, Musisi approached the old man. "Sit down, son," Pius waved him to a chair at his side. "Miriamu feeds me so well it's all I can do to keep awake."

"I am glad you are having a rest, sir." Musisi fumbled in the pocket of his jacket. "There is another telegram for you. Shall I read it?" The old man sat up expectantly and said, "If you'll be so kind."

Musisi first read the telegram in silence, then he looked at Pius and commented, "Well, sir, I'm afraid it isn't good news."

"Not good news? Has somebody died?"

Musisi smiled. "Well, no. It isn't really as bad as that. The thing is, the pools firm say that owing to an unfortunate oversight they omitted to add, in the first telegram, that the prize money is to be shared among three hundred other people."

Pius was stunned. Eventually he murmured, "Tell me, how much does that mean I shall get?"

"Three hundred into seventeen thousand pounds won't give you much over a thousand shillings."

To Musisi's astonishment, Pius sat back and chuckled. "More than a thousand shillings!" he said. "Why, that's a lot of money!"

"But it's not, when you expected so much more."

"I agree. And yet, son, what would I have done with all those thousands of pounds? I am getting past the age when I need a lot."

Miriamu brought a mat onto the verandah and she and Cousin Sarah made themselves comfortable near the men. "What a disappointment!" cried Miriamu, but Cousin Sarah sniffed and said, "I agree with Cousin Pius. He wouldn't know what to do with seventeen thousand pounds, and the family would be hanging round his neck forevermore."

At mention of Pius's family, Musisi frowned. "I should warn you, sir, those relatives of yours have made a terrific mess of your shamba—your plantains have been stripped—and Mrs. Kivumbi here," nodding at Sarah, "was only just in time to prevent them digging up your sweet potatoes."

"Yes, Cousin Pius," added Sarah. "It will take us some time

to put the *shamba* back in order. They've trodden down a whole bed of young beans."

"Oh, dear," said Pius weakly. "This is dreadful news."

"Don't worry. They will soon disappear when I tell them there is no money, and then I shall send for a couple of my grandsons to come and help us do some replanting." Pius could not help but admire the way Sarah took things in her stride.

Musisi rose from his chair. "I'm afraid I can't stay any longer, so I will go now and help Cousin Sarah clear the crowd, and see you tomorrow to take you home." He and Sarah climbed back into the landrover and Sarah waved energetically until the vehicle was out of sight.

"Your cousin is a fine woman," Miriamu told Pius, before going indoors. Pius merely grunted, but for some odd reason he felt the remark to be a compliment to himself.

All was quiet at Pius's home when Musisi brought him home next day. He saw at once that his *shamba* was well-nigh wrecked, but his drooping spirits quickly revived when Sarah placed a mug of steaming tea before him, and sat on a mat at his feet, explaining optimistically how matters could be remedied. Bit by bit he began telling her what he planned to do with the prize money, ending with, "Of course, I shan't be able to do everything now, especially since I promised Salongo something for the tomb."

Sarah poured some more tea and said, "Well, I think the roof should have priority. I noticed last night that there are several leaks. And whilst we're about it, it would be a good idea to build another room on and a small outside kitchen. Mud and wattle is cheap enough, and then the whole place can be plastered. You can still go ahead and extend your coffee. And as for hens, well, I have six good layers at home, as well as a fine cockerel. I'll bring them over!"

Pius looked at her in silence for a long time. She is a fine-looking woman, he thought, and that blue *busuti* suits her. Nobody would ever take her for a grandmother—but why is she so anxious to throw herself at me?

"You sound as if you are planning to come and live here," he said at last, trying hard to sound casual.

Sarah turned to face him and replied, "Cousin Pius, I shall

117

be very frank with you. Six months ago my youngest son got married and brought his wife to live with me. She's a very nice girl,
but somehow I can't get used to having another woman in the
house. My other son is in Kampala, and although I know I would
be welcome there, he too has a wife, and three children, so if I
went there I wouldn't be any better off.

"When I saw that bit about you in the paper, I suddenly remembered—although I don't expect you to—how you were at my
wedding and so helpful to everybody. Well, I thought to myself,
here is somebody who needs a good housekeeper, who needs somebody to keep the leeches off, now that he has come into money.
I came along right away to take a look at you, and I can see I did
the right thing. You do need me." She hesitated for a moment, and
then said, "Only you might prefer to stay alone. . . . I'm so used to
having my own way, I never thought about that before."

Pius cleared his throat. "You're a very impetuous woman,"
was all he could find to say.

A week later, Pius wandered over to the tomb and found
Salongo busily polishing the Ssabalangira's weapons. "I thought you
were dead," growled the custodian, "it is so long since you came
here—but then, this tomb thrives on neglect. Nobody cares that one
of Buganda's greatest men lies here."

"I have been rather busy," murmured Pius. "But I didn't
forget my promise to you. Here! I've brought you a hundred shillings, and I only wish it could have been more. At least it will buy
a few cement blocks."

Salongo took the money and looked at it as if it were crawling
with lice. Grudgingly he thanked Pius and then remarked, "Of
course, you will find life more expensive now that you are keeping
a woman in the house."

"I suppose Nantondo told you, " Pius smiled sheepishly.

"Does it matter who told me?" the custodian replied. "Anyway, never say I didn't warn you. Next thing she'll want will be
ring marriage!"

Pius gave an uncertain laugh. "As a matter of fact, one of
the reasons I came up here was to invite you to the wedding—it's
next month."

Salongo carefully laid down the spear he was rubbing upon

a piece of clean barkcloth and stared at his friend as if he had suddenly grown another head. "What a fool you are! And all this stems from your scribbling noughts and crosses on a bit of squared paper. I knew it would bring no good! At your age you ought to have more sense. Well, all I can advise is that you run while you still have a chance."

For a moment Pius was full of misgivings. Was he, after all, behaving like a fool? Then he thought of Sarah, and the wonders she had worked with his house and his *shamba* in the short time they had been together. He felt reassured.

"Well, I'm getting married, and I expect to see you at both the church and the reception, and if you don't appear, I shall want to know the reason why!" He was secretly delighted at the note of authority in his voice, and Salongo's face was the picture of astonishment.

"All right," he mumbled, "I shall try and come. Before you go, cut a bunch of bananas to take back to your good lady, and there might be some cabbage ready at the back. I suppose I've got to hand it to her. She's the real winner!"

Upper Volta Women at Work   GUIRMA

The Epic of Liyongo

by MUHAMMED KIJUMA

Muhammed Kijuma is a twentieth-century Swahili poet who has written in traditional verse about the Swahili hero, Liyongo. *The Epic of Liyongo,* one of the most famous Swahili legends, is often compared to the King Arthur cycle in English. Both are a mixture of myth and history. The theme of the Liyongo epic is a family feud, a struggle between Liyongo and his cousin for the sultanate of Shaka, or Shagga, in the thirteenth century.

The word *Swahili,* which literally means "coast people" in Arabic, describes the people of Kenya, Tanzania, and Zanzibar, who are descendants of native Bantu tribes and Arab traders. Their language is a mixture of Bantu and Arabic that has evolved over a long period. Swahili is the *lingua franca* of East Africa and is also used in Tanzania as the official language of the National Assembly. It is spoken by more people than any other indigenous language.

Swahili poetry exists in its own right as an important cultural heritage. Originally, it was used to teach the spirit and practice of the Islamic religion. There are many Swahili proverbs, homilies, praise-songs, love songs, serenades, and legends which have been preserved orally for hundreds of years. Among all these *The Epic of Liyongo* is a favorite, a sad and tragic story which brings tears to the eyes of its listeners, no matter how many times they hear it.

As Liyongo grew in perfection   he became a mature man   he
    was a true man   and his beauty of appearance increased.
He was of glorious stature   very broad and tall   he became
    famous in the provinces   and people came to behold him.
If he should stare at you   you would faint right off   death
    would be near   because of the fear that has entered into you.

Rumours came   to the Sultan a thousand of them   and he
    determined with guile   to kill him (Liyongo), understand.

And the Sultan, let me say   feared this man   that he would rob
    him of his kingdom   and he thought of him with suspicion.
Liyongo understood   that they looked for a way to kill
    him   and so he withdrew himself from Pate   and jour-
    neyed on the mainland.
And when the Sultan perceived   that he (Liyongo) had fled
    to the forest   he made contact with the Sanye tribes-
    men   and with Dahalo as well . . .
One day they said   Now let us eat like gentlefolk   the
    kikoa feast is very delicious   a feast that does not fail.
And for the *kikoa* let us eat the dum-palm fruit   we will not
    come to the end of being satisfied with it   those who eat
    the dum-palm fruit   one man shall climb each day.
When their plan was finished   they went their way   for
    those who get the fruit   one man climbs up (alone).
And their idea was   that on the day when he (Liyongo) would
    climb up   they would all shoot him   with one swift volley.
They all made their contribution   and only Liyongo re-
    mained   it is you now, they told him   we want (the fruit),
    understand.
Liyongo spoke quickly   Choose a dum-palm   the fruits that
    you like   so that I may pluck them down for you.
Walking in single file   to choose a tall tree   until they saw
    it   they said to him, It is this one.
When Liyongo saw it   (that) it was a very tall tree   he
    understood the meaning   of those (things) that he had
    thought about them.
For he was always cautious   (even) while he slept he was on
    guard   he knew that they purposed evil   all of them
    together.
And he said to them, Wait   and he took from a shaft   arrows
    and put (one) in the bow-string   and brought down the
    fruit for them.
He brought down the ripe topmost cluster   a cluster with many
    fruits   and they were all agape   and wonder filled their
    hearts.
And they murmured in their hearts   Who can get the better
    of him?   This man is undefeatable   and (to try to best
    him) is to want to be destroyed . . .

Liyongo, what I tell you now   was Shaha of the *gungu* tourneys and of the *mwao* dance   he was their leader   he excelled them all.

The Sultan explained   to the leaders of the town   and said to them in private   Proclaim a *gungu* tourney, he told them.

(A dance) for men and women   and invite Liyongo   I intend to seize him   and this is a secret that I have told you.

And if he gets wind of this   and he Liyongo runs away   (if) you have told him of this   I will slay you all.

And this Sultan   (if he sought) to slay, (no man) could gainsay him   for when he spake it was with certainty   he would fulfil his word at once.

The leaders sent out the invitation   to Liyongo they proclaimed   we will prepare a *mwao* dance   so that we may all be together.

And they prepared the *mwao* dance   with every customary due   the Sultan sent   his men-at-arms about a hundred in number.

They marched in column   with spears and bows and battlestaves   and they seized Liyongo   and he was put in jail.

He was put in jail   and was shut up in a cell   with soldiers at the door   taking turn to watch.

Then there was debate   whether he should be killed   (they said) Let us keep away from this evil of his   I am afraid of Liyongo.

The Sultan thought   It is better to kill him   for if he is spared there would be danger   for he would embroil me in some scheme.

Let him deprive me of my kingdom   and I would gnaw the finger of repentance   it is better for me that this fellow   be killed at once.

His kinsmen then he called   to plan with them the slaying   and they agreed, Indeed, that is the thing to do   we are of the same opinion.

They sent a slave-messenger   to Liyongo and said   Death is certain   they have sent me to tell you.

What is there that you wish?   The Sultan has sent me   you will receive it most certainly   so that you may make your farewells to the world.

He has told you, our Lord   and he has sent me as messenger   that in the space of three days   understand you will be killed.

And he replied, Do not be sure   tell the Sultan   that I wish for a *mwao* dance   and for a *gungu* tourney as well.

And when the Sultan's messenger   had left the cell   there entered a servant-maid   and she brought him food.

And when his (Liyongo's) mother for certain   sent good food   the soldiers would deprive him of it   and would eat the food.

Whenever they brought food to him   the soldiers confiscated it   but on this day he said (to the slave-girl)   Greet my mother for me.

And he spoke (in secret) rhyme   Go and tell her   let my mother prepare   these things that I have told you of (i.e. in the following poem).

O maiden, I send you, for you have not yet been sent, Tell my mother, who is innocent and guileless.

Let her make a loaf for me and put inside a file   So that I can cut through these handcuffs and break my chains.

Let me cross these walls and the roof shall be broken through,   Let me kill men and as they fight I will laugh.

Let me go into the reeds and creep like a fierce snake,   Let me enter the forest and roar like a fierce lion.

I am like a lone tree alone in the treeless wilderness   Without kinsfolk or friends, alone I am left an orphan.

Only my mother is left, to whose whelp's cry her answering will be lent.

Saada perceived his plan   and his mother set the fires   to make a loaf of bran   and sent him the bread.

This bread, understand was of about eight pounds weight and she placed the file inside   and Liyongo received her (the slave-girl).

When the soldiers saw   that it was made of bran they

cursed   Only slaves eat loaves of bran   take it to him, go
    on, get in.
But Liyongo in his cell   broke the loaf in secret   and he saw
    the file inside   and was filled with joy.
And when night was come   and they made ready for the
    dances   and according to custom prepared   the gongs,
    horns, and trumpets.
With the drums and much hand-clapping   and no one being
    absent   it was just like a wedding   and the people watched.
They spread out (rugs) of thread of gold   with silken (fabrics)
    of great beauty   and they sang poems   midst handclaps
    and drumming.
And the poems are these   which they sang together   the
    people sang the chorus   and Liyongo sang the air.

"Mringwari, drummers and chorus, come, you are called by the
    Lord Liyongo   come, Lord Liyongo calls you and his kins-
    man Shaha Mwengo.
Sit on the ceremonial divan, let them gather the dancers of the
    pirouette   let them gather the graceful dancers skilled in
    composing enigmas.
Who know how to rhyme and to dance with the straining of the neck
    you are called, hurry, arise and go, you nobles of high place.
There is a *gungu* ceremony, a nuptial dance, Liyongo's sister is
    being wed   what time people cannot pause in the hall be-
    cause of the crowd.
And when you go don your fine robes and sprinkle yourselves
    with perfume   perfume yourselves with choice *tibu*, fine-
    ground with admixtures of perfuming powders.
And with incense of ambergris and of aloe-wood, cense your spot-
    less garments   cense your silken garments and cloths for
    your loins free from all blemish.
Take the young girls with great show and receive the young men
    with united chorus   and the hand-clappers and singers, take
    the young girls in groups.
Haste, haste, rise up, you are called, today the door is wide   there
    are baskets and baskets of presents and gifts by the hundred.
Of silver and Indian crystal and chains for adorning the

neck   and baskets and baskets of garments in the great hall
    of the Lord Liyongo.

No sooner the people arrive in the hall than there is a great
    throng   with the tall folk on tip-toe and the short ones
    straining their necks.

And everyone says, This is joyful; both those who walk upright
    and those who are bent   for gaining the best of the matter
    without surfeit of strolling about.

At that moment Liyongo arose and calmed his heart and sup-
    pressed his rage   and he calmed himself as he sang while the
    maidens and youths danced around.

And those people cried out all together, It is Liyongo the poet,
    of that there is no mistake   it is the poet chieftain, the poet
    who came to the coastland with battle.

When he beat with a bone on the platter, those with food licked
    china bowls   and those who had food feasted greatly, sitting
    at leisure.

His verses of song were forty, perhaps more   they exceeded four
    tens and that is correct, for let me not state what is wrong.

By the grace of Allah, take these, take these, for the Shah has
    come to the dancing   The Shah has come to the dance; arise
    everyone and let me play."

When the songs' refrain increased   and the drumming loudly
    swelled   he was cutting away there   at his handcuffs and
    chains.

While the clapping increased   he was cutting away quickly   until
    when the clapping stopped   he said to them, Lift up your
    eyes.

And pausing in their dance   Liyongo appeared   and fear fell
    upon them   and they were lost in fright as they ran away.

For they all ran away   there was no one left   Liyongo came
    forth   and returned once again to the mainland . . .

PART 4

PEOPLE OF THE CITY

Whatever else a man does in this world,

let him avoid greed.

—HAUSA PROVERB

In the Streets of Accra

by ANDREW AMANKWA OPOKU

Andrew Amankwa Opoku is a sculptor, farmer, educator, and poet. He was born in the Ashanti region of Ghana in 1912 and grew up there. Trained as a teacher in local schools, he served as headmaster of a primary and middle school for several years.

His literary talents led to his appointment as an editor for the Vernacular Literature Bureau. Later he joined the Ghana Broadcasting System, but before that he did a good deal of writing, including a festival play and several informational books on such subjects as food, travel, and ethics.

He maintains a farm at Aburi and belongs to a group of sculptors called the Akwapin Six.

This is the road!
This is the main highway!
Shouters, we are in the street!
Shooters, restrain your guns!
This is Accra.

This is the town,
The street of the municipality.
Strangers, we are in the streets.
Townsmen, stretch out your sleeping mats
This is Accra.

This is the beach,
This is the pilgrim's haven—
A vast town, but where is the sleeping place?
A great crowd but where is an acquaintance?
This is Accra.

Why this tumult in the street?
Where are the pursuers
That harry every one so?
Let me join the throng.
This is Accra.

Why this head turning
Or is something approaching
That makes you turn jerkily
To look round about you?
This is Accra.

What is this buzzing noise?
What means this paa! paa!
Is this where you walk daily?
And you have lived so long!
This is Accra.

Stay let me have a look.
If such a collection of merchandise
Crowd even the streets so,
What of the market?
This is Accra.

What does this ringing of the bell signify?
This shouting and tinkling noise
This running in the blazing sun
This sweat that is skimmed off with the hands?
This is Accra.

Could women monopolize a street so?
In vain you try to elbow your way through
If you stop they will roll over you
If you turn away a vehicle is knocking you down.
This is Accra.

If it is like this on the edge, how will it be in the depth?
So grand as it is at the backyard

How will it be inside at the dance?
How the electric lights scintillate!
This is Accra.

The dance has become grand indeed!
If you would permit my going in
I should join in too.
No one denies himself his favorite unto death.
This is Accra.

Madam, make room for me to sit!
I only came to have a look
The stranger does not carry the head side of the corpse,
Neither does one go to a strange place to proclaim oneself a savior.
This is Accra.

The Crooks

by GABRIEL OKARA

Gabriel Okara is identified with the eastern region of Nigeria where he was born in the early twenties. He has written short stories and film scripts, and his poems have been published in England, the United States, Sweden, West Germany, and Italy. Before the Biafran war he worked for the Ministry of Information in Enugu, Nigeria. He is now living in Port Harcourt, working for a newspaper syndicate.

His best known work is his novel *The Voice* (1964), in which a young man challenges the Elders of his tribe. The narrative is developed in poetic language which attempts to reproduce the rhythms and idioms of his native Ijaw.

In the story which follows, as in most of his other writing, he is concerned not with black-white relations and conflicts but with African characters in African situations.

人 Their hair was all brown with dust. The clothes they had on were dirty and torn. Their bare feet were as dirty and as brown as their hair. The only luggage they had was a bulging haversack. It was neatly buckled down, and one of them carried it on his shoulder as they walked along the bridge towards Idumota. They were two men who had apparently just arrived from the provinces by lorry.

Traders arriving dirty and dusty from head to foot, and carrying haversacks, are a familiar sight in Lagos. But these two had an air about them of being in a strange place. They walked one behind the other as if they were picking their way in a forest. They avoided bodily contact with the people walking briskly to and fro past them, and were startled over and over again by the strident horns of the cars. They gaped at the lagoon and at the stream of cars, motorcycles and bicycles rushing in both directions across the gigantic bridge.

On the other side, a man was cycling leisurely along on a brand-new bicycle from the Idumota end of the bridge. His shirt and trousers were a dazzling white, and his two-tone black and white shoes were spotless. Tilted over his forehead was a white cork helmet. He put on his brakes as his practiced eyes caught the two men on the other side, stopping now and again to allow people to pass, or looking for an opening through the milling throng on the pavement. The man on the bicycle studied them for a few minutes from his side of the bridge and waited for a break in the traffic. His eyes never left them. An old car wheezed past. He looked quickly left and right. Another car was approaching, but he dashed across narrowly missing death. Safe on the other side he cycled up to the two men.

"Hallo," he said, with a broad smile.

The two men were startled and moved on faster. But the cyclist stuck to them.

"I know you from somewhere," he said, smiling. "I tink na Enugu. I get friend dere and you resemble 'am."

The man carrying the haversack moved to the railings and his partner, turning to the cyclist, said, "Yes, na from Enugu we come. You go for Enugu before?"

"Yes," the cyclist said, "I stay for Enugu long time. Okonkwo be my big friend an' you resembl'am for face. You be him broder?"

"Yes," said the stranger, "one Okonkwo be one farder one moder with me. He be big contractor for Enugu an' we stay for Asata. Na him be your frien'?"

"Ah, na him!" said the cyclist, "we be big frien's. All the lorry wey he get na me arrange for 'am. I be agent for lorry. Dis na firs' time you come for Lagos?"

"Yes, dis na firs' time an' na lorry I wan buy sef."

"Ah, you be lucky man!" said the cyclist. "Waiten be your name?"

"Okonkwo."

"An' your friend?"

"Okeke."

"You be lucky, man. Na lorry I go give person for Ebute

Metta jus' now. Na God say make you meet me. Wayo plenty for here. They wayo you an' take your money for nothin'. How many lorry you wan' buy?"

"Na only one," said Okonkwo.

"Na only one you want. I go fit arrange ma quick for you if na today or tomorrow. Only today late small. But tomorrow I go fit getam for you easy. . . . You get place for stay?"

"The person wey I know, I no know the place he stay. But we go look for am," said Okonkwo.

"Make you no worry," said the cyclist, "you stay for my place. Your broder be my big frien' and he go vex when he hear say I see you an' no keep you for my house. Come we go."

At this invitation Okonkwo shook his head and said, "I fear for dis town. They tell me say wayo plenty. I no know you. You say you be my broder frien' but I dey fear."

"You right," said the cyclist, "you right for fear. But your broder an' me be big frien's an even 'e write me letter say him broder dey come. I forget for tell you de firs' time I see you. So make you no fear. Na God make wey I see you."

"I dey fear O," said Okonkwo, "I dey fear but make I tell Okeke firs'."

With this he went over to Okeke and told him. But Okeke replied with a vigorous shake of his head and said loudly that it was all a trick to get their money. But after much persuasion he reluctantly agreed and they went with the cyclist.

It was evening. Okonkwo and Okeke had eaten a well-pounded *foofoo* and *egusi* soup specially prepared for them and were sitting close together with the haversack between them in their host's parlour. The latter, who had been out for some little time, had just come in with a party of other people. The newcomers were dressed in heavily embroidered *agbadas* and slippers.

"Dis na my frien's," their host said, introducing the people to Okonkwo and Okeke. "I tell dem say I get big 'tranger so they come salute you. All be big people. Na we dey sell motor for dis town."

As the men went forward to shake hands with them, Okonkwo and Okeke looked awed and fidgeted. The hand shaking over, their host beckoned one of his friends into his bedroom.

"You see how them be?" he said, after shutting the door. "They be moo-moo and they get plenty money for bag. Now listen, as I say before we go play big. We go make them win hundred 'redboys.'" When you wan' kill big fish you use big hook and big bait. So you know waiten you go do. Tomorrow we go rich." Then he opened a small wooden box and bringing out three cards, said, "Dis na the cards," as he handed them over to his partner who took them and put them in his pocket. Then the two men went back into the parlor to join the others. Soon drinks were produced from their bag-like pockets and as they drank and boasted of their riches the cards were brought out. They invited Okonko and Okeke to play, but they refused as they didn't know how.

"Very easy," said the man with the cards. "When I cutam putam for ground, you pick dis one," showing them an ace of spades as he continued, "you pick dis one you win, you pick another I win, easy you see."

Still Okonkwo and Okeke were reluctant, but they soon seemed to be impressed by the easy way some of the people won money and joined the game.

"Na one one poun'," said the man with the cards. "Put your money for ground. You take dis you win, you take dis you lose." Okonkwo and Okeke watched carefully as the man cut the cards and put them face downwards on the floor. After studying them for a minute or two Okonkwo picked one card. It was the ace of spades and so he won. So it went on until Okonkwo and Okeke won one hundred pounds between them.

"E do now," said the host as the hundredth pound was being handed over to Okonkwo and Okeke. "E do now. You be lucky people. Tomorrow you go get lorry."

So they stopped playing and the people left. The host also went to bed after showing Okonkwo and Okeke a place to sleep in the parlor.

When he thought that Okonkwo and Okeke would be asleep, their host opened the door quietly and peered in. The haversack was chained to a chair. He shut the door. But soon he was back again unable to resist the anticipation of the money he would trick them out of the next day. Okonkwo and Okeke snored. They were the greenest things he'd ever come across, he thought. He already felt the seven hundred and fifty pounds in the haversack in his palms. Tomorrow, tomorrow, he thought, and shutting the door gently, went to bed a rich man. . . .

But when he went to greet his guests in the morning, the room was empty!

In the lavatory of the "Up Limited" train, Okonkwo and Okeke were grooming themselves.

"Free food, free lodging, and a gift of a hundred pounds!" Okonkwo was saying, as he washed his face.

"When he was peeping in again and again, I thought he was going to be tough," said Okeke, as he rubbed his chin before the mirror.

"They'll never learn," said Okonkwo, as he wiped his face. "They are green as peas, the whole batch of them. See how they left the door only bolted."

So they bantered as the train jogged along. Swaying on the handle of the door was their haversack now emptied of the stones and old rags that had won them the hundred pounds.

A Day Off

by ANTHONY M. HOKORORO

Anthony M. Hokororo came to Makerere University College in Kampala from Tanzania. He graduated in 1959, took a diploma in Education in 1960, and continued his studies at Carleton University in Ottawa, Canada.

While at Makerere, Hokororo was one of a group of young authors from Kenya, Tanzania, and Uganda whose writings were published in the anthology, *Origin East Africa,* edited by David Cook. James Ngugi collaborated with David Cook in the selection of material and its preparation for publication.

David Cook says, "English is not a mother tongue in Africa; nor, however, is it foreign—it has let down its roots here; technically speaking, it is a second language. What a positive power Africans enjoy in thus possessing two fundamentally different languages! Sometimes Africans choose to write in Swahili or Yoruba, Luganda or Kikuyu. At other times, they choose to write in East African English."

人   The kitchen at six in the morning was bright and cheerful, but Zale was scarcely aware of that, as she washed her breakfast dishes and laid a fresh place for Abdu. She noticed, instead, the freshly laundered curtains. Everything showed what a good housekeeper she was.

Abdu gave very little thought to such things. He liked comfort, a regular routine and familiar objects where he expected to find them. He took them for granted, going off cheerfully each day to his job at the carpentry-shop, coming back at night tired, but still cheerful, accepting Zale and the dinner she served him with the same equanimity with which he took over his big chair and reading lamp, his pipe, and the *Tanganyika Standard.*

With one last look around, Zale tiptoed up to the spare-room where she had laid out her new suit the night before. She

137

dressed quickly, put on her wide-brimmed hat with a pink rose on it and picked up her plastic handbag.

At the door of the spare room, she paused to peer through a partly open bedroom door. Abdu lay in a tangle of sheets, with one dusky arm over his head. He looked young and defenseless, with his flushed face and parted lips. Earlier in their marriage Zale could never resist kissing him awake at such moments. But now her mind registered only the fact that he was dead to the world and that he needed a shave.

Back in the kitchen, she quickly thumbed through the pages of a recent *Drum*, tore out what she wanted and thrust it into her purse. Then she scribbled a note for Abdu: "I've decided to take a day off," it said. "There's rice and meat in the cupboard if I'm not back for supper. Love, Zale." And then she slipped out the side way.

The ticket office was not open when Zale reached the station, so she had time to get her breath and tighten the elastic on her hat, which now and then slid back on her head, loosening the knot of her hair. She steadied it with extra pins, somewhat reassured by the face which stared back at her from the mirror which she kept in her handbag.

The office now being open, Zale stepped in briskly. "Dar, second class, please," she said, putting her money on the counter.

The ticket clerk was Saudari. He smiled as soon as he saw her. He had earlier on pursued her but to no effect. Zale had never paid attention to men until Abdu came along.

"Goin' on a toot, baby?" he asked softly. "In such a fairy hat, too. Somebody ought to put a flea in Abdu's ear."

"You owe me twenty cents change," said Zale, rather stiffly, and turned in relief at the sound of the incoming train.

Once settled, with a seat to herself, she took out the page which she had torn from *Drum* and studied the heading: SOME WOMEN GET INTO GROOVES, ARE YOU ONE OF THEM? Then she read the article for the fourth time. Such women, the article said, had only themselves to blame. For husbands had a way of just accepting unthinkingly what was done for them. That was why a wife ought to take a day off every now and then: do what she wanted to do and see what she wanted to see. The experience would be beneficial to her and to her family.

She put down the paper and sighed. The trouble was she had

no idea what she wanted to do or see, at least she had not made up her mind as to what she was going to do, because for three years now her interests had been purely domestic. She was in a groove, no doubt, a household groove, and Abdu had reached the point of accepting everything without thinking, just as the article said.

At ten o'clock the train stopped at her destination. Now for the first time she felt a quiver of excitement and wished she had made a definite plan for the day. The sun shone very brightly, but the wind blew gustily from the Indian Ocean. Zale clutched her purse with one hand, and with the other steadied the big hat on her heavy hair.

From the station, she moved with the crowd across Acacia Avenue to Kariakoo, a large market place surrounded with Indian bazaars. Young people in Id El Fitr finery and with cameras swarmed in and out. The air was full of the sound of gay voices, and from the center of the market-building could be heard trickling water running on the freshly caught fish. The smell of oriental perfumes was almost intoxicating.

Zale stood, entranced. Then suddenly, a gust of wind sent her hat spinning towards one of the rows of shops. She ran after it, conscious of the shower of hair-pins, and of the knot of hair at the back of her head slipping lower and lower. The bystanders watched her, amazed at her beauty and amused with her hat-racing. At that moment, a tall, elderly man stepped from one of the doorways, picked up the hat and held it out with a smile.

"Thank you," murmured Zale, struggling with the remaining hair-pins, while he flicked the pink rose with an immaculate handkerchief. "Please, don't bother," she added, in a confused state of mind.

"You're all excited, aren't you? Having a holiday from school, perhaps?"

He helped her put on the hat and then made her sit on a bench. As he sat beside her she noticed that he was not old, really. It was just because his hair had gone grey that he looked old.

The strange thing was that at that moment Zale did not at all feel disturbed by the knowledge that she was being "picked up," something—her Mama had often told her—no girl ever permitted.

"Not from school," she laughed. "I'm a married woman, but I've been here only once, and—well, there's an awful lot to see in a short time. I've got to go home by the three forty-five train."

He smiled. "What will you see first?" he asked.

"I've got a plan," she said firmly, and paused. "I—I guess I'll just have to take things as they come." It was then that she began to think she *was* being "picked up."

"There's the King George V's Memorial Museum," he said, "but it's too nice a day to spend indoors. How about the Mission Quarters, including the Cathedral?"

Her eyes widened. "A monastery!" But, her embarrassment forgotten, she listened very eagerly while he explained that it was a kind of museum. She hesitated, but only for a second, and then off they went.

As they were coming out of the Cathedral, Zale sighed delightedly. "I never thought that I'd be doing this," she said.

"The nicest things are the unexpected ones," her escort answered. "I found that out a long time ago; so I'm often in a receptive mood. And sometimes"—his eyes twinkled—"I even nudge at fate, speak to a stranger, buy a ticket to an unknown destination and do something I've always wanted to do and never have."

Zale nodded quickly. Now for the first time she remembered what she had always wanted to do. "I've always wanted to cut my hair," she said, "only I've never had the courage to do so."

"Hair is sure to grow again," he said, "not like a finger or an ear."

"Abdu might not like it," murmured Zale.

"Your husband?" he asked, and, when she nodded, said, "Well, you never can be sure about husbands until you confront them with the fact, can you?"

Zale remembered the article she had read that morning and found out that what it said was surprisingly similar to what her companion was saying.

He grew grave again. "I'm afraid I was cross with Kate for letting her hair grow," he said. "But I liked it later."

"Kate, your wife?"

He nodded.

They were now in the Rainbow Hotel where, as they talked over dessert and coffee, Zale mentioned the article that had inspired her day off, and that led to other thngs, so that before she knew it she had said enough about Mama and her marriage to give her listener a fair knowledge of her life.

She told him that it was her Mama's sudden death five years before that had led to her marriage. She and Abdu had been living in the same house and after her Mama's death Abdu had watched her helplessly trying to keep the place in good condition. One awful night when Zale, having burnt the dinner beyond salvaging, had announced between sobs that she could not go on, and proposed that the house should be sold, Abdu had quietly objected to the proposition. This was her home, he had said, and she must stay in it. He would see to that. Then, gulping once or twice, he had asked her to marry him. He was doing well at the carpentry-shop and would be assistant master the next year.

Zale had then wept in incredulous relief, grateful for his arm around her. Being married, she said, had been very great fun at first, looking after the house, making curtains and learning to cook. Abdu had shown himself to be quite a contented husband. "But," she concluded, "it seems that he is too contented to—to—" She stopped, "it seems that he is too contented to—to—" She stopped, remembering the article in *Drum*.

"Husbands are always like that," he helped her out. "There comes that time when they take their wives for granted."

"By the way," he spoke again, "you haven't told me your name. Mine is Richard, or Dick if you wish."

"My name is Zale."

And then his own story followed.

"Kate and I were married when we were young," he explained, "years ago. We lived together in our childhood. We played together. We particularly like dancing, swimming and——" He hesitated.

The change in tone perplexed Zale. Presently he told her of the accident that had changed his life. Kate had been crippled so badly while playing that she had never walked again. Her husband, of course, could not give her the care she needed. Only qualified doctors could do that. He was then working as an office boy, but, finding the wages insufficient to maintain the family, he had taken another job instead.

"It's a kaolin concern," he said, "and I've done well financially."

"But being away from her," said Zale, quite amazed at the story, "how can you bear it?"

"I suppose it's a sort of game I play with myself," he admitted,

141

"finding bits of fun and beauty here and there to take to her. Like today"—he shot a mischievous look at her—"seeing the Mission Quarters and having luncheon with a pretty girl."

As they went out of the hotel, the clock above the information booth struck the quarter.

"I'm afraid I must go," said Zale, hurriedly. "Good-bye, Mr. Richard, and thank you very much for your kindness. I'll always remember how good you've been. It's been a very beautiful day to me. Only that, all of a sudden, it's—it's over."

"Beauty, Mrs. Abdu, hasn't anything to do with time," he said. "A great deal can be crowded into a small space, you know."

They shook hands and parted.

As Zale walked away, the idea suggested in the article once again came before her mind, and, encouraged by Dick's words: "You never can be sure about husbands until you confront them with the fact," she resolved to do what she'd always wanted to do—her hair, she must have her hair cut. There was a barber's shop on the concourse. She ran off to find it. Luckily the place was empty. "King Salon" was at her service, and, in a wink, her gleaming knot was lying on the floor. Experienced fingers snipped and shaped, fluffed and patted, and at 3:30 the barber stood inspecting his work with pride. She had no time to listen to compliments. She just smiled and placed a shilling on his palm.

She flew now, hat in hand, her heart pounding, afraid that she might miss the 3:45 train. With only one minute to spare she sank back in her seat and closed her eyes.

She felt as if she had been cast between two worlds, and was part of neither. Her mind still glowed with the memory of the day with Dick; and yet there was an excitement in the thought that she was on her way to Abdu.

When she entered the house, there was a silence long enough to make her wonder what questions she would have to answer, what words she could possibly find to tell Abdu everything that was in her heart. But when her husband appeared, all that she could say was, "You didn't eat your supper, Abdu, and I fixed just what you like."

"I wasn't hungry," he muttered. But his look of injured dignity struck a comic note, since he held a razor in his hand and one side of his face was fringed with lather. "I heard the train coming," he went on. "Knew you'd be along, so——" He broke off crossly. "Oh, the heck with it, Zale, who wants to eat alone?"

She smiled to herself, feeling suddenly older and wiser than he, for she had done what she had always wanted to do and what she had not had the courage to do before, and now he had confirmed a fundamental truth about husbands.

"O.K.," she said, "we'll have supper together."

As they sat down to eat, Abdu said, in a husky voice, "You're back and I'm glad. Only you seem different. I've missed you. Don't go away again like that without warning me. It upset me, sort of— I can't explain."

Zale's laughter had a catch in it. "All right, Abdu," she said, "I promise not to." And she turned away to hide the new secret knowledge in her eyes.

With Strings

by KULDIP SONDHI

Kuldip Sondhi is an Asian who has made his home in Africa. He was born in Lahore, India, in 1924. He received his early schooling in India, then emigrated with his family to Kenya. Later he studied aeronautical engineering in the United States. When he received his master's degree, he returned to Mombasa, where he is now employed in an engineering firm.

Writing is his hobby. He has written plays and also short stories, several of which have been published. His play *The Undesignated* won first prize in the Kenya Drama Festival of 1963.

Most African playwrights have chosen traditional themes for their plays. Sondhi, however, chose a very modern theme—the romance between an African boy and an Asian girl whose fathers are business associates—for his play *With Strings*.

CHARACTERS

DEV	Retired Indian Engineer, in 50's
SAVITRI	His wife, in 40's
MOHAN	Dev's son, late 20's
NJEROGE	Retired African administrator, in 50's
CYNTHIA	African girl, early 20's

SAVITRI: Don't you believe it?

DEV: Frankly, no.

SAVITRI: No? (*Takes letter. Scans it briefly.*) Why not? There's his signature. There's the stamp from America. And here he says clearly: "I will give £ 10,000 to the family if your son Mohan gets married and produces an heir within the next twelve months."

DEV: Produce an heir! Who does he think he is—God?

SAVITRI: Don't be silly. How many times haven't we said ourselves

144

that it's time the boy got married. He's doing it for Mohan's own good.

DEV: Mohan's own good! He hasn't even met our boy yet. Do you know what this is?

SAVITRI: What?

DEV: This—(*Grimaces at letter.*)—this is aid with strings!

SAVITRI: Is it? Well, no one's forcing you to accept it. If you don't want the aid, just say so.

DEV: You can't "just say so" about something so big. It's been offered to us and whether we accept it or not now our lives will never be the same again. Whatever happens to us from now will be his responsibility.

SAVITRI: Your pride's been touched, so you're thoroughly prejudiced against him now; but if Mohan turns out to be like cousin Sobod I'll be proud of the boy.

DEV: Nonsense. The two can never be alike. Mohan's a chemist, and an educated man. Your cousin is just a fruit-picker—made good. He's even given us his telephone number in case we want to show our appreciation!

SAVITRI: Let's not argue any more, Dev. You are giving me a head-ache with your talk. We have been offered a very generous gift and it's up to us to take it or leave it. To me it's like a dream come true. It no longer matters if Mohan gets a dowry with his marriage or not. All he needs is an educated girl with the right background. How much easier that makes everything.

DEV: It doesn't. We will have sold ourselves into the bargain. Don't forget that. Your soul will no longer be your own.

SAVITRI: I don't think cousin Sobod buys souls.

DEV: This is a different kind of soul.

SAVITRI: The difficulty with you is, you read too many books. That's why you get confused so easily. But wait till Mohan hears the news. He will be delighted.

DEV: Of course. Who wouldn't be at the thought of getting so much money. He may not want to pay the price for it though.

SAVITRI: Pay the price!—(*Telephone rings. Picks up the receiver.*) Hallo. Oh, Mohan, is that you—where are you speaking from? Back at your flat—good! Well, you must be tired after that long drive from Mombasa. No, don't take a taxi, I'll come over. (*Pause.*) In about 15 minutes. I have some exciting news for you, Mohan. No, not on the phone. I'll tell you as soon as we meet. Goodbye. (*To Dev.*) He's given his car for washing.

DEV: Has he? The difficulty with your son is he doesn't take life seriously enough. He has a nice little shop in the center of Nairobi but half the time he's out of it. I'm sure he could increase his trade if he paid as much attention to his customers as he does to his own pleasures. Last year he must have made at least ten trips to the coast.

SAVITRI: He has business down there.

DEV: What business? Have you ever asked him?

SAVITRI: Yes. He told me that as a chemist he deals in every branch of chemistry, or whatever he calls . . .

DEV: (*Looks doubtfully at his wife.*) He probably meant anatomy. Well, never mind, you're his mother. If this money does tempt him to get married, it will at least have done some good. Actually there are a few good families from our community on the coast and if he has eyes on someone suitable in Mombasa there is no harm in it.

SAVITRI: I wish he would choose Laxman's daughter. They are big people and Veena is a beautiful girl.

DEV: Yes, it would be an ideal match. He used to be very friendly with her once, I remember. Perhaps he still is. But you can never tell what that boy is up to from day to day. (*Looks at watch.*) Now don't be long, you know I expect Njeroge this evening. If he brings his niece with him you should be here to meet her.

SAVITRI: The one who's just returned from England, is it?

DEV: I believe so, though I haven't met her, they're good people; and Njeroge is a sound man. I like him. (*Becomes reflective.*) You know, Savitri, I have great hopes about this new business I'm after.

SAVITRI: The one with Mr. Njeroge?

DEV: Yes. (*Pause.*) You have some doubts about it, don't you? Why?

SAVITRI: Not about the business.

DEV: I see.

SAVITRI: I know you like Mr. Njeroge, Dev, but are you sure you can trust him?

DEV: You can't forget that he's an African, can you?

SAVITRI: That's true, I can't. And why should I? Do you think he forgets that you are an Indian, or an Asian as he probably calls you?

DEV: He doesn't call me anything but Dev.

SAVITRI: I'm not criticising him. I'm wondering how well you know him.

DEV: (*Shrugs and paces as he thinks aloud and talks.*) As well as I know any other man. Better I'd say. We worked in the same department for fifteen years. He also retired as a superintendent in the Post and Telegraphs. We are about the same age and citizens of the same country. How much closer can I get to Njeroge without one of us changing colour?

SAVITRI: No one's asking you to change your colour. All I'm saying is do you trust him? Do you know how he thinks?

DEV: Sometimes, Savitri, I don't even know how you think. When Njeroge and I are together we forget our racial differences. Isn't that a sign of trust?

SAVITRI: No, that's only a sign of your thinking. Do you realise, Dev, that you are going to risk a part of our life savings in this new business.

DEV: I do, yes I do, Savitri, but I'm sure I'm doing the right thing. Njeroge is an African and if I am to make a proper start in business, I want an African with me. Don't forget this is his country.

SAVITRI: It's also supposed to be our country. Mohan was born in Kenya, and everything we have is here now. But none of that will help if you lose your money simply because you want to trust Njeroge.

DEV: But I do trust him, Savitri. I couldn't trust him any more if he were an Indian. And the business is a very simple one really. All we need are a few touring cars. With a good contract from the Tourists' Association to start us off, we are in. Anyhow, aren't we soon going to have another £ 10,000.

SAVITRI: We haven't got it yet, and have you forgotten your son? (*Starts bustling in her bag and looking for keys.*) Now, enough of this. Mohan's waiting.

DEV: You are in a difficult mood. (*Bell. Dev opens door. Njeroge enters with niece.*) Come in, Njeroge, come in. So this is your niece.

147

NJEROGE: Yes, this is Cynthia. She arrived from London last night. (*Shakes hands. Cynthia is pretty, refined, self-assured but quiet.*)

DEV: How do you do, Cynthia. I'm glad he brought you along. This is my wife.

CYNTHIA: (*Shaking hands.*) How do you do.

NJEROGE: I'm a bit early, Dev, but I've brought some news for you.

DEV: Good news I hope.

NJEROGE: Judge for yourself. I found out that one of the directors of the Tourists' Association is an old school friend of mine. I rang him up just before I came and he asked me to come over to his house, straightaway, for a chat. Will you come with me?

DEV: Of course. This is good news. Now maybe things will start moving. But sit down for a few minutes. Let's have a drink to celebrate Cynthia's arrival while Savitri fetches Mohan from his flat. We can leave after that.

SAVITRI: I'd better bring Mohan now if you're in a hurry.

DEV: Yes, all right. He must be ready by this time. (*Leaves. Dev pours out drinks standing on tray.*)

NJEROGE: Mohan lives nearby, doesn't he?

DEV: Not far away. At the end of this road, actually.

CYNTHIA: Is he all right?

DEV: (*Surprised.*) Yes, I think so.

NJEROGE: (*To niece.*) Do you know Mohan?

CYNTHIA: I met him last year before I left for England. Didn't I tell you at the time?

NJEROGE: Not that I remember.

CYNTHIA: Well, I met him when I was working at the General Hospital in Mombasa. He used to come there to sell his drugs.

DEV: (*Smiles.*) Ah, so he was at work on those trips.

CYNTHIA: I don't know what you mean, but the hospital did place orders with him.

NJEROGE: (*Chuckles.*) That boy you know . . . the stories I hear of him! But take it from me, Mohan is a very bright, enterprising young man. There's no harm if he gets around a bit. I wish I had a son like him.

DEV: (*Pleased.*) Do you, really?

NJEROGE: Well, yes . . . What does he lack!

148

DEV: A wife.

NJEROGE: (*Laughs.*) True, though I'm sure he could remedy that easily enough if he wanted to.

DEV: If he wanted to—exactly.

NJEROGE: You're behind the times, Dev. These days young people only marry if they have something to gain by it. I shouldn't be saying this in front of Cynthia of course.

CYNTHIA: Why not? As a rule I think that what you say is correct. There is no point in marrying if you get nothing from it.

DEV: You can take it from me that Mohan has quite a lot to lose if he doesn't get married within the next twelve months. (*Thoughtful momentarily.*) No, in the next three months.

NJEROGE: What's this, you planning the boy's future for him or something?

DEV: Not me, but I'll tell you about it later. Well, Cynthia, how does it feel to be back in Kenya?

CYNTHIA: Wonderful. I will not want to go back, but I'll have to, of course.

NJEROGE: Cynthia is studying to become a midwife. She has another year to go for her degree.

DEV: Really, that's wonderful. Well, we must see more of you while you're here.

CYNTHIA: You probably will. One month's a long time. (*Laughter in corridor. Door opens. Mohan and mother enter.*)

MOHAN: Good evening, Mr. Njeroge. Hello, Cynthia. (*Holds out hand to her. Their eyes meet for a moment.*) You've told them that we know each other, haven't you?

CYNTHIA: I have.

DEV: What will you have, Mohan?

MOHAN: I would prefer tea, actually.

SAVITRI: I'll make some for you just now.

MOHAN: No hurry, mother. So you're back, Cynthia?

CYNTHIA: (*Smiling.*) Yes, here I am, Mohan. (*Savitri glances from one to the other with a perplexed smile.*)

DEV: (*Amiable and relaxed, lighting cigarette for Njeroge and himself.*) England must have been a change after this country, eh, Cynthia?

CYNTHIA: In some ways, though in my work there are few surprises. Babies and mothers act the same everywhere. (*All laugh.*)

NJEROGE: But the people are different surely, Cynthia.

CYNTHIA: Under their reserve I don't think they are so different to us. I don't mean their customs and habits now. These come from the environment, not the heart.

SAVITRI: It's a comfortable theory.

NJEROGE: I agree with you, Mrs. Dev. Of course, people are different, Cynthia. We are all friends here but look at us, aren't we different?

CYNTHIA: Aside from our colors I don't see any difference.

DEV: (*Smiles.*) But you admit then there are some differences.

CYNTHIA: Of course. How boring it would be if we all looked and thought exactly alike! See how different Mohan is to you.

MOHAN: I'm glad you learnt so much during one year. You must have been working hard in England.

CYNTHIA: I was. Your father's also been telling us how hard you work. (*All laugh.*)

DEV: Be careful what you say to this young lady, Mohan. I think you've met your match.

SAVITRI: The only difficulty with a woman going in for a profession is that it usually goes to waste after she gets married. And if it doesn't, she hardly remains a woman at all.

CYNTHIA: I think it's better to take that risk than becoming a cabbage at home.

DEV: (*Laughs.*) Yes . . . yes, quite right! Well, Mohan, when you choose you had better be careful what you get. We don't want a cabbage or a woman who wears pants.

MOHAN: I don't think you'll get either.

DEV: Well, the quicker we know the better! Now if you'll excuse us.

NJEROGE: Can I leave Cynthia with you till we return, Mrs. Dev?

SAVITRI: Of course. You carry on now. I'll look after her.

NJEROGE: Thank you. (*Goes out with Dev.*)

SAVITRI: How would you like to try some Indian masala tea, Cynthia? It's Mohan's favorite.

CYNTHIA: Oh, I'd love some of that, Mrs. Dev. I've had it before.

SAVITRI: Well, just sit down then and make yourself comfortable while I prepare it. I won't take long. (*Cynthia sits and Savitri leaves through inside door. Then Cynthia rises swiftly and Mohan turns to her, crushing out his cigarette.*)

MOHAN: At last! I thought we would never be alone.

CYNTHIA: Nor did I. It's been a whole year, Mohan.

MOHAN: The longest year of my life.

CYNTHIA: Really? I missed the sound of your voice. You used to phone me every weekend at the hospital, remember?

MOHAN: I remember everything.

CYNTHIA: Everything?

MOHAN: (*Uncertainly.*) Yes, why?

CYNTHIA: What about Mr. Laxman's daughter!

MOHAN: What about her?

CYNTHIA: You liked Veena once, didn't you?

MOHAN: That was before I met you.

CYNTHIA: I know, and I'm just being jealous. From now on I'll believe everything you say and refuse to listen to gossip. But Mohan . . . have you really been behaving yourself?

MOHAN: No one believes it, but I have. My trip to Mombasa this time was the first one since you left and it was a genuine business trip. But all the time I kept thinking of you and what you've done to my life.

CYNTHIA: Tell me what I've done, Mohan.

MOHAN: Don't you know? Because of you I'm going to break from convention. Because of you I no longer see life constricted in narrow bands of color and feeling. I am possessed by a new sense of freedom and sometimes it is like walking on air. I warn you, I've changed this past year and hold you responsible for any transformation. You realise you are guilty, don't you?

CYNTHIA: Yes!

MOHAN: All right then, you stand paroled for the rest of your life in my custody.

CYNTHIA: Mohan, you don't talk like this to other girls, do you?

MOHAN: No, I don't, and there aren't any other girls, not now.

CYNTHIA: In that case I won't appeal against your sentence, but, Mohan . . . do your parents know anything about us?

MOHAN: I haven't told them yet.

CYNTHIA: I think we'll have to soon. This isn't really fair on them or on us.

MOHAN: Cynthia, there's something I must tell you.

CYNTHIA: Yes?

MOHAN: I want you to stay. I can't bear the thought of you going back.

CYNTHIA: I'm here a whole month, Mohan. We can meet every day.

MOHAN: Yes, of course we will, but . . . this is ridiculous.

CYNTHIA: What is?

MOHAN: This secrecy. We love each other. It's not a sin. I want you to marry me immediately.

CYNTHIA: (*Happy.*) You mean now, just like that?

MOHAN: Yes.

CYNTHIA: Oh, this is the happiest day of my life! Let me confess it, Mohan, I've always been a bit doubtful about you, but now it's all blown away. No one can really separate us again. But for the sake of the others, let's just wait a little longer. There's no harm done by it.

MOHAN: But there is! Why should we wait? I'm going to tell my parents everything tonight. They'll have to agree.

CYNTHIA: They may not if you go at them like that.

MOHAN: You take care of your side and I'll take care of mine. I tell you, there is no time to be lost!

CYNTHIA: (*Laughs.*) I must say you are in a hurry. I'm not running away tomorrow morning, Mohan.

MOHAN: You're not, but time is.

CYNTHIA: Mohan, is there something that I should know?

MOHAN: (*Cautious.*) How do you mean?

CYNTHIA: Shall I tell you what I really think?

MOHAN: Of course.

CYNTHIA: I believe your parents have someone else in view for you and to beat them at their own game you're in this hurry to marry me. Isn't that so? Why are you laughing?

MOHAN: At you because you may be right too. That's why I say let's get married before you return to England. What's wrong with it anyway?

CYNTHIA: Nothing's wrong when you're with me, Mohan. But I want our marriage to meet with their approval. Especially uncle's approval. He's been so good to me. My parents died when I was very young, but he's never allowed me to feel an orphan. Now I must take his feelings into account.

Market Stall in Nigeria   ODITA

MOHAN: Your uncle is as conventional and old fashioned as my parents are, even if he doesn't know it, Cynthia.

CYNTHIA: I know and that's what I'm afraid of. Uncle's got a minister in my future.

MOHAN: A minister?

CYNTHIA: Yes.

MOHAN: Which one?

CYNTHIA: Oh, any one of them will do. It's just some sort of dream he had.

MOHAN: Well, he can stop dreaming. No minister's getting you, unless I become one. (*Glances at photo.*) Anyhow, I'll soon be as rich as one.

CYNTHIA: (*Catches his glance.*) What do you mean?

MOHAN: Oh, nothing.

CYNTHIA: I'd still like to know, Mohan. Your father was mysterious about something and so are you now. Does it concern us in any way?

MOHAN: It's a silly whim this old uncle of mine's suddenly got. I've never met the old boy, but he's written a letter to say that if I get married and have an heir within twelve months the family gets £10,000.

CYNTHIA: What . . . I see . . . Why didn't you tell me this before?

MOHAN: I haven't had time to. We've hardly been alone ten minutes. You know that!

CYNTHIA: I don't know anything. So that's why you're in such a hurry to marry me?

MOHAN: Of course not. I want to—

CYNTHIA: You mean you want the money!

MOHAN: I want you, I said. But if the money's also thrown in, what's the harm?

CYNTHIA: What's the harm? You can get someone else for this kind of bargaining. My God, to drag me into something so wicked!

MOHAN: But what's so wicked about it, Cynthia? I knew you wouldn't understand.

CYNTHIA: It was agreed between us some time back that we'd not think of marriage for some time yet. Now you no sooner see me than you can talk of nothing else. And I was fool enough to think it was all for my sake.

MOHAN: But it is, Cynthia. Don't you see—

CYNTHIA: No, that's just what I don't see. I don't want to have anything to do with that money.

MOHAN: But it's stupid to throw it away. It's a fortune, Cynthia.

CYNTHIA: I'm not for sale.

MOHAN: Look, if you think I'm only after the money, I could easily get someone in a matter of days.

CYNTHIA: You mean Veena; well, why don't you?

MOHAN: Because I don't want to. I want you.

CYNTHIA: But only on condition I help you to get the money, isn't that so?

MOHAN: Of course not, but I don't want to lose a fortune either.

CYNTHIA: Well, for God's sake, don't. Get your saried beauty.

MOHAN: No, no, Cynthia, this is all wrong. You are making it sound crude.

CYNTHIA: I am making it sound crude? You have the cheek to tell me that?

MOHAN: I'm sorry, I didn't mean it that way.

CYNTHIA: That's enough now. I won't hear any more of this. Thank God I've found out in time. I'm not a breeding machine that I can guarantee to produce heirs for your family. Get someone else for that kind of nonsense.

MOHAN: Calm down, Cynthia; just listen to me.

CYNTHIA: No, never! If we get married it's after my studies in a year's time or not at all. But I think it's better if you find someone else. Your money can buy her. Not me. Goodbye. (*Cynthia runs out. Mohan stands frowning.*)

CURTAIN

The Truly Married Woman

by ABIOSEH NICOL

Abioseh Nicol was born in Sierra Leone and educated in that country and in Nigeria. He later studied natural sciences and medicine in England.

Dr. Nicol writes under two names. Under his African name, Abioseh Nicol, he has written short stories and poetry. As Dr. Davidson Nicol, he has written on scientific and medical topics and has edited political and historical essays, including *Black Nationalism in Africa, 1867*, extracts from the writings of Africanus Horton, a revealing chapter in the history of nineteenth-century Africa. In 1952 he was awarded the Margaret Wrong Prize and Medal for African Literature.

Dr. Nicol's creative writing has a conscious purpose. He explains: "I started writing partly because I wanted to and partly because I found that most of those who wrote about us seldom gave any nobility to their African characters unless they were savages or servants faced with impending destruction. I knew differently. I saw all around me worthy Africans who lived and worked with varying degrees of success, distinction, and happiness. I began to write about them."

In *The Truly Married Woman* Dr. Nicol suggests that we cannot understand Africa without taking into consideration the personality and status of the women. This story, like all his stories, is also enormously revealing of the everyday details of African life—the food, the clothing, the work habits, and the marriage customs of a great majority who are neither rich or poor, but simply ordinary, respectable members of the community.

人　Ajayi stirred for a while and then sat up. He looked at the cheap alarm clock on the chair by his bedside. It was six-fifteen, and light outside already; the African town was slowly waking to life. The night-watchmen roused from sleep by the angry crowing of cockerels were officiously banging the locks of stores and houses to assure themselves and their employers, if near, of their efficiency. Village women were tramping through the streets to the market place with their wares, arguing and gossiping.

Ajayi sipped his cup of morning tea. It was as he liked it, weak and sugary, without milk. With an effort of will, he got up and walked to the window, and standing there he took six deep breaths. This done daily, he firmly believed, would prevent tuberculosis. He walked through his ramshackle compound to an outhouse and took a quick bath, pouring the water over his head from a tin cup with which he scooped water from a bucket.

By then Ayo had laid out his breakfast. Ayo was his wife. Not really one, he would explain to close friends, but a mistress. A good one. She had borne him three children and was now three months gone with another. They had been together for twelve years. She was a patient, handsome woman. Very dark with very white teeth and open sincere eyes. Her hair was always carefully plaited. When she first came to him to the exasperation of her parents— he had fully intended marrying her as soon as she had shown satisfactory evidence of fertility, but he had never quite got round to it. In the first year or so she would report to him in great detail the splendor of the marriage celebrations of her friends, looking at him with hopeful eyes. He would close the matter with a tirade on the sinfulness of ostentation. She gave up after some time. Her father never spoke to her again after she had left home. Her mother visited her secretly and attended the baptismal ceremonies of all her children. The Church charged extra for illegitimate children as a deterrent; two dollars instead of fifty cents. Apart from this, there was no other great objection.

Occasionally, two or three times a year, the pastor would preach violently against adultery, polygamy, and unmarried couples living together. Ajayi and Ayo were good church-people and attended regularly, but sat in different pews. After such occasions, their friends would sympathize with them and other couples in similar positions. There would be a little grumbling and the male members of the congregation would say that the trouble with the Church was that it did not stick to its business of preaching the Gospel, but meddled in people's private lives. Ajayi would indignantly absent himself from Church for a few weeks but would go back eventually because he liked singing hymns and because he knew secretly that the pastor was right.

Ayo was a good mistress. Her father was convinced she could have married a high-school teacher at least, or a pharmacist, but instead she had attached herself to a junior Government clerk. But Ayo loved Ajayi, and was happy in her own slow, private way. She cooked his meals and bore him children. In what spare time she had she either did a little petty trading, visited friends, or gossiped with Omo, the woman next door.

With his towel round his waist, Ajayi strode back to the bedroom, dried himself and dressed quickly but carefully in his pink tussore suit. He got down the new bottle of patent medicine which one of his friends who worked in a drug store had recommended to him. Ajayi believed that to keep healthy, a man must regularly take a dose of some medicine. He read the label of this one. It listed about twenty diseased conditions of widely differing pathology which the contents of the bottle were reputed to cure if the patient persevered in its daily intake. Ajayi underlined in his own mind at least six from which he believed he either suffered or was on the threshold of suffering: dizziness, muscle pain, impotence, fever, jaundice, and paralytic tremors. Intelligence and courage caused him to skip the obviously female maladies and others such as nervous debility or bladder pains. It said on the label too that a teaspoonful should be taken three times a day. But since he only remembered to take it in the morning and in any case believed in shock treatment, he took a swig and two large gulps. The medicine was bitter and astringent. He grimaced but was satisfied. It was obviously a good and strong medicine or else it would not have been so bitter.

He went in to breakfast. He soon finished his maize porridge, fried beans, and cocoa. He then severely flogged his eldest son, a ten-year-old boy, for wetting his sleeping-mat last night. Ayo came in after the boy had fled screaming to the backyard.

"Ajayi, you flog that boy too much," she said.

"He should stop wetting the floor, he is a big boy," he replied. "In any case, no one is going to instruct me on how to bring up my son."

"He is mine too," Ayo said. She seldom opposed him unless

158

she felt strongly about something. "He has not stopped wetting, although you beat him every time he does. In fact, he is doing it more and more now. Perhaps if you stopped whipping him he might get better."

"Did I whip him to begin doing it?" Ajayi asked.

"No."

"Well, how will stopping whipping him stop him doing it?" Ajayi asked triumphantly.

"Nevertheless," Ayo said, "our own countrywoman Bimbola, who has just come back from England and America studying nursing, told us in a women's group meeting that it was wrong to punish children for such things."

"All right, I'll see," he said, reaching for his sunhelmet.

All that day at the office he thought about this and other matters. So Ayo had been attending women's meetings. Well, what do you know. She would be running for the Town Council next. The sly woman. Always looking so quiet and meek and then quoting modern theories from overseas doctors at him. He smiled with pride. Indeed Ayo was an asset. Perhaps it was wrong to beat the boy. He decided he would not do so again.

Towards closing-time the chief clerk sent for him. Wondering what mistake he had made that day, or on what mission he was to be sent, he hurried along to the forward office. There were three white men sitting on chairs by the chief clerk, who was an aging African dressed with severe respectability. On seeing them, Ajayi's heart started thudding. The police, he thought; heavens, what have I done?

"Mr. Ajayi, these gentlemen have enquired for you," the chief clerk said formally.

"Pleased to meet you, Mr. Ajayi," the tallest said, with a smile. "We represent the World Gospel Crusading Alliance from Minnesota. My name is Jonathan Olsen." Ajayi shook hands and the other two were introduced.

"You expressed an interest in our work a year ago and we have not forgotten. We are on our way to India and we thought we would look you up personally."

It transpired that the three Crusaders were *en route* and that their ship had stopped for refuelling off the African port for a few hours. The chief clerk looked at Ajayi with new respect. Ajayi tried desperately to remember any connection with W.G.C.A. (as Olsen by then had proceeded to call it) whilst he made conversation with them a little haltingly. Then suddenly he remembered.

Some time ago he had got hold of a magazine from his subtenant who worked at the United States Information Service. He had cut a coupon from it and posted it to W.G.C.A. asking for information, but really hoping that they would send illustrated Bibles free which he might give away or sell. He hoped for at least large reproductions of religious paintings which, suitably framed, would decorate his parlor or which he might paste up on his bedroom wall. But nothing had come of it and he had forgotten. Now here was W.G.C.A. as large as life. Three lives. Instantly and recklessly he invited all three and the chief clerk to come to his house for a cold drink. They all agreed.

"Mine is a humble abode," he warned them.

"No abode is humble that is illumined by Christian love," Olsen replied.

"His is illumined all right, I can assure you," the chief clerk remarked drily.

Olsen suggested a taxi, but Ajayi neatly blocked that by saying the roads were bad. He had hurriedly whispered to a fellow clerk to rush home on a bicycle and tell Ayo he was coming in half an hour with white men and that she should clean up and get fruit drinks.

Ayo was puzzled by the message as she firmly imagined all white men drank only whisky and iced beer. But the messenger had said that there was a mixture of friendliness and piety in the visitors' mien, which made him suspect that they might be missionaries. Another confirmatory point was that they were walking instead of being in a car. That cleared up the anomaly in Ayo's mind and she set to work at once. Oju, now recovered from his morning disgrace, was dispatched with a basket on his head to buy soft drinks. Ayo whisked off the wall all their commercial calendars with suggestive pictures. She propped up family photographs which had fallen face downwards on the table. She removed the Wild West novels and romance magazines from the parlour and put instead an old copy of Bunyan's *Pilgrim's Progress* and a prayer-book which she believed

160

would add culture and religious force to the decorations. She re-membered the wine glasses and the beer-advertising table-mats in time and put those under the sofa. She just had time to change to her Sunday frock and borrow a wedding ring from her neighbor when Ajayi and the guests arrived.

The chief clerk was rather surprised at the changes in the room—which he had visited before—and in Ayo's dress and ring. But he concealed his feelings. Ayo was introduced and made a little conversation in English. This pleased Ajayi a great deal. The children had been changed too into Sunday suits, faces washed and hair brushed. Olsen was delighted and insisted on taking photo-graphs for the Crusade journal. Ayo served drinks and then modestly retired, leaving the men to discuss serious matters. Olsen by then was talking earnestly on the imminence of Christ's Second Coming and offering Ajayi ordination into deaconship.

The visit passed off well and soon the missionaries left to catch their boat. Ajayi had been saved from holy orders by the chief clerk's timely explanation that it was strictly against Govern-ment regulations for civil servants to indulge in non-official organi-zations. To help Ajayi out of his quandary, he had even gone further and said that contravention might result in a fine or imprisonment. "Talk about colonial oppression," the youngest of the missionaries had said, gloomily.

The next day Ajayi called at the chief clerk's office with a carefully wrapped bottle of beer as a present for his help generally on the occasion. They discussed happily the friendliness and inter-est the white men had shown.

This incident and Ayo's protest against flagellation as a spe-cific against enuresis made Ajayi very thoughtful for a week. He decided to marry Ayo. Another consideration which added weight to the thought was the snapshot Olsen took for his magazine. In some peculiar way Ajayi felt he and Ayo should marry, as millions of Americans would see their picture—Olsen had assured him of this— as "one saved and happy African family."

He announced his intention of marrying her to Ayo one eve-ning, after a particularly good meal and a satisfactory bout of belch-ing. Ayo at once became extremely solicitous and got up looking at him with some anxiety. Was he ill? she asked. Was there anything

161

wrong at the office? Had anyone insulted him? No, he answered, there was nothing wrong with his wanting to get married, was there? Or had she anyone else in mind?

Ayo laughed. "As you will," she said, "let us get married, but do not say I forced you into it."

They discussed the wedding that night. Ajayi wanted to have a white wedding with veil and orange blossoms. But Ayo with regret decided it would not be quite right. They agreed on grey. Ayo particularly wanted a corset to strap down her obvious bulge; Ajayi gave way gallantly to this feminine whim, chucking her under the chin and saying, "You women with your vanity!" But he was firm about no honeymoon. He said he could not afford the expense and that one bed was as good as another. Ayo gave way on that. They agreed, however, on a church wedding and that their children could act as bridal pages to keep the cost of clothes within the family.

That evening Ajayi, inflamed by the idea and arrangements for the wedding, pulled Ayo excitedly to him as they lay in bed.

"No," said Ayo, shyly, pushing him back gently, "you mustn't. Wait until after the marriage."

"Why?" said Ajayi, rather surprised, but obedient.

"Because it will not somehow be right," Ayo replied seriously and determinedly.

Ayo's father unbent somewhat when he heard of the proposed marriage. He insisted, however, that Ayo move herself and all her possessions back home to his house. The children were sent to Ayo's married sister. Most of Ajayi's family were in favor of the union, except his sister, who, moved by the threat implicit in Ayo's improved social position, had advised Ajayi to see a soothsayer first. As Ayo had got wind of this through friends met at market on Saturday, she saw the soothsayer first and fixed things. When Ajayi and his sister called at night to see him, he had, after consulting the oracles, pronounced future happiness, avoiding the sister's eye. The latter had restrained herself from scratching the old man's face and had accepted defeat.

The only other flaw in a felicitous situation had been Ayo's neighbor Omo, who had always on urgent occasions at short notice loaned Ayo her wedding ring. She had suddenly turned cold. Especially after Ayo had shown her the wedding presents Ajayi intended to give her. The neighbor had handled the flimsy nylon articles with a mixture of envy and rage.

"Do you mean you are going to wear these?" she had asked.

"Yes," Ayo had replied simply.

"But, my sister," she had protested, "you will catch cold with these. Suppose you had an accident and all those doctors lifted your clothes in hospital. They will see everything through these."

"I never have accidents," Ayo answered, and added, "Ajayi says all the Hollywood cinema women wear these. It says so there. Look—'Trademark Hollywood.'"

"These are disgraceful; they hide nothing, it is extremely fast of you to wear them," the jealous girl said, pushing them back furiously over the fence to Ayo.

"Why should I want to hide anything from my husband when we are married?" Ayo said triumphantly, moving back to her own kitchen and feeling safe in future from the patronizing way the wedding ring had always been lent her.

The arrangements had to be made swiftly, since time and the corset ribs were both against them; Ajayi's domestic routine was also sorely tried, especially his morning cup of tea which he badly missed. He borrowed heavily from a moneylender to pay the dowry and for the music, dancing, and feasting, and for dresses of the same pattern which Ayo and her female relations would wear after the ceremony on the wedding day.

The engagement took place quietly, Ajayi's uncle and other relations taking a Bible and a ring to Ayo's father and asking for her hand in marriage, the day before the wedding. They took with them two small girls carrying on their heads large hollow gourds. These contained articles like pins, farthings, fruit, kola nuts, and cloth. The articles were symbolic gifts to the bride from the bridegroom, so that she might be precluded in future marital disputes from saying, "Not a pin or a farthing has the blackguard given me since we got married."

On arrival at Ayo's father's house, the small procession passed it first as if uncertain, then returned to it. This gave warning to the occupants. Ajayi's uncle then knocked several times. Voices from within shouted back and ordered him to name himself, his ancestry, and his mission. He did this. Argument and some abuse followed on either side. After his family credentials had been seriously examined, questioned, doubted, and disparaged, Ajayi's uncle started wheedling and cajoling. This went on for about half an hour to the enjoyment and mock trepidation of Ajayi's relations. He himself had remained at home, waiting. Finally, Ayo's father opened the door. Honor was satisfied and it was now supposed to be clearly evident to Ajayi's relations, in case it had not been before, that they were entering a family and household which was distinguished, difficult, and jealous of their distinction.

"What is your mission here?" Ayo's father then asked sternly.

Ajayi's uncle answered humbly:

"We have come to pluck a red, red rose
That in your beautiful garden grows.
Which never has been plucked before,
So lovelier than any other."

"Will you be able to nurture our lovely rose well?" another of Ayo's male relations asked?

Ajayi's family party replied:

"So well shall we nurture your rose
Twill bring forth many others."

They were finally admitted; drinks were served and prayers offered. The gifts were accepted and others given in exchange. Conversation went on for about thirty minutes on every conceivable subject but the one at hand.

All through this, Ayo and her sisters and some young female relations were kept hidden in an adjoining bedroom. Finally with some delicacy, Ajayi's uncle broached the subject after Ayo's father had given him an opening by asking what, apart from the honor of being entertained by himself and his family, did Ajayi's relations seek. They had heard, the latter replied, that in this very household there was a maiden chaste, beautiful, and obedient, known to all by the name of Ayo. This maiden they sought as wife for their kinsman Ajayi.

Ayo's father opened the bedroom door and brought forth Ayo's sister. Was this the one? he asked, testing them. They examined her. No, it was not this one, they replied, this one was too short to be Ayo. Then a cousin was brought out. Was this she? No, this one is too fat, the applicants said. About ten women in all were brought out. But none was the correct one. Each was too short or too fat or too fair, as the case was, to suit the description of the maiden they sought.

At this point, Ajayi's uncle slapped his thigh, as if to show that his doubts were confirmed; turning to his party, he stated that it was a good thing they had insisted on seeing for themselves the bride demanded, or else the wrong woman would have been foisted on them. They agreed, nodding. All right, all right, Ayo's father had replied, there was no cause for impatience. He wanted to be sure they knew whom they wanted. Standing on guard at the bedroom door, he turned his back to the assembly, and with tears in his eyes beckoned to Ayo sitting on the bed inside. He kissed her lightly on the forehead to forgive the past years. Then he led her forth and turned fiercely to the audience. Was this then the girl they wanted, he asked them sternly?

"This *is* the very one," Ajayi's uncle replied with joy.

"Hip, hip, hip, hooray," everybody shouted, encircling Ayo and waving white handkerchiefs over her head. The musicians smote their guitars instantly; someone beat an empty wine bottle rhythmically with a corkscrew; after a few preliminary trills the flutes rose high in melody; all danced round Ayo. And as she stood in the center, a woman in her mid-thirties, her hair slightly streaked grey, undergoing a ceremony of honor she had often witnessed and long put outside her fate, remembering the classic description of chastity, obedience, and beauty, she wept with joy and the unborn child stirred within her for the first time.

The next morning she was bathed by an old and respected female member of her family and her mother helped her to dress. Her father gave her away at the marriage service at church. It was a quiet wedding with only sixty guests or so. Ajayi looked stiff in dinner jacket with buttonhole, an ensemble which he wore only on special occasions. Afterwards they went to Ayo's family home for the wedding luncheon. At the door they were met by another of Ayo's numerous elderly aunts, who held a glass of water to their lips for them to sip in turn, Ajayi being first. The guests were all gathered outside behind the couple. The aunt made a conveniently long speech until all the guests had foregathered. She warned Ayo not to be too friendly with other women as they would inevitably steal her husband; that they should live peaceably and not let the sun go down on a quarrel between them. Turning to Ajayi, she told him with a twinkle in her eye that a wife could be quite as exciting as a mistress, and also not to use physical violence against their daughter, his wife.

After this they entered and the western part of the ceremony took place. The wedding cake (which Ayo had made) was cut and speeches made. Then Ajayi departed to his own family home where other celebrations went on. Later he changed into a lounge suit and called for Ayo. There was weeping in Ayo's household as if she were setting off on a long journey. Her mother in saying goodbye, remarked between tears, that although she would not have the honor next morning of showing the world evidence of Ayo's virginity, yet in the true feminine powers of procreation none except the blind and deaf could say Ayo had lacked zeal.

They called on various relations on both sides of the family and at last they were home. Ayo seemed different in Ajayi's eyes. He had never really looked at her carefully before. Now he observed her head held erectly and gracefully through years of balancing loads on it in childhood; her statuesque neck with its three natural horizontal ridges—to him, signs of beauty; her handsome shoulders. He clasped her with a new tenderness.

The next morning, as his alarm clock went off, he stirred and reached for his morning cup of tea. It was not there. He sprang up and looked. Nothing. He listened for Ayo's footsteps outside in the kitchen. Nothing. He turned to look beside him. Ayo was there and her bare ebony back was heaving gently. She must be ill, he thought; all that excitement yesterday.

"Ayo, Ayo," he cried, "are you ill?" She turned round slowly still lying down and faced him. She tweaked her toes luxuriously under the cotton coverlet and patted her breast slowly. There was a terrible calm about her.

"No, Ajayi," she replied. "Are you?" she asked him. "Are your legs paralysed?" she continued.

"No," he said. He was puzzled and alarmed, thinking that her mind had become unhinged under the strain.

"Ajayi, my husband," she said, "for twelve years I have got up every morning at five to make tea for you and breakfast. Now I am a truly married woman you must treat me with a little more respect. You are now a husband and not a lover. Get up and make yourself a cup of tea."

The Invitation

by T. M. ALUKO

T. M. Aluko, born in Nigeria in 1918, grew up under the British colonial system. After graduating from Government College, Ibadan, he continued his education in Lagos and London, specializing in two related fields, engineering and town planning. In 1960, when independence came, he was appointed Director of Public Works for Western Nigeria.

His first two novels, *One Man, One Wife* (1959) and *One Man, One Matchet* (1964), draw on his own experiences to develop the theme of the educated youth who tries to apply modern ideas in a situation dominated by family practices and loyalties. Mr. Aluko treats serious problems with a light touch.

Kinsman and Foreman (1966), the novel from which the following episode is taken, is the story of Titus Oti, English-educated engineer, who does not wish to offend the family elders but neither does he wish to follow the old ways of idleness and corruption. The extended family co-operated in sending him abroad for an education, and they intend to control his activities on his return. Titus may "know book" but they have their prestige in the community to defend. Both young and old were stubborn.

ᚠ   Titus was cross with his mother and he told her so. "How many times will I tell you that if you want to come and see me you should send someone to tell me. I'll come to fetch you in my car. Do you have to walk from one end of the town to the other to get to me here at the Government Reservation? And now you are soaking wet."

His mother in her turn was cross with him. "Whenever I come to you, you scold me as if I'm a little child of yesterday. I'm not. If it was not important for me to come, I would not have come. And do I complain to you that I'm tired of walking? It's my feet and not yours that I use—why do you have to complain?" She paused to concentrate on the important business of unstrapping an infant from her back. It clung for security to the part of her *buba* round her bosom. She succeeded in depositing it on the floor. It took immediate possession of its new kingdom and crawled all over the place. It had no clothes on whatsoever.

Titus followed the baby round with a disapproving eye. "Whose child is it, Mother?"

"The child of Rachel, the daughter of your father's elder sister. You remember her; she was at the thanksgiving service." Deborah was in the habit of measuring dates and describing people from the time of the thanksgiving service and the attendance at the thanksgiving service.

"But look at that, Mother. See what a mess the baby has made on the floor," Titus cried in anger. The baby had first urinated on the carpet and then had proceeded to play with the mess.

"But, Titus, why must you be angry that a baby has done this? Does it know any better—does it know that it is wrong?"

"I don't care what it knows and what it does not know. I want you to take it away from here, now."

"Did you not do worse when you were a child?"

He opened his mouth and without saying a thing snapped it shut in anger.

She smiled in triumph, and proceeded to press home her obvious advantage. "Is it not the prayer of everybody that he may have the good fortune of having a child that will both urinate and evacuate its bowels on his clothes and on his mat? And when you have settled down sufficiently and Bola has come back from the white man's country too and you are both married, will you not pray to have a child like this that will urinate and vomit all over the house?"

"No," he said in monosyllabic finality.

"My God, Titus," she cried in anguish. "You must not curse yourself. You will have a child. You will have not just one but several children. And I am going to tend them all on this back of mine."

"Yes, I pray I'll have children, but not the sort we are talking about now. Not one without a napkin on. And tell me now what the important matter is that has brought you here."

"This letter," she said. She untied the knot at one corner of

168

her head-tie. She brought out a crumpled envelope which she handed to him. He frowned; he noticed that half the address on the envelope had been rendered illegible by water. He tore it open and brought out the sheet of paper inside.

"Pastor and Foreman told me it is very important," she said as he began to read the note. "So I decided to bring it myself."

Very important, sure enough. Addressed to Titus Oti, Esq., B.Sc. (Eng.) (London), it was from the Harvest Committee of All Souls Church. It said that the Committee had unanimously elected him to be the Chief Opener at the Bazaar Sale that year. They were writing him formally to acquaint him with this decision. The Committee would be calling on him at his convenience to discuss details. The note ended with a reminder of the good things that the Lord of the Harvest had in store for those who contributed generously to both the Harvest and the Bazaar.

She noticed the frown on his face. "What has Pastor written in the letter, Titus?"

"He and his Harvest Committee want me to open the Bazaar Sales."

"They want you to open the Bazaar Sales!" she echoed. "That is going to be serious. I don't want you to be exposed to the glare of the public yet, Titus."

Titus shared her anxiety. For once mother and son appeared to agree.

"When women who are older than I see you performing this very important function they will be jealous, because their own sons are not as important as my son. That is why I am anxious. I am afraid of witches and evil-doers."

Titus listened to her, but said nothing.

"But wo must accept the invitation since it has something to do with the church"—she appeared to be having second thoughts. "If we don't, they will think we are running away from spending money. We must begin to prepare for it now."

"What do we prepare—and how many of us?" he asked, staring at the baby who at that time was laying waste everything movable in its path.

"Well, must we not begin to prepare for it now? Is it not going to cost money, much money?"

"About how much?"

"Can you do it for less than £30? When your kinsman, the Foreman, did it last year he opened it with more than that. He spent about £40."

"More than £30! Where did he get the money from?" he asked without really expecting her to give the answer.

"He is quite rich, Titus. And you too will soon be rich. You both do the same work and people who do this work have plenty of money. Everyone say so. And I know it's true."

"But, Mother, I don't want you to talk like this," he stopped her. "I have no money, and I'm going to be honest. I'm not going to steal any money, to please anyone. If the Church people want £30 from me for opening Bazaar Sales, they will be disappointed. I just haven't got it."

"But, Titus, you mustn't talk like that. You mustn't let down the family. We shall find the money."

"And please pick up the child, Mother. It's messed up the floor enough. Thomas has brought some food for you. Drink the Ovaltine. It will do you good. After that I'll drive you back home. How's my great-aunt today?"

"She is well. But people of her age die without warning— without being ill. So you must begin to put money aside now for the funeral expenses."

"Money for Bazaar Sales! Money for funeral expenses! Money for this, money for that. Christ in heaven! It's nothing but money, money, and yet more money ever since I came back from England!"

"Titus!"

On the drive back to his mother's home Titus pondered the problem of money and allied matters. Before he left England he had been told at the Colonial Office that his salary on arrival in Nigeria would be forty-two pounds ten shillings a month. He and Bola had thought that that was a reasonably good salary and that he should be able to save at least twelve pounds ten shillings out of this every month. Surely one pound a day was sufficient to live on.

He had been back from England five months now. And in every one of these five months there had been demands on his purse. One pound a day had not been sufficient to live on at all. What really made the cost of living higher than he expected was

170

the extra expenses of a cook-steward, Thomas. He paid him four pounds a month; but he made nearly as much again on the purchases he made at the market and in pilfering. He resented intensely Deborah's attempts to take over the buying of foodstuffs for her son. In this he was well supported by his master! Finally, Titus himself ate only a mere fraction of the food Thomas cooked. Thomas saw to it that more than enough was cooked—the rest being eaten by him and his tribal brothers.

"Look out, look out," his mother shouted in panic. He saw it, nearly too late, and swerved sharply to the left bringing the car to a screeching stop mere inches short of a telegraph pole on the off-side of the road. He had narrowly avoided a head-on collision with a lorry. He had mistaken the oncoming vehicle for a motorcycle because it had only a single headlamp, which the driver had not dipped. It was at the last minute that the "motorcycle" had suddenly materialized into a lorry—with near-disastrous consequences.

"Jesu! Jesu!" Deborah cried in fright.

Titus climbed out of his car, fuming. The driver of the lorry had stopped. He too came out, and shouted: "Why won't you drive carefully? You nearly ran into my lorry."

"You must be mad, you senseless idiot," Titus answered him, shaking with rage and from the shock of the averted accident.

"Don't you call me an idiot, I tell you," the driver cried. "And don't you tell me I'm mad. There is no madness in my family history. You appear to be a big man. This is the only reason why I refrain from calling you mad yourself."

"Why on earth don't you have both headlights working properly?"

"The other one is not working. The mechanic tried to get it working but it just wouldn't work. And what am I to do, Mother?" he appealed to Deborah as if to say: I know you are his mother or his aunt but this case here is so straightforward that even you, his relative, cannot but agree that I'm right and he is wrong! "What can I do? Can I pluck out one of my eyes to fix it on the lorry, can I? I tell you I will not. Not even if my master pays me ten pounds a month."

"You are talking rubbish," Titus said helplessly. "Absolute rubbish. You've broken the law."

"Don't you start abusing me again, I warn you."

"Let us go now," Deborah entreated.

The driver continued: "Yours is not the first car that I have met on this journey. I tell you all the others had not made the bad mistake of thinking that I was a motorcycle; only amateur drivers cannot tell the sounding of a motor-car engine from that of a motorcycle's."

"Do let us go, Titus," his mother again pleaded. He wasn't getting anywhere. The rascal was unrepentant.

" I want to see your licence," Titus demanded.

"You don't need to see my licence. Everyone knows my vehicle in Ibadan and in Lagos. Safe Journey. Write it down in your book and go and report me to the police. Who makes you a policeman, anyway?" The man climbed into the driver's seat and started to fumble with its controls.

The crowd that had gathered round both of them persuaded Titus to break up the argument and go his way. The lorry was not a local one and no one knew the driver. One of the men told him that drivers belonged to a breed that did not care for anyone, not even for engineers. Except, of course, the policeman. They feared policemen, with good reason!

Later on that evening a little girl from the Oti household delivered a letter at the vicarage. After reading it a second time the Rev. Morakinyo sent for both Pa Joel and Simeon Oke. To both of them he read out Titus's letter first in English before translating it into Yoruba for the benefit of the old man:

"I am writing to thank you and through you the members of the Harvest Committee for inviting me to open the Bazaar Sales on 27 May next.

"I have given much consideration to this. While appreciating the great honor done me I have reluctantly come to the conclusion that I have to decline it for reasons I shall now endeavor to explain.

"I understand that this role is usually played by an influential member of the Church who usually donates a respectable sum of money, thereby setting a good example for the supporters and the generality of the church members at the ceremony to follow. The truth is that, as it is only five months since I came back from England, my financial position is still quite bad and I shall be unable to make a donation worthy of a chairman.

"I also consider that it will be better practice not to choose a young man for this role. I respectfully suggest therefore that the Committee should now look round for someone else who in age and affluence and, above all, in Christian piety is more deserving of the honor.

"I enclose herewith a check for two guineas as my own contribution to the Bazaar.

"I wish you and your Committee every success."

After he had translated the letter to Pa Joel, the vicar folded it and put it back in the envelope. He puffed at his pipe.

Pa Joel spoke: "I do not believe Titus wrote it, Pastor." He stretched out his hand to Rev. Morakinyo. The latter handed the envelope to the old man. He drew out of it the sheet of paper and purred at it.

Simeon chuckled. "Why are you staring at the paper as if you can read it? You should say whatever you have to say to this serious matter now that Pastor has read out the letter from Engineer."

"It is a very serious matter, Pastor. I do not believe that the sons of my nephew Samuel could write those words that you have read to my ear this evening, Pastor. I do not believe it, Pastor."

"I thought I should bring it to your notice, Elder, and to yours, Brother Simeon, before I summon a meeting of the Harvest Committee."

All three were silent. Pa Joel's bald head shone in the little light of the kerosene lamp on the table. He coughed preparatory to his next observation: "These young men! There is no limit to what they will do. Not only has he brought shame to our family and to the memory of his father, he now thinks that he knows better than the members of the Harvest Committee by teaching them how to go about their business. Pastor, is it not every year that we form a Committee to organize the harvest and the Bazaar?"

Pastor Morakinyo puffed at his pipe rapidly and nodded his head rapidly to signify assent.

"Have we not been doing it this way long before Titus was born? It is you I blame for suggesting his name at all."

"But all the Committee thought that he is the most suitable person," Simeon said. "Look, Pa, the important thing is for you to speak to him. He will not refuse you. Speak to him and tell him to reconsider the matter."

Pastor Morakinyo puffed at his pipe rapidly. He nodded his head rapidly.

"Speak to him? I shall order him to do it. That's what I shall do. He may have been to the white man's country. He may have been to Jerusalem in heaven. He is still Titus. And I am going to tell him that. If he insists on bringing dishonor to the family, and disgrace to the memory of his father, I shall have nothing to do with him. Simeon, we go. And, Pastor, please do not be vexed with him. He is only a small boy. That's what he is. Leave him to me. I shall knock some sense into his head."

Pa Joel did not succeed in his determination to knock sense into the head of Titus. There were angry scenes between the old man and the young rebel. There were angry scenes between Deborah and her erring son. At each scene between Pa Joel and Titus and between mother and son, Simeon was present; cool, saying little but leave no doubt as to which side he supported.

But Titus stood his ground. He had paid two guineas towards the Harvest Fund and he was not going to pay a penny extra. As for being the chief opener at the Bazaar he would have nothing whatever to do with it.

After a final family meeting a compromise was announced to the world. Engineer Titus and the whole family appreciated very much the honor done to them by the church congregation in considering Titus suitable for performing the most important function at the Bazaar. Titus had, however, decided to transfer this great honor to the dearly respected head of the family Pa Joel Tobatele. Unfortunately Titus himself would be away, on the day, as he would be having important consultations with the Director of P.W.D. in Lagos. But both his mother, Sister Deborah, and his kinsman, Brother Simeon Oke, would be there to support the head of the family.

From Kinsman and Foreman, *by T. M. Aluko, Heinemann Educational Books Ltd., 1966.*

The Suitcase

by EZEKIEL MPHAHLELE

Ezekiel Mphahlele was born in 1919 in the slums of Pretoria, South Africa, in the worst type of urban ghetto. With his mother's help, he managed to spend three years at St. Peter's School in Johannesburg, which was closed in the late 1950's by the Bantu Education Act.

While teaching high school, he studied for the B.A. and M.A. and was awarded these degrees by the University of South Africa. Banned from teaching because of his political activities, he held several menial jobs as clerk and messenger and finally served as editor for *Drum,* the black magazine of sports, music, and politics, when it was first published in Johannesburg.

In 1957, he chose exile: first in Nigeria, then Paris, then Nairobi, holding various teaching positions and beginning his career as a writer. His autobiography, *Down Second Avenue* (1959) has been translated into eight languages, including Japanese and Hungarian. His short stories appeared in *Drum, Kenyan Review, New World Writing,* and other magazines. He edited two anthologies of stories and poems by his contemporaries: *Modern African Stories* (1964) and *African Writing Today* (1967). He is now Associate Professor in the Department of English at the University of Denver.

His most recent publications are a one-man collection of fourteen short stories, *In Corner B* (1970), and a novel, *The Wanderers* (1971).

One of these days he was going to take a desperate chance, Timi thought. He would not miss it if it presented itself. Many men had got rich by sheer naked chance. Couldn't it just be that he was destined to meet such a chance?

He sat on a pavement on a hot afternoon. It was New Year's Eve. And in such oppressive heat Timi had been sitting for over an hour. An insect got into his nostril and made him sneeze several times. Through the tears that filled his eyes the traffic seemed to dance about before him.

175

The grim reality of his situation returned to him with all its cold and aching pain after the short interlude with the insect. Today he had been led on something like a goose chase. He had been to three places where chances of getting work were promising. He had failed.

At one firm he had been told, "We've already got a boy, Jim."

At the second firm a tiny typist told him, "You're too big, John. The boss wants a small boy—about eighteen you know." Then she had gone on with her typing, clouding her white face with cigarette smoke.

At the third place of call a short pudgy white man put down his price in a squeaking voice: "Two pounds ten a week." Three pounds ten a week, Timi had said. "Take it or leave it, my boy," the proprietor had said as his final word, and snorted to close the matter. Timi chuckled softly to himself at the thought of the pudgy man with fat white cheeks and small blinking eyes.

He was watching the movements of a wasp tormenting a worm. The wasp circled over the worm and then came down on the clumsy and apparently defenseless worm. It seemed to stand on its head as it stung the worm. The worm wriggled violently, seeming to want to fly away from the earth. Then suddenly the worm stretched out, as though paralysed. The winged insect had got its prey. Timi felt pity for the poor worm. An unequal fight, an unfair fight, he thought. Must it always be thus, he asked—the well armed and agile creature stings the defenseless to death? The wasp was now dragging the worm; to its home, evidently.

He remembered he had nothing to take home. But the thought comforted him that his wife was so understanding. A patient and understanding wife. Yes, she would say, as she had often said, "Tomorrow's sun must rise, Timi. It rises for everyone. It may have its fortunes"; or "I will make a little fire, Timi. Our sages say even where there is no pot to boil there should be fire."

Now she was ill. She was about to have a baby, a third baby. And with nothing to take home for the last two months, his savings running out, he felt something must be done. Not anything that would get him into jail. No, not that. It wouldn't do for him to go to jail with his wife and children almost starving like that. No, he told himself emphatically.

A white man staggered past him, evidently drunk. He stopped a short way past Timi and turned to look at him. He walked back to Timi and held out a bottle of brandy before him, scarcely keeping firm on his legs.

"Here, John, drink this stuff. Happy New Year!" Timi shook his head.

"C'mon, be—be a s-sport, hic! No p-police to catch you, s-s-see?"

Timi shook his head again and waved him away.

"Huh, here's a bugger don't want to have a happy New Year, eh. Go t-to hell then."

The white man swung round, brandishing his bottle as he tripped away.

If only that were money, Timi thought bitterly.

He remembered it was time he went home, and boarded a bus to Sophiatown. In the bus he found an atmosphere of revelry. The New Year spirit, he thought; an air of reckless abandon. Happy New Year! one shouted at intervals.

Timi was looking at a man playing a guitar just opposite him across the aisle. Here a girl was dancing to the rhythm of the music. The guitarist strummed away, clearly carried away in the flight of his own music. He coaxed, caressed and stroked his instrument. His long fingers played effortlessly on the strings. He glowered at the girl in front of him with hanging lower lip as she twisted her body seductively this way and that, like a young supple plant that the wind plays about with. Her breasts pushed out under a light sleeveless blouse. At the same time the guitarist bent his ear to the instrument as if to hear better its magic notes, or to whisper to it the secret of his joy.

Two young women came to sit next to Timi. One of them was pale, and seemed sick. The other deposited a suitcase in front between her leg and Timi's. His attention was taken from the music by the presence of these two women. They seemed to have much unspoken between them.

At the next stop they rose to alight. Timi's one eye was fixed on the suitcase as he watched them go towards the door. When the bus moved a man who was sitting behind Timi exclaimed. "Those young women have left their case."

"No, it is mine," said Timi hastily.

"No. I saw them come in with it."

This is a chance. . .

"I tell you it's mine."

"You can't tell me that."

Now there mustn't be any argument, or else . . .

"Did you not see me come in with a case?"

I mustn't lose my temper, or else . . .

"Tell the truth, my man, it bites no one."

"What more do you want me to say now?"

The people are looking at me now. By the gods, what can I do?

"It is his lucky day," shouted someone from the back, "let him be!"

"And if it is not his, how is this a lucky day?" asked someone else.

"Ha, ha, ha!" A woman laughed. "You take my thing, I take yours, he takes somebody else's. So we all have a lucky day, eh? Ha, ha, ha." She rocked with voluble laughter, seeming to surrender herself to it.

"Oh, leave him alone," an old voice came from another quarter, "only one man saw the girls come in with a suitcase, and only one man says it is his. One against one. Let him keep what he has, the case. Let the other man keep what he has, the belief that it belongs to the girls." There was a roar of laughter. The argument melted in the air of a happy New Year, of revelry and song.

Timi felt a great relief. He had won.

The bus came to a stop and he alighted. He did not even hear someone behind him in the bus cry, "That suitcase will yet tell whom it belongs to, God is my witness!" Why can't people mind their own affairs? He thought of all those people looking at him.

Once out of the bus he was seized by a fit of curiosity, anxiousness and expectancy. He must get home quickly and see what is in the case.

It was a chance, a desperate chance, and he had taken it. That mattered to him most as he paced up the street.

Timi did not see he was about to walk into a crowd of people. They were being searched by the police, two white constables. He was jolted into attention by the shining of a badge. Quickly he slipped into an open backyard belonging to a Chinaman. Providence was with him, he thought, as he ran to stand behind the great iron door, his heart almost choking him.

He must have waited there for fifteen minutes, during which he could see all that was happening out there in the street. The hum and buzz so common to Good Street rose to a crescendo; so savage, so cold-blooded, so menacing. Suddenly he got a strange and frightening feeling that he had excited all this noise, that he was the center around which these angry noises whirled and circled, that he had raised a hue and cry.

For one desperate second he felt tempted to leave the case where he squatted. It would be so simple for him, he thought. Yes, just leave the case there and have his hands, no, more than that, his soul, freed of the burden. After all, it was not his.

Not his. This thought reminded him that he had done all this because it was not his. The incident in the bus was occasioned by the stark naked fact that the case was not his. He felt he must get home soon because it was not his. He was squatting here like an outlaw, because the case was not his. Why not leave it here then, after all these efforts to possess it and keep it? There must surely be valuable articles in it, Timi mused. It was so heavy. There must be. It couldn't be otherwise. Else why had Providence been so kind to him so far? Surely the spirits of his ancestors had pity on him, with a sick wife and hungry children.

Then the wild, primitive determination rose in him; the blind determination to go through with a task once begun, whether a disaster can be avoided in time or not, whether it is to preserve worthless or valuable articles. No, he was not going to part with the case.

The pick-up van came and collected the detained men and women. The police car started up the street. Timi came out and walked on the pavement, not daring to look behind, lest he lose his nerve and blunder. He knew he was not made for all this sort of thing. Pitso was coming up the pavement in the opposite direction. Lord, why should it be Pitso just at this time? Pitso, the gasbag, the notorious talker whose appearance always broke up a party. They met.

"Greetings! You seem to be in a hurry, Timi?" Pitso called out in his usually noisy and jovial fashion. "Are you arriving or going?"

"Arriving." Timi did not want to encourage him.

"Ha, since when have you been calling yourself A. J. B.?"

"Who says I'm A. J. B.?"

"There my friend." Pitso pointed at the large initials on the case, and looked at his friend with laughing eyes.

"Oh, it's my cousin's." Timi wished he could wipe a broad stupid grin off the large mouth of this nonentity. He remembered later how impotent and helpless he felt now. For Pitso and his grin were inseparables, like Pitso and his mouth. Just now he wished he wouldn't look so uneasy.

"I'm sorry, Pitso, my wife isn't well, and I must hurry." He passed on. Pitso looked at his friend, his broad mouth still smiling blankly.

The Chevrolet came to stop just alongside the pavement. Then it moved on, coasting idly and carelessly.

"Hey!" Timi looked to his left. Something seemed to snap inside him and release a lump shooting up to his throat. "Stop, *jong!*" The driver waved to him.

There they were, two white constables and an African in plain clothes in the back seat. Immediately he realized it would be foolish to run. Besides, the case should be his. He stopped. The driver went up to him and wrenched the suitcase from Timi's hand. At the same time he caught him by the shoulder and led him to the car, opening the back door for Timi. The car shot away to the police station.

His knees felt weak when he recognized the black man next to him. It was the same man who was the first to argue that the case was not Timi's in the bus. By the spirits, did the man have such a strong sense of justice as to call God to be the witness? Even on New Year's Eve? Or was he a detective? No, he could have arrested him on the bus. The man hardly looked at Timi. He just looked in front of him in a self-righteous posture, as it struck Timi.

Timi got annoyed; frantically annoyed. It was a challenge. He would face it. Things might turn round somewhere. He felt he needed all the luck fate could afford to give him.

At the police station the two constables took the case into a small room. After a few minutes they came out, with what Timi thought was a strange communication of feelings between them as they looked at each other.

"*Kom, kom, jong!*" one of them said, although quite gently. They put the case in front of him.

"Whose case is this?"

"Mine."

"Do you have your things in here?"

"My wife's things."

"What are they?"

"I think she has some of her dresses in it."

"Why do you say you *think*?"

"Well, you see, she just packed them up in a hurry, and asked me to take them to her aunt; but I didn't see her pack them."

"Hm. You can recognize your wife's clothing?"

"Some of it." Why make it so easy for him? And why was there such cold amusement in the white man's eyes?

The constable opened the suitcase, and started to unpack the articles singly.

"Is this your wife's?" It was a torn garment.

"Yes."

"And this? And this?" Timi answered yes to both. Why did they pack such torn clothing. The constable lifted each one up before Timi. Timi's thoughts were racing and milling round in his head. What trick was fate about to play him? He sensed there was something wrong. Had he been a dupe?

The constable, after taking all the rags out, pointed to an object inside. "*And is this also your wife's?*" glaring at Timi with aggressive eyes.

Timi stretched his neck to see.

It was a ghastly sight. A dead baby that could not have been born more than twelve hours before. A naked, white, curly haired image of death. Timi gasped and felt sick and faint. They had to support him to the counter to make a statement. He told the truth. He knew he had gambled with chance; the chance that was to cost him eighteen months' hard labor.

181

Coin Diver

by CYPRIAN EKWENSI

Cyprian Ekwensi was born in Northern Nigeria in 1921. He studied forestry at Ibadan and pharmacy in London. In Lagos, he taught biology and chemistry before joining the Nigerian Broadcasting Corporation. Later he became Director of Information in the Federal Ministry of Information in Nigeria. His hobbies include photography and sports.

Ekwensi is especially perceptive in his portrayal of African city life. With characters like Jagua Nana, Nancy of the Grand Palm Hotel, and Charlie the Coin Diver, he weaves an unforgettable picture of the chaotic social life of the modern African metropolis. His theme is often the destructive impact of the city on the man-woman relationship. Many of his short stories and articles have been published, as well as several novels: *People of the City* (1954), *Jagua Nana* (1961), and *Beautiful Feathers* (1963).

†   In the bright sunlight of the Freetown afternoon, Nancy came down the lane. Charlie, the coin-diver, pushed aside the flower-bush and gazed at her. Tall she was, with a rich black skin and eyes big and black and lips made red, so red, with lipstick. Her ear-rings—big golden loops—dangled in rhythm with her light foot-steps. Dust rose lightly from her white sandals but her eyes were bright as the ribbons in her straw hat. *Fine gal*, thought Charlie. *Like say dem born am for America, not Sa Leone!* For a moment he forgot why he had been waiting for her behind the bush: to ask her to be his wife.

And she was alone too—alone! He was in a flutter. "How I will tell her this thing? I got no money like de rich men who come for Grand Palm. An' I want dis gal who sing like canary. Because of Nancy, everybody who come to Freetown mus' go to Grand Palm Hotel to lodge—white man, black man, all de stranger!"

He stepped forward, hopefully. "Nancy . . ." Her smile encouraged him. "Nancy, I got to tell you somethin' . . ."

She was smiling even more sweetly, but her eyes bored right through him and beyond. Charlie, confused, turned to see what she was gazing at.

In the path behind him stood Diamond Joe, his bitter rival. Joe's gold tooth gleamed. He extended a heavily ringed hand and clasped Nancy's delicate and shapely fingers. Charlie boiled with envy. He saw them walk away; saw Nancy slip a parcel she had been carrying into Joe's hands. He was disgusted at the way they held hands and whispered into each other's ears and even looked back over their shoulders to laugh—at him, no doubt. He watched them till they turned the corner, and even then his eyes still focused on the bush that had hidden them; his ears still strained for sounds of their happiness, for their sneering contempt of him.

He looked down at his canvas shoes, tunic shirt and white drill shorts. He knew now why he had failed. He had come to court a girl like Nancy, the singing star of the Grand Palm, the most exclusive social spot in Freetown, and he was unimpressively dressed. *But, if this gal like me, she no go worry 'bout my dress.*

He remembered the night when he first heard Nancy sing, and how since then he had known no peace of mind. He had even succeeded once in entering her dressing-room. It was shortly before she went on stage, and her girls were helping her adorn herself. Charlie was ill at ease. Things destined for her ears only would be heard by others. Why did she not send the maids away? Perhaps they were mocking him now. Why did she keep glancing at her watch, slim and expensive though it was?

"What is it now, Mister?" She was marking out her brows with a pencil.

Charlie averted his gaze. "I—got a little money I been savin'."

"And you want me to marry *you*," she flashed, serving up his most secret thoughts in a manner which made nonsense of his ambition.

"No . . . No, not so! I—I think say you will like to improve you voice . . ." What was wrong with telling her the truth? This was not what he meant to say, but it had now been said.

She frowned. "You mean to tell me I don' sing well?"

183

"Not so!" Charlie's hands rose in protest. "I beg pardon, Madam. No, you sing like canary. Like canary! But you know . . . nowadays, anybody in Africa who do anythin' fine mus' travel an' see de world." Charlie had forgotten the two maids present. For one brief moment, he saw how intently Nancy was listening. Then the spark died out of her eyes. She sighed.

"Thank you for the offer, Mr. —"

"Them call me Charlie . . . Am one of de people who dive into de sea when de mail boat come. I kin dive for your sake. Lord works wonders! Your voice! . . . I never hear the like!"

"Flattery, eh? I'm sorry I can't accept your offer."

Did he see tears in her eyes? No . . . pure imagination. Even so he could not concentrate on his work. More cargo boats and passenger liners were calling at Freetown. More coins were spinning into the Atlantic while sun-burnt men and women from the outside world thronged the gangways, laughing. But Charlie knew that less and less money was finding its way into his own pockets. He stood in his paper-light canoe and hailed:

"A penny? . . . How you, Ma'am! A penny? I kiant sell this boat to you. I bought it to try my luck. . . . Whenever a boat comes in, I come aboard and try my luck. . . ."

Those words. Where was their music? Deftly he guided his paper-light canoe on the jumping surface of the bight, trying desperately to be light-hearted. "What about a tanner, Ma'am? What about it, Ma'am . . . Well, you kin have a look . . . I just goin' over other side . . . The ship's getting ready to movin' . . . What about a good-bye, Ma'am?"

Looking up at the rearing wall of the side of the vessel, at the tangled skeins of rope dangling downwards, Charlie knew he was not the same man without Nancy. As he could not have Nancy, he must have something—a symbol of her. Nancy to him meant music. If he had music! If he had . . . music . . . But how? Not for him the gramophones and the radiograms. No. His music must be different, natural as Nancy's; fresh and clean—like a canary. That was it! A canary. He should have thought of it before.

He told no one of his plans because he knew they would call him "silly." They would laugh and say, "Charlie, you done gone craze? You mean, you goin' to Cape Verde on you canoe—jus' to catch canary, because woman refuse you?" They would discourage him and so he told no one. He tied up his money in an old cloth belted to his waist. He went to market and bought food; he put fresh water in a kerosene tin. And at night, when no one saw him, he slid quietly northwards in his bigger canoe.

For days he was on the wide Atlantic. Sun and wind bit into his face and back. Hunger clawed at his stomach. The porpoises leapt about and the sharks waited for him to drown while the whales tossed his canoe. But when he finally eased off in the Canary Islands, Charlie felt that nothing could be more romantic than capturing a wonderful canary—one that sang like Nancy.

At the bazaar Charlie found just what he wanted—a canary with a voice like Nancy. But she cost him all he had in the world. With no means of returning to Freetown, Charlie told his hard-luck story to the captain of a cargo boat who had seen him at the bazaar. The captain was so impressed by Charlie's courage and the magic of Nancy the canary that he signed Charlie on his boat for the homeward journey to Freetown.

His duties on deck did not give him much time, but Charlie never forgot to take the greatest care of the canary. He called her Nancy. Her cage was never without red pepper and water. All through the stormy passage Nancy delighted the crew with ceaseless gymnastics of song. Holding the cage at arm's length Charlie's heart swelled with joy. "Now, when I want to hear good music, I don't go no more to the Grand Palm. I got me own Nancy in the house!" He laughed. "Wait till Diamon' Joe see this! . . ."

Back in Freetown, Charlie found it impossible to hide such talent. In a week, everyone had heard of Nancy, the coin-diver's canary. Tourists touching Freetown went first to the Grand Palm, then came straight to Charlie's little shack to hear Nancy sing. Once a white woman brought Charlie a packet of rare seeds. An American tourist, on hearing the price Charlie had paid for the bird, offered double for it: in dollars. Charlie would not sell. He was quite sure that Nancy of the Grand Palm had heard of the bird; and so also must Diamond Joe.

A new passenger liner had come into port, and as Charlie prepared to go down for the day's work, he heard a knock on his door. It was Nancy, and Diamond Joe was with her. Charlie had not seen her since his trip to Cape Verde and now it seemed to him that she had become even more desirable. Nancy, the bird, could only sing. It could not replace the love he had in his heart for Nancy of the Grand Palm. He watched her eyes for signs of envy. He saw only admiration. An eager joy had given vitality to her cheeks, and her teeth shone with laughter. But Diamond's eyes, red as Nancy's new frock, depicted greed, envy . . . jealousy. All the meanness in his nature seemed to bubble up at the sight of Nancy's innocent happiness.

"I want your canary," he said shortly.

"Not for sell, Diamon' Joe. I tell you so yesterday when we workin' in de wharf."

"Ah'll pay you what you spen' three times!"

"They awready offer me more, Joe. I no sell."

Nancy's eyes darted from one to the other. "Now, you two men, don't fight now!"

She made the bird sing. She stared at it in rapt admiration, cooing all the time. Charlie flattered himself that her enthusiasm had some faint far-off connection with affection for its owner. Or was she merely trying to annoy Diamond Joe? He observed the disgruntled look on Joe's face as they left. He knew also that his journey to Cape Verde had been in vain. He still loved Nancy; more so than ever before. And by bringing this bird back to Freetown, was he not harming her reputation in some way?

All through his work that day, the dreadful thought remained with him: he was undermining Nancy's position in the Grand Palm. So engrossed was he with his own thoughts that he did not notice the absence of Diamond Joe. He was glad when the boat sailed away and he could go home. As he turned the key of his front door, a queerness came to him. Someone had been in this room. The cage appeared to have been shifted. He whistled. He walked straight to the cage and took it down. At the bottom of it was a lifeless form. Nancy, the canary, was dead.

The very air about him froze into silence. Charlie lost count of time. Slowly it dawned on him that his canary had not died a natural death. Someone who disliked its existence had destroyed it. He remembered now how Diamond Joe had looked at the bird in the morning, how he had not been seen at work.

Charlie rolled up his shirt-sleeves and walked towards the beach, talking to no one. Children called out, "Charlie!" and one of them came and said, "You lookin' for somebody?"

"Yes, Diamon' Joe . . ."

They said: "He jus' went dat way. . . ."

Charlie caught up with him in a drinking house. He smashed his way into the room and seized Diamond Joe by the coat-collar, smashing his face with his mallet of a right hand.

"Where's my canary? Talk!"

Tables were overturned as both men fought. It broke up in disorder when Diamond threatened to send for the police, but Charlie was making for the Grand Palm in search of Nancy. He did not find her, and all through the day he walked the streets, searching for her.

When evening came, he guessed that she must have left. He felt terribly depressed as he turned his steps homewards to his hut without music. Why had fate conspired to deny him his simple pleasure?

He pushed his door open. A shadowy form slipped towards him and he stepped backwards, fists clenched. It was a woman.

"Charlie! . . ."

"Nancy, sorry. I think is Diamon' come to murder me."

"Charlie, I beg you to—forgive me! Is my mistake."

"What's matter, Nancy? You done me wrong?"

"Is jealousy, Charlie. I come here with Diamon' Joe. I told him; jus' change the canary. Put another one an' open the cage let Nancy fly away. Instead, you know what Diamond do? He's too mean. He jus' strangle Nancy."

Charlie stood confused. Dimly he realized that something new was happening to his world. A light was glowing in the dark. Nancy was sobbing now.

"You see, everybody loved your Nancy better than me. Even you! Since you got your Nancy, you don' come to see me in the Grand Palm! Tha's why Joe killed your bird."

"He kill the happy I get in my belly too. How can man be happy without music? I mean—*natural* music!"

"Charlie, I—I think I kin sing as well as the canary. Will you put me in your cage, I mean—your house—" And Nancy smiled

187

at the comparison. "Will you? I promise to sing for you every day and for ever as my voice is good—"

Charlie looked into her face to see if she meant it. But the tears veiled her eyes and she could not stand his gaze. "Don' cry, Nancy," he said, reaching out in the dark and touching her soft shoulders.

Her face buried itself in his rough shirt and he could feel the fragrance of her hair and the warmth of her as she sobbed against his breast. He took her arm and they walked out towards the beating surf of the Gulf of Guinea. Charlie asked himself, looking out over the wide horizons: is this Nancy whose hand I hold, or am I dreaming? She sighed and he knew he was wide awake—and happy.

A Street in Ouagadougou, Capital of Upper Volta   GUIRMA

The Apprentices

by SEMBENE OUSMANE

Sembene Ousmane, born in 1923, was the son of a Senegalese fisherman. At the time of his birth, his country was part of Western Sudan, a French colonial province, now the independent African state of Senegal. As a youth, he drifted from one job to another until he recognized his vocation as a writer, specializing in material with social or political implications. His first novel was *The Black Dockman* (1956). He has also written short stories and produced films. His film *The Money Order* was shown in the 1969 Film Festival at Lincoln Center in New York.

God's Bits of Wood, published in 1962, is a novel based on the Dakar-Niger Railway strike of 1947–48. Its background is well documented, but the power of the book lies in the author's dramatization of the human struggle. It is a story of social action, of men, women, and children who pit their strength against the French colonial officials.

The workers who began the strike were not well organized at first. The strike was an act of desperation, springing from stark poverty. They wanted a living wage, sick pay, and pensions—demands which the French called nonsense.

人 In all this period, there was one group in Thiès that lived entirely apart, separated from both the workers and their wives and the closed circle of the company itself. It was the group of the apprentices, and because of them a series of momentous events was building up at the very moment when the deceptively calm city seemed just to be sinking deeper into the apathy caused by the strike.

Magatte, Doudou's apprentice, had rapidly become the unquestioned leader of the little band. There were twelve of them, of whom the youngest was fourteen and the oldest seventeen. In the beginning, the strike had seemed to them to be just a sort of prolonged holiday; the older people appeared to have forgotten them completely, and they savored their freedom as if it were a new and exciting game. Then, as money ran out and the days grew harsh, it occurred to their families that they could be useful, and they were sent out to search for chickens that had wandered off or to pick the "monkey bread" of the baobab trees, the only fruit available at that season of the year. For a time it amused their elders to see them running and jumping from one compound to another, ferreting out anything that was edible and happy with the task; but soon there were no more chickens to be recaptured, and even in the ravine which led to the airfield the baobab trees had been stripped of their fruit. Every morning then their shouting and running through the courtyards was broken up with cries of, "Go and amuse yourselves somewhere else!"

On the outskirts of N'Ginth, the largest suburb of Thiès, there was an old baobab tree standing by a path that led into the fields. Its enormous trunk was completely hollow, and its leafless branches made it look like some gigantic old woman waving her arms in the air. No one knew exactly how old it was, but it was certainly the oldest tree in the district. The moment the apprentices discovered it they knew that this would be their future home. They scraped out the inside of the trunk to form a secret hiding place and built an elaborate ladder of huge nails up the side of the tree. They would sit in there for hours, talking or sleeping, but one of them was always on guard, astride a great branch just outside the entrance. Their discussions were invariably concerned with the same subject—the films they had seen in the days before the strike. They told the stories of every one of them over and over again, but never without feverish interruptions: "You're forgetting the part where . . ." or, "No, that's not the way he killed the Indian!" Next to Western films, war films were their favorites. Sometimes, as a change from their enforced inactivity, they played war games themselves. The old baobab became the enemy, and they bombarded it with stones, but after a time this became too simple and they turned their attention to the swarms of little snakes and lizards in the fields around them. Occasionally they had killed as many as a hundred of them in a single day. They would gather the dead animals together in one place, shouting to each other with each new addition to the pile, "That one didn't say his prayers today!" for they had always been taught that any serpent who neglected his daily prayers would die before the night.

One day, when they were playing idly with a hedgehog in the field beside the baobab tree, Souley came and sat down beside Magatte.

"We ought to have some slingshots," he said.

Magatte chewed thoughtfully on a blade of grass. "Where would we get the rubber to make them?"

Sène, the son of Sène Masène, joined them, carrying the hedgehog, which had curled itself into a spiny little ball. "It's a good idea," he said. "We should have some slingshots."

"I saw some inner tubes for bicycles at Salif's," Gorgui said, scratching his egg-shaped head. He still had a bad case of ringworm, and his forehead and the back of his neck were painted blue again.

"Automobile inner tubes would be better," Magatte said.

"Maybe we could find some at Aziz's shop. He has a truck."

"That's true—I saw it last week in the court behind his shop."

"But how could we get in?" Sène asked, rolling the hedgehog about in the palm of his hand.

"Put that animal down," Magatte said, chopping at his wrist. "We have to make a plan."

The hedgehog fell to the ground and vanished almost instantly, and the apprentices gathered in a circle around Magatte. Their conference went on all through the afternoon.

The next morning they set to work on the execution of their plan. The shop of Aziz the Syrian was located on one of the corners of the Place de France, and behind the shop was a large courtyard surrounded by a bamboo fence. Magatte opened a small gap between some of the stalks and peered through. The truck was standing in the center of the yard.

"I'll go in, with Souley and Sène," he said. "Gorgui, you stay in front of the shop and watch out for Aziz. If you see him coming this way, you whistle to warn us. The rest of you keep an eye on the square."

"Look out," one of the boys said suddenly, "there's a policeman now."

The group promptly improvised a noisy game to distract attention from Magatte and his two assistants, who were cutting a space in the bamboo wall large enough to pass through. The policeman, however, was watching the passers-by in the square. His red tarboosh was set precisely above his ears and he carried his heavy night stick with military precision. A band of noisy children was of no interest to him. At last he walked off, and the game subsided as quickly as it had begun.

Magatte finally succeeded in cutting through the wires that held the bamboo stalks together and crawled into the courtyard, motioning to his two lieutenants to follow him.

"There's no one here," he whispered hoarsely.

"I'm scared," Sène said.

They made their way slowly across the courtyard, walking on their toes and holding their arms tautly at their sides, like tightrope walkers. The wheels of the truck, an ancient Chevrolet, had been dismounted, and the chassis rested on some large wooden cases, serving as blocks. They had almost reached it when the sound of an opening door made them hurl themselves to the ground. They scrambled on their stomachs into the shelter of the cases.

Aziz's wife had come out on the porch at the back of the house. She was wearing no veil, and in the shelter of a flimsy mosquito net she began to take off her clothes. When she was completely naked she began to bathe her body with a glove of toweling material. The color of her skin, which was as white as chalk, was not the least of the surprises to the frightened boys. They were observing her every movement, in silent astonishment, when they heard a warning whistle, followed almost immediately by the sound of Aziz's voice, talking to his wife from the interior of the house. The conversation seemed to last for an eternity, but finally the woman put on her robe and went back inside.

Gorgui breathed a sigh of relief. "There's an inner tube in there," he said, gesturing to the driver's compartment of the truck.

Magatte opened the door on their side of the truck, seized the rubber tube, and dropped back beside the others. "Let's get out of here," he said.

The three lithe little bodies never stood up from the dust of the ground until they reached the fence. Sène, who was last, kept glancing fearfully over his shoulder, but the porch was empty.

A half hour later the whole group was gathered again beside the baobab tree. They set to work in an atmosphere of lazy triumph, and that day the anatomy of the Syrian woman replaced the films as the topic of discussion.

The following morning a band of lighthearted apprentices went hunting, armed with brand-new slingshots and little balls of lead. Hummingbirds were the targets of their first expedition, and then it was the turn of the lizards again. Anything that showed itself in the grass or moved in the wind was fair grame. At the slightest movement or sound, a dozen projectiles were zeroed in on the suspected enemy. By noon they had collected several crows, two magpies, and a bird none of them could identify.

"We have to learn to shoot these things properly," Magatte said.

"Yes, general," replied the eleven soldiers of an army whose lowest-ranking member was a lieutenant.

The dead birds were hung from the branches of the baobab, and stones and lead pellets began whistling through the air in an organized drill. Each time a goal was scored, the victor marked a stripe on his naked arm with the point of a charred stick.

At night they would return to their homes tired but happy. Their parents, preoccupied with their own troubles, paid no attention to their wandering, and since they got their own meals out at their tree no one even bothered about feeding them. Sometimes they would be seen with the groups of the other children, but they rarely took part in their games any more. They wore the slings around their necks as though they were strings of prayer beads and behaved like guardians of a secret which had set them apart from ordinary humans.

One day, however, Dieynaba, who had noticed their constant absences, stopped her son as he was on his way to join the others.

"Where are you going, Gorgui?" she demanded.

"I'm going to look for Magatte, Mother."

"What do you do all day, you and the others?"

"Nothing much—we usually go walking in the fields."

"Well, instead of wandering around doing nothing, like a bunch of dumb animals, why don't you do your wandering in the *toubab's* district? Some of them have chickens running around loose . . ."

It took Gorgui a minute to realize what his mother meant, but then he went off like a shot and didn't stop running until he reached the baobab tree. The idea of raiding the chicken coops of the white men took their breath away at first, but the more they thought about it the more exciting it became.

"Do we go, general?"

"We go, soldiers!"

The first expedition was so successful that they didn't even have to use their slingshots. They were back at home before noon, and each one of them was carrying at least one or two chickens. They were overwhelmed with praise for their daring, and their chests swelled proudly above the sharp-boned cage of their ribs. From that moment on they had found a new reason for their existence.

Each morning one of them would go out on a scouting trip, and that night the whole band would pay a visit to the selected spot. On their return, the women would be waiting and sometimes would even come out to meet them, crying, "Our men are back!" Thus exonerated from any feelings of guilt, they redoubled their zeal in the hunt and only the failure of a mission caused them any misgiving.

Following their success with Dieynaba's idea, Penda conceived another one. She summoned the apprentices to her cabin, and, when they came out after a long conference, their faces were marked with the expression of men who have embarked on a serious venture. Penda herself was carrying two large cloth bags. Dieynaba was sitting alone in the courtyard at the time, puffing at a new mixture of leaves in her pipe. She couldn't help smiling as she watched the little band walk off in the direction of the shop of Aziz, the Syrian.

The shopkeeper's father-in-law was stretched out on a chaise longue, sleeping, and Aziz himself was dozing behind the counter, occasionally inhaling deeply from a Turkish water pipe. The early afternoon heat seemed to have overcome him completely. Penda had chosen her time well. She went into the shop with her "crew," as she called the apprentices, close on her heels.

Without moving an inch, Aziz said, "What do you want?"

Acting as if she had already made her choice, Penda indicated a pile of cloth on the shelf behind the counter.

"The print?" Aziz said, turning his head, but without removing the tube of the water pipe from his mouth.

"No, the one next to it."

"The muslin?"

"Is that really muslin?"

"You can see for yourself, woman!"

While this dialogue was taking place, the "crew" had wasted no time. Three of them stood behind Penda, forming a screen, and behind them Magatte had pierced a hole in one of two enormous sacks of rice that stood between the glass doors of the shop. Into the opening he thrust a long tube whose other end he had placed in one of the bags Penda had been carrying.

"Well?" the Syrian said.

"No—don't bother getting up—but, tell me, is the muslin really good quality?" Penda glanced over her shoulder in time to see one of the boys dash off, with a well-filled bag on his shoulder.

The shopkeeper looked at her irritably, and the water in the bowl of his pipe gurgled as he inhaled again. "Look, if you don't want anything, at least don't bother me."

Sène had noticed that the shrinking sack of rice was beginning to fall off balance, and he gestured frantically. Penda took a few steps backward.

"Well, never mind about it. I just wanted to know how much it cost."

"I don't sell anything at this hour. Come back at two o'clock," Aziz said.

Penda had reached the door safely. "He doesn't want to sell anything now," she said. "Let's go, children."

It was high time. Just as she spoke, the sack of rice collapsed completely and fell over on its side. The band scattered through the alleys like a flight of quail.

The rice lasted for two days of a feasting and gaity they had almost forgotten, but the exploit of Penda and her "crew" was talked about for a week, and the Syrian shopkeeper was the butt of all kinds of jokes. After that, however, Penda seemed to lose interest in the apprentices; she had other ideas in her head now and was working to create a "committee of women." So the boys went back to the baobab tree, the hedgehogs, and marksmanship drills and boredom.

They had tasted the bitter fruits of danger and now nothing else had any flavor.

But one night, destiny, which has an infallible sense of timing, called out to them again.

The shadows were lengthening on the ground as the sun went down. From somewhere in the distance the mournful notes of a bugle could be heard, signaling the changing of the guard. The apprentices were walking across the field of the watchmen's camp in the twilight. No one paid any attention to them, and at the end of the field they came to the district administrator's house, standing in the center of a well-tended garden. Not far from them some automobiles were parked beside the gateway.

Souley, the smallest of the group, was swinging his slingshot back and forth in his hand. Suddenly he stopped, picked up a stone, and placed it carefully in the leather sling. The rubber strips on either side stretched taut, the stone whistled through the air, and a headlight on one of the cars shattered noisily. For an instant the other boys were dumbfounded, but only for an instant. Then they began searching through their pockets, and the air was filled with the whistling of stones and pellets of lead, and the explosion of headlights, windshields, and windows. The watchmen came running out of their tents to see what was happening, but the band had already scattered. An hour later the windows, the showcases, and even the electric light bulbs of the station were serving as targets.

They had found a game to replace all the others. They waited until darkness had enlisted on their side, and then, moving in little groups to throw the guards and the soldiers off their track, they invaded the European quarter. Hidden behind the trunk of a tree, flattened against a wall or crouched in a ditch, they adjusted their slings, fired, and vanished into the shadows. Everything that shone in the night was a target, from windows to lamp posts. At daybreak the bulbs and the glass might be replaced, but it was a wasted effort. The following night the ground would again be littered with sparkling splinters.

They even pushed their luck so far as to attack the police station. Some of the older people did not approve of this latest manifestation of the "crew's" activities, and there were even parents who forbade their sons to go out on the expeditions, with the result

196

that General Magatte's army was reduced to seven soldiers. Others, however, could not help thinking that every window that broke, every light that went out, helped to establish a kind of balance: they were no longer alone in carrying the burden of the strike.

As for the Europeans, the feeling of constraint and uneasiness they had known for weeks gave place to panic. The patrols on the streets were reinforced, but, in spite of this, fear was an unwelcome guest in every house in the quarter. It was not so much the stones or the little balls of lead themselves as the thought of those black bodies slipping through the shadows that transformed every home into a fortress as soon as darkness came. Native servants were sent home, and men and women went to bed with weapons at their sides. At the slightest sound, nervous fingers reached out for the trigger of a pistol or the stock of a rifle. And, in the meantime, the members of the "crew," exhausted from their work, slept the sleep of the just.

In between their nocturnal expeditions, they had acquired the habit of practicing their marksmanship constantly, since they were determined to remain masters of their craft. Anything, living or dead, that could serve as a target was put to use. It was as a result of this that one evening, as they were wandering along the siding which connected with the main line from Saint-Louis, little Kâ, the youngest of the group, happened to notice a lizard basking in the last rays of the sun. His sling was already in his hand, and the child pulled back slowly on the rubber bands, sighted through the branches of the stick, and fired. The lizard leaped slightly and fell over on its back. They saw its little white belly twitch for a second against the crushed stones between the rails and then lie motionless. A second lizard thrust his nose from behind the wheel of a car and arrowed in the direction of a near-by wall. Seven projectiles instantly smashed into the dust around him or clattered against the rail he had leaped.

It was at this moment that Isnard appeared from behind the same car that had sheltered the lizard. His hand went to his pocket, and three shots rang out. Little Kâ received the first bullet and dropped without uttering a sound. Sène fell while he was still in the act of turning around, and the other children fled, screaming. Isnard's arm was trembling, but he continued firing until the magazine of the revolver was empty. One of the last bullets struck Gorgui in the leg, and he collapsed in the middle of the tracks.

For a moment Isnard just stood there, dazed, his arm still stretched out in front of him, holding the smoking gun. Then, with a mechanical gesture, he put it back in his pocket and began to run toward the European quarter, muttering breathlessly to himself, "They were shooting at me! They were shooting at me!"

Magatte ran straight to the union office to tell the men what had happened. Breathless, his lips trembling, his eyes swimming with tears of shock, he tried to explain how he and his comrades had been hunting lizards when Isnard had suddenly appeared with a revolver, fired on them, and killed them all. At his first words everyone in the office moved out to the street, where there would be room for the others to join them. Lahbib and Boubacar, Doudou and Sène Masène, the father of one of the dead boys, were there already. They were joined almost immediately by Penda, who had taken to wearing a soldier's cartridge belt around her waist since she had been made a member of the strike committee.

The news spread like fire through the courtyards of the district, traveling from compound to compound and from main house to neighboring cabins. Men, women, and children flowed into the streets by the hundreds, marching towards the railroad yards. The crowd swelled at every step and became a mass of running legs and shouting mouths, opened on gleaming white teeth or blackened stumps. The headcloths of the women fluttered convulsively, and a few lost scarves floated above the crowd for a moment before falling and being trampled in the dust. The women carried children in their arms or slung across their backs, and as they walked they gathered up weapons—heavy pestles, iron bars, and pick handles— and waved them at the sky like the standards of an army. On their faces, hunger, sleeplessness, pain, and fear had been graven into the single image of anger.

At last the crowd arrived at the siding, and the bodies of the two dead children were wrapped in white cloths, which were rapidly stained with blood. Gorgui was carried away, weeping and moaning, and the long cortège turned in the direction of home. This time the women were at its head, led by Penda, Dieynaba, and Mariame Sonko. As they passed before the houses of the

European employees, their fury reached a screaming peak; fists were waved and a torrent of oaths and insults burst from their throats like water through a shattered dam.

In front of the residence of the district administrator the two corpses were laid out on the ground, and the women began to intone a funeral dirge. Watchmen, soldiers, and mounted policemen were hastily summoned and formed a protective cordon around the house. When the last mournful notes of the dirge no longer hung in the air, the entire crowd simply stood there silently. But the silence was heavier with meaning than the oaths or the clamor: it was a witness to the unlit fires, the empty cooking pots, and the decaying mortars, and to the machines in the shops where the spiders were spinning their webs. For more than an hour they stood there, and the soldiers themselves remained silent before these silent people.

At last the cortège formed up again, but the ceremony was repeated, and the bodies of the children laid out, four times again —in front of the station, in the suburbs of N'Ginth and Randoulène, and in the market square in the heart of Thiès.

It was not until almost nightfall, when the mass of this human river was already indistinguishable from the shadows, that the funeral procession ended and the remains of the two children returned at last to their homes.

Three days later, the directors of the company notified the strikers that their representatives would be received.

From God's Bits of Wood, *by Sembene Ousmane, Doubleday and Company, Inc., 1962; Anchor edition, 1970.*

Guest of Chief Nanga

by CHINUA ACHEBE

Chinua Achebe is a Nigerian writer, literary critic, and editor. Born in 1930 in Iboland, he is a graduate of University College, Ibadan, and he also studied in England. He has played an important role in the development of Nigerian broadcasting programs, but his major contribution has been in the literary world. (See page 86.)

His novels have many important themes—politics, social justice, conflict between generations, and tribal history. He is primarily a stylist and storyteller. A character in one of his books explains what is really his own personal point of view: "In all great compounds, there must be people of all minds—some good, some bad, some fearless, some cowardly: those who bring in wealth and those who scatter it, those who give good advice and those who speak the words of palm wine."

The following selection is taken from his novel *A Man of the People*. It shows the dilemma of the young educated African who returns home to enter politics, contrasting the role of the self-interested politician and the inexperienced intelligentsia.

𝕏 As it turned out I arrived in the capital, Bori, exactly one month after Chief Nanga's unexpected invitation. Although I had written a letter to say when I would be arriving and had followed it up with a telegram, I still had a lingering fear as I announced the address rather importantly and settled back in the taxi that morning. I was thinking that a man of Chief Nanga's easy charm and country-wide popularity must throw out that kind of invitation several times each day without giving it much thought. Wasn't I being unreasonable in trying to hold him down to it? Anyhow I had taken the precaution of writing to an old friend, a newly qualified lawyer struggling to set up in private practice. I would watch Nanga's reaction very closely and if necessary move out smartly again on the following day as though that had always been my intention.

When we got to the Minister's residence my fear increased as his one-eyed stalwart stopped the car at the gate and began to look me over.

"Who you want?" he scowled.

"Chief Nanga."

"He give you appointment?"

"No, but . . ."

"Make you park for outside. I go go haskam if he want see you. Wetin be your name?"

Fortunately the Minister, who was apparently relaxing with his family in the lounge, came to the door, and on seeing us rushed outside and threw his arm round me. Then his wife and three of his children trooped out and joined in the excited welcoming.

"Come right inside," said the Minister. "We have been wait- ing for you all morning. The house is yours."

I hung back to pay the taxi-driver. "No, no, no!" cried my host. "Go right inside. I will settle with the driver. He na my very good friend, no be so, Driver?"

"Yes, sir, master," said the driver, who had hitherto seemed a most unfriendly man to me. Now he broke into a broad smile showing smoke- and kola-stained teeth.

For a mother of seven, the eldest of whom was sixteen or seventeen, Mrs. Nanga was and still is very well kept. Her face, unlike her husband's, had become blurred in my memory. But on seeing her now it all came back again. She was bigger now of course—almost matronly. Her face was one of the friendliest I had ever seen.

She showed me to the Guest's Suite and practically ordered me to have a bath while she got some food ready.

"It won't take long," she said, "the soup is already made."

A small thing, but it struck me even as early as this: Mr. Nanga always spoke English or pidgin; his children, whom I dis- covered went to expensive private schools run by European ladies, spoke impeccable English, but Mrs. Nanga stuck to our language— with the odd English word thrown in now and again.

My host did not waste time. At about five o'clock that afternoon he told me to get ready and go with him to see the Hon. Simon Koko, Minister for Overseas Training. Earlier that day one of those unseasonal December rains which invariably brought on the cold harmattan had fallen. It had been quite heavy and windy and the streets were now littered with dry leaves, and sometimes half-blocked by broken-off tree branches; and one had to mind fallen telegraph and high-voltage electric wires.

Chief Koko, a fat jovial man wearing an enormous home-knitted red-and-yellow sweater, was about to have coffee. He asked if we would join him or have some alcohol.

"I no follow you black white-men for drink tea and coffee in the hot afternoon," said Chief Nanga. "Whisky and soda for me and for Mr. Samalu."

Chief Koko explained that nothing warmed the belly like hot coffee and proceeded to take a loud and long sip followed by a satisfied Ahh! Then he practically dropped the cup and saucer on the drinks-table by his chair and jumped up as though a scorpion had stung him.

"They have killed me," he wailed, wringing his hands, breathing hard and loud and rolling his eyes. Chief Nanga and I sprang up in alarm and asked together what had happened. But our host kept crying that they had killed him and they could now go and celebrate.

"What is it, S.I.?" asked Chief Nanga, putting an arm around the other's neck.

"They have poisoned my coffee," he said, and broke down completely. Meanwhile the steward, hearing his master's cry, had rushed in.

"Who poisoned my coffee?" he asked.

"Not me—o!"

"Call the cook!" thundered the Minister. "Call him here. I will kill him before I die. Go and bring him."

The steward dashed out again and soon returned to say the cook had gone out. The Minister slumped into his chair and began to groan and hold his stomach. Then his bodyguard whom we had seen dressed like a cowboy hurried in from the front gate, and hearing what had happened dashed out at full speed to try and catch the cook.

"Let's go and call a doctor," I said.

"That's right," said Chief Nanga with relief and, leaving his friend, rushed towards the telephone. I hadn't thought about the telephone.

"What is the use of a doctor?" moaned our poisoned host. "Do they know about African poison? They have killed me. What have I done to them? Did I owe them anything? Oh! Oh! Oh! What have I done?"

Meanwhile Chief Nanga had been trying to phone a doctor and was not apparently getting anywhere. He was now shouting threats of immediate sacking at some invisible enemy.

"This is Chief the Honorable Nanga speaking," he was saying. "I will see that you are dealt with. Idiot. That is the trouble with this country. Don't worry, you will see. Bloody fool. . . ."

At this point the cowboy bodyguard came in dragging the cook by his shirt collar. The Minister sprang at him with an agility which completely belied his size and condition.

"Wait, Master," pleaded the cook.

"Wait your head!" screamed his employer, going for him. "Why you put poison for my coffee?" His huge body was quivering like jelly.

"Me? Put poison for master? Nevertheless!" said the cook, side-stepping to avoid a heavy blow from the Minister. Then with surprising presence of mind he saved himself. (Obviously the cowboy had already told him of his crime.) He made for the cup of coffee quickly, grabbed it and drank every drop. There was immediate silence. We exchanged surprised glances.

"Why I go kill my master?" he asked of a now considerably sobered audience. "Abi my head no correct? And even if to say I de craze why I no go go jump for inside lagoon instead to kill my master?" His words carried conviction. He proceeded to explain the mystery of the coffee. The Minister's usual Nescafé had run out at breakfast and he had not had time to get a new tin. So he had brewed some of his own locally processed coffee which he maintained he had brought from OHMS.

There was an ironic twist to this incident which neither of the ministers seemed to notice. OHMS—Our Home Made Stuff— was the popular name of the gigantic campaign which the Government had mounted all over the country to promote the consumption of locally made products. Newspapers, radio and television urged every patriot to support this great national effort which, they said, held the key to economic emancipation without which our hard-won political freedom was a mirage. Cars equipped with loud-speakers poured out new jingles up and down the land as they sold their products in town and country. In the language of the ordinary people these cars, and not the wares they advertised, became known as OHMS. It was apparently from one of them the cook had bought the coffee that had nearly cost him his life.

The matter having been resolved to everyone's satisfaction I began to feel vicariously embarrassed on behalf of Chief Koko. If anyone had asked my opinion I would have voted strongly in favor of our leaving right away. But no one did. Instead Chief Nanga had begun to tease the other.

"But S.I.," he said, "you too fear death. Small thing you begin holler 'they done kill me, they done kill me!' Like person way scorpion done lego am for him prick."

I saw his face turning towards me no doubt to get me to join in his laughter. I quickly looked away and began to gaze out of the window.

"Nonsense! Why I go fear? I kill person?"

They carried on in this vein for quite a while. I sipped my whisky quietly, avoiding the eyes of both. But I was saying within myself that in spite of his present bravado Chief Nanga had been terribly scared himself, witness his ill-tempered, loud-mouthed panic at the telephone. And I don't think his fear had been for Chief Koko's safety either. I suspect he felt personally threatened. Our people have a saying that when one slave sees another cast into a shallow grave he should know that when the time comes he will go the same way.

Naturally my scholarship did not get a chance to be mentioned on this occasion. We drove home in silence. Only once did Chief Nanga turn to me and say: "If anybody comes to you and wants to make you minister, run away. True."

That evening I ate my supper with Mrs. Nanga and the children, the Minister having gone out to an embassy reception after which he would go to a party meeting somewhere.

"Any woman who marries a minister," said his wife later as we sat watching TV, "has married worse than a night-watchman."

We both laughed. There was no hint of complaint in her voice. She was clearly a homely, loyal wife prepared for the penalty of her husband's greatness. You couldn't subvert her.

"It must be very enjoyable going to all these embassy parties and meeting all the big guns," I said in pretended innocence.

"What can you enjoy there?" she asked with great spirit. "Nine pence talk and three pence food. "Hallo, hawa you. Nice to see you again.' All na lie lie."

I laughed heartily and then got up pretending to admire the many family photographs on the walls. I asked Mrs. Nanga about this one and that as I gravitated slowly to the one on the radiogram which I had noticed as soon as I had stepped into the house earlier in the day. It was the same beautiful girl as in Chief Nanga's entourage in Anata.

"Is this your sister?" I asked.

"Edna. No, she is our wife."

"Your wife? How?"

She laughed. "We are getting a second wife to help me."

The first thing critics tell you about our ministers' official residences is that each has seven bedrooms and seven bathrooms, one for every day of the week. All I can say is that on that first night there was no room in my mind for criticism. I was simply hypnotized by the luxury of the great suite assigned to me. When I lay down in the double bed that seemed to ride on a cushion of air, and switched on that reading lamp and saw all the beautiful furniture anew from the lying down position and looked beyond the door to the gleaming bathroom and the towels as large as a lappa I had to confess that if I were at that moment made a minister I would be most anxious to remain one for ever. And maybe I should have thanked God that I wasn't. We ignore man's basic nature if we say, as some critics do, that because a man like Nanga had risen overnight from poverty and insignificance to his present opulence he could be persuaded without much trouble to give it up again and return to his original state.

A man who has just come in from the rain and dried his body and put on dry clothes is more reluctant to go out again than another who has been indoors all the time. The trouble with our new nation—as I saw it then lying on that bed—was that none of us had been indoors long enough to be able to say "To hell with it." We had all been in the rain together until yesterday. Then a handful of us—the smart and the lucky and hardly ever the best—had scrambled for the one shelter our former rulers left, and had taken it over and barricaded themselves in. And from within they sought to persuade the rest through numerous loudspeakers, that the first phase of the struggle had been won and that the next phase—the extension of our houses—was even more important and called for new and original tactics; it required that all argument should cease and the whole people speak with one voice and that any more dissent and argument outside the door of the shelter would subvert and bring down the whole house.

From A Man of the People, *by Chinua Achebe, The John Day Company, Inc., 1966.*

One More Step   ODITA

Butcherboy

by ALEX LA GUMA

Alex la Guma, like Peter Abrahams, is a South African writer now living in exile. Born in 1925 in a Cape Town ghetto, he grew up in the shadow of his father's political activity and became a champion of rights for the Cape-Colored people. He was one of 156 South Africans rounded up for the famous Treason Trial of 1956, aimed at those who had helped to formulate the Freedom Charter, or Bill of Rights, in 1955.

La Guma had no special training as a writer but was a constant reader and served on the staff of the Cape Town newspaper, *The New Age,* from 1956 to 1962. Between 1962 and 1966 he was a prisoner under house arrest because of repeated political activity, and he endured solitary confinement for months at a time. While he was in prison or under house arrest, he continued his writing.

Based on his bitter personal experiences, La Guma's novels and short stories are all concerned with the victims of apartheid and are highly charged with emotion. His first short novel, *A Walk in Night,* was followed by a longer one, *And a Threefold Cord.* In *The Stone Country,* the source of the following selection, he takes the reader inside the walls of a South African prison.

George Adams was a newcomer to the South African prison, that world of stone and steel. He was a "political" arrested for handing out leaflets against the "apartheid" policy of the government. He was guilty of another crime, too: he was colored. He was thrown in prison with hardened offenders: Butcherboy Williams, the tough bully who exacts tribute from the weaker prisoners, Yusef the Turk who dares to challenge Butcherboy, and all the others, from Solly the clown to the Casbah Kid, sentenced to hang for murder. George Adams didn't quite fit in. He talked back to the guards. He didn't acknowledge Butcherboy's right to tribute. When

207

he received some gifts from outside—a tin of beef, a tin of cocoa, 50 cigarettes and a tube of toothpaste—he accepted them happily.

On his way towards his cell once more, he felt a thick hand laid casually on his shoulder and halted, feeling hot, sour breath against his neck, while a thick voice, distorted by a damaged throat, said, "Howsit, pally? You got something nice there for us?"

George Adams looked aside and up and into the blood-flecked, gorilla eyes and the heavy, red, rubbery lips peeled back to reveal broken, stained and mossy teeth like desecrated tombstones, grinning out of the bludgeoned and badly repaired, stubbly face.

"You got something nice there for us, pal?"

The harsh, carious breath fanned him, and George Adams was reminded of overturned dustbins in the grime-slippery lobbies of moldering tenements and the smell of latrine buckets in hot cells. He said carefully, "Just some stuff my people sent me."

"That's real wake-up," Butcherboy said huskily, and George Adams felt the big hand close like an iron grab on his shoulder. He stood very still and waited for the next move.

"Well, *ou* pal, let us see what you got for us in that bag, *ou* pal."

Around them the muttered conversation of the squatting prisoners evaporated slowly and the atmosphere became taut as a harp-string as all eyes turned on them. In the stretched silence somebody giggled nervously, and the sound took on an exaggerated character, like the smashing of crockery, and George Adams, exploding into anger, glared into the bloodshot eyes as he shouted, "———— off!"

Something like a sigh now swept through the onlookers, and everybody seemed to tense with the anticipation of violence.

George Adams could feel his mouth quivering with rage, and his shoulder had gone numb, clamped in the steel-wire fingers. He heard the throaty voice ask mockingly curious: "What was that what you said, pal?"

"———— off," George Adams said, raising his voice again, so that everybody could hear, thinking at the same time, This bastard can break your neck like a match, why don't you just play it small?

"So. *Ach so*," the throaty voice laughed, and the hard, blunt head turned towards the group of henchmen who lounged, grinning, in a doorway, with even the face of the Casbah Kid twisted into a reluctant grimace as he slouched on the fringes.

"This little man, he like to talk back," Butcherboy told them, laughing hoarsely. "He's *mos* a clever. Like to talk back to big johnnies."

The horrid face turned back to George Adams. The ape-like eyes moved in their deep sockets, and discovered the bulge of the cigarette-box in the shirt pocket.

"Let's see now, man. Tobacco, hey?" And the free hand came up towards the pocket and George Adams saw the tattooed arm, ropy with muscle, and fingers thick as cables with their half moons of dirt under the nails. "You's a shot, *mos*. Cigarettes and all."

And then somebody else said jovially, "What do you need, Butcherboy? Picking on respectable people, like."

Both Butcherboy and George Adams recognised the voice, and looked aside to where the tall, lean, knife-blade form of Yusef the Turk had moved up. The sleek handsome head was cocked and the face smiled, showing the even dentures, white as new enamel in the swarthy face.

"Turk," Butcherboy said, without relaxing his hold on George Adams. "Turk, this is not your business, *mos. Ou* Turk, man, you's in the wrong place, man."

"Why, Butcher?" Yusef the Turk asked easily. "Wrong place? Hell, man, we's all here together in the wrong place, don't I say?"

"You know what I mean, man. Me and this *juba*, we's *mos* got business."

"Business," Yusef the Turk laughed. "This is good people, man. Not your kind, not my kind, even. You know this john? No." The easy voice changed suddenly, and the Turk said dangerously, "Leave him."

Butcherboy did not move, but the reddish eyes contracted into their folds of grimy flesh, and peered out between the narrowed lids like predatory creatures in ambush. "Turk, I'm just giving you a fair warning, hey." The husky voice was menacing.

In the yard the watching prisoners stirred again, and Butcherboy's henchmen, Brakes Peterson, Squinteye Samuels, Pinks, Moos and others, straightened and edged instinctively into line of battle. The Casbah Kid flicked out his tongue and licked his battered lip, his eyes on Butcherboy, and a hand closed over the skewer in his pocket.

But Yusef the Turk ignored them and said, "Butcher, you been bossing this yard a long time, don't I say?"

"*Ja*, and so?"

"You *mos* catch wire with the small boys, don't I say?"

"*Ja*, and so?"

"So I'm telling you this is a pally of mine. Leave him."

Butcherboy released a gust of bad breath and shook his head slowly. "Turk," he said. "Turk, I's sorry for you. Turk, you getting too big for this yard, so I'm going to do something about it, hey."

"Any time you say, Butcherboy."

"Maybe you might *mos* move over to my cell one night."

Yusef the Turk smiled a dangerous smile. "Why not, then?"

"Is okay, then."

George Adams now said to the lean man, "Forget it, Yusef, man."

"Is okay, pal," Yusef the Turk said. "And maybe *ou* Butcherboy will let go your shoulder now, hey?"

The tiny eyes stared at Yusef the Turk who smiled back, and just then the triangle outside the square clanged and clanged, and the guard was shouting, "Fall in, fall in," so that the general movement of the prisoners, rising to assemble, broke the tension like the snap of a fishing-line.

Butcherboy relaxed his grip on George Adams's shoulder and removed his hand. He said, "We will talk about it some more, Turk," and Yusef the Turk chuckled.

The morning was bright in the yard, and the iron grille which formed the end wall threw its pattern of parallel grey lines and garish rectangles onto the concrete floor. Overhead the sky was a hard enamel blue smudged with a coppery smear of sun. There was no sign of a breeze, and beyond the stern hard stone and PWD paint of the prison, the outline of the flat mountain was clear and sharp as a cleaver against the sky.

The tap at the upper end of the yard had been opened and water ran along the shallow trench down the middle of the concrete floor where the prisoners were busy washing their clothes. The slapping sounds of wet material beaten on the stone, flop-flop-

flopped through the murmur of voices and occasional laughter. Some of the men were stark naked, having decided to wash every scrap of rag they possessed, others squatted in shorts or trousers, everybody scrubbing and pummelling in two lines, facing each other across the running trench. Those who were not washing lounged about and smoked or talked.

Yusef the Turk wrung out the shirt he had washed and rose stiffly from his place at the gutter, and carried it over to the wash-line of wire which had been strung between the banister of the gallery steps and the grille. Having draped the shirt over the line, he sat down with his back to the wall, and proceeded to watch it.

He watched it unwaveringly and intently, for he knew that to move his gaze for only a few seconds might mean its complete and utter disappearance. Others who had also hung up washing were sitting around, staring at their clothes with trance-like devotion, waiting for the summer sun to do its work. While he was sitting there, thinking, he became aware of the anthropoid bulk of Butcherboy, who had slunk up beside him.

"Turk," Butcherboy said, and his voice was a growl deep down in the cavernous chest. "Turk."

"Ja," replied Yusef the Turk, without taking his eyes from the shirt suspended from the line. "You got something on your min'?"

"Turk," Butcherboy said, still grinning balefully, "Turk, this yard is *mos* getting too small for us two together. You one of them big-shot burgs, hey. And I reckon to myself, is *mos* time you got to show what kin' of a big-shot you is. Don't I say?"

"Any time you say, Butcherboy."

"Okay, *ou* Turk. Tonight I reckon one of those baskets from my cell will move over to yours. Then you can move into mine, likely. Then we can settle this business. Okay?"

Yusef the Turk smiled at his shirt. He said, "Okay, pally."

"Tonight then, hey?"

"Tonight," said Yusef the Turk.

The heat in the cell was solid. As Yusef the Turk would have said, you could reach out in front of your face, grab a handful of heat, fling it at the wall and it would stick. With over forty prisoners locked up in the middle of summer, the smell of sweat was heavy and cloying as the smell of death. The heat seemed packed in between the bodies of the men, like layers of cotton wool; like a thick sauce which moistened a human salad of accused petty thieves, gangsters, rapists, burglars, thugs, brawlers, dope peddlers, few of them strangers to the cells, many already depraved, and several old and abandoned, sucking hopelessly at the bitter, disintegrating butt-end of life.

Everybody was quiet that night, hardly noticing the heat. Words passed in whispers, instead of in an uproar which usually preceded the settling down for the night. Tension held the caserne in its taut grip.

George Adams did not like it. He felt nervous, and he did not like it at all. This was the country behind the coastline of laws and regulations and labyrinthine legislation; a jungle of stone and iron, inhabited by jackals and hyenas, snarling wolves and trembling sheep, entrapped lions fighting off shambling monsters with stunted brains and bodies armored with the hide of ignorance and brutality, trampling underfoot those who tried to claw their way from the clutch of the swamp.

And Butcherboy said, "Turk, I reckon we got to put you on trial."

Yusef the Turk stood loosely against the wall at one end of the caserne, with George Adams by him. He was smiling faintly with drooping lids, but despite the ease and the smile, his eyes were alert as sparks, and he was now sharp and tough and dangerous as a polished spear.

"Trial?" asked Yusef the Turk. "Hell, *ou* Butcher, I thought this was going to be a fair fight. Man to man."

A not uncommon occurrence in prison was the "trial," by the most depraved and brutalised inmates, of some unfortunate who might have raised their ire by rebellion, by boot-licking a guard, by squealing on fellow prisoners, or by provoking vengeance in some way or other. Mock courts, much more dangerous than real ones, were held in the cells and "sentence meted out."

There had been a "case" of a prisoner who had given offence to a cell boss and his gang. It had been said that he had complained to a guard, an unpardonable "crime." The gangsters "tried" him, found him guilty and sentenced him to—he was not told. That, as some sadistic refinement, they kept secret among themselves.

The terrified man died a thousand times over before, finally, unable to hold back weariness, he was forced to collapse in sleep. As he lay quaking through some unknown nightmare, a blanket was pressed over his head and face, and a half-dozen knives driven through the one in which he slept.

The next morning the guards found a dead man wrapped in a bloody blanket. No trace of blood on any of the rest of the packed humanity in the cell. There was no sign of a knife. Nobody had a knife, in spite of searches. The prison enquiry revealed nothing.

Butcherboy laughed. He was at the other side of the cell, backed by his coterie of toadies, Pinks, Moos, Brakes Peterson, Squinteye Samuels, Noor, and on the fringes of the gang, such satellites as Crip, Little Johnny, Solly and the Casbah Kid. They waited for the giant's reaction.

"Fair fight," Butcherboy laughed hoarsely, looking around at the faces of the onlookers. "The basket want a fair fight. Man to man."

And to his surprise there came a mutter from most voices, "Fair fight, fair fight." A murmur echoed even by his immediate henchmen. He peered about again. So it was like that, was it? He would have to get things in hand as soon as he had dealt with this big-mouthed skinny basket over there.

The battered face darkened and the stained and broken teeth were bared in a sneer. "Right," Butcherboy said. "Is a fair fight, hey." The hard round head turned on the thick neck and he ordered, "You, Brakes, stand by the door and listen when the guard comes around." He stared around at the others. "Clear this place and get over to the wall, all of you. And everybody stay quiet, understand? Not a sound. Dead still."

In a moment the crowd commenced pulling blankets and mats out of the way, piling them along the back wall of the caserne. That done, the spectators crowded onto the piled bedding or stood along the walls, everybody hushed and expectant, faces taut with excitement.

Butcherboy peeled off his shirt, and displayed the great torso, knotted with muscle and fat and cicatriced with old wounds, decorated with a gallery of tattooing. He flexed his biceps and slapped his chest, grinning with his bad teeth, displaying the pictures needled into his flesh; the skull-and-cross-bones, the flags and crossed daggers, the nude women who wiggled as his muscles writhed, and on

213

the left side of the wide back, an eagle in full flight, its beak agape and wings spread, eyes glaring and talons hooked and poised for the kill.

He laughed cruelly, "Come on, *ou* pal, and let me squash you like a louse." His voice rumbled from his damaged larynx. "Fair fight, hey."

And now Yusef the Turk moved away from the wall where he had been leaning, and unbuttoned his shirt. In peg-topped trousers and brogues he appeared tubercular in comparison with the uncouth bulk of Butcherboy, but under the smooth, tan skin, muscles rippled like lizards and the long body was really as tough and as flexible as a *sjambok*.

He put a hand to his mouth and slipped out his dentures. His face became thin and sunken. "Hold these for me, Professor," he said.

George Adams took the damp teeth, feeling somewhat ridiculous, and gingerly dropped them into a coat pocket.

Silence fell on the caserne in a dead weight. Over at the end of the room Butcherboy's henchmen waited, their eyes bright and evil in their treacherous faces. The Casbah Kid was as quiet and unemotional as a mummy, except that one eyelid twitched and narrowed as if winking slyly. Over by the iron-clad door, his ear to the judas-hole, the fried face of Brakes Peterson wore a fixed and ghastly grin.

Butcherboy shuffled forward. Below his stained khaki shorts, his legs were thick and ugly and knotted like tree-stumps. He growled, and as the sound rolled out of him, he thrust his huge right hand forward, as though to seize the other man in a wrestling hold.

With a lightening grab Yusef the Turk seized the extended hand, gave a swift jerk and released it before Butcherboy could free it and fasten upon him in turn. The swift tug upon his arm swung the giant half left and before he could recover his balance, Yusef the Turk drove at the side of his face with a chopping blow of the edge of his flat and rigid hand, laying open the flesh along the cheek-bone.

The spectators gasped and bodies grew stiff with tension as the giant reeled, and like the skilled master of innumerable street fights, Yusef the Turk gave him no chance to recover. The lean, plaited-leather body whirled sideways on the left foot while, at the same time, the right leg jerked up, knee high and the foot shot out like a projectile, parallel with the floor. It caught the tottering Butcherboy in the belly with the force of a shell.

His eyes popped and a gust of breath belched from the gaping circle of his mouth with a sound like a hiccough. The knotted face worked as he gasped for breath, and the great body rocked like a boulder, but did not topple, and Yusef the Turk kicked him again, savagely, against the knee.

Butcherboy stumbled, his arms gyrating as he sought for balance. For years he had depended upon his size and ferocity to intimidate his victims; nobody lighter than he had ever attempted to challenge him to single combat, and the result was that now the swift onslaught of Yusef the Turk had both advantages of surprise and experience. Nevertheless, Butcherboy was only moderately hurt and shaken, and exasperated to the point of madness.

He roared and charged. Dodging clumsily under a swing, he reached out to fling his massive arms around the other's waist. As arms shot out for the deadly embrace, Yusef the Turk's knee flew up with terrific force to smash into the face so temptingly appearing above it. The face jerked aside in a flash, the knee missed it, and the leg was instantly seized in a grip like a vice. A sigh passed through the watchers.

But Yusef the Turk had been involved in too many fights of this kind. He snapped his left arm around Butcherboy's neck, getting it into the crook of the elbow, slipping the hand under his own right biceps, hooking it there. Then he slid the right forearm up and across the throat of his enemy, the side of the wrist against the Adam's apple, and with all his wiry strength he started to throttle the big man. Certainly, Butcherboy would throw him, but that would not free his throat from the garotte of sinew, bone and muscle that was relentlessly squeezing the air-pipe shut.

With a heave, Butcherboy threw Yusef the Turk and fell heavily on top of him. The latter's arms tightened, bone crushing the Adam's apple, and Yusef the Turk saw the face gradually turn blue, the tongue bulging. Swiftly Butcherboy changed his hold. Keeping one arm around the other's leg at the knee, he seized the foot with his other hand and drew it backwards with all his brute strength. As the leg bent backwards, he pressed the other arm tightly into the back of the knee. In a moment the leg would snap like a stick. Yusef the Turk knew it, and the sweat sprang like dew across his face, his eyes bulging from their sockets, toothless gums bared in a grunt of pain.

George Adams wanted to cry. He wanted to rush forward and kick the snarling face of Butcherboy to a pulp. Everybody waited, staring, for the sound of snapping bone.

Then Brakes Peterson, at the door, was hissing through the pregnant silence. "The guard. Here come the —— guard."

In a moment the antagonists parted, the spectators scrambled to the floor in positions of relaxation, looking at anything else but the door. Butcherboy slid flat, glaring at Yusef the Turk, his breath working like bellows. Yusef the Turk's face had assumed a greenish tinge under the tan skin, and his own lungs panted like those of a weary dog. His leg ached and he was worried about whether he would be able to use it against Butcherboy again. They were both slippery with sweat.

All heard the step of the guard in the yard outside. He was whistling as he went from peep-hole to peep-hole, and they could hear the tune of *Lili Marlene* through the crunch of his boots. The heat was soaked with silence inside the caserne, and when a man coughed suddenly, it sounded like the explosion of a faulty engine.

The whistling reached the cell door, and stopped. They heard the clink of the peep-hole cover being moved. Then a second clink as it fell back into place after the guard had looked in. The whistling started up again and moved away from the door, heading towards the gallery staircase.

"Brakes," asked Butcherboy, wheezing slightly, "Is it awright?"

"He's gone upstairs," the man with the burnt face said, sprawled at the foot of the door.

After a while the guard came downstairs again, and now he was whistling *It's a hap-hap-happy day*. They listened to him reach the foot of the stairs and then head down the yard towards the gate.

"Okay," Brakes said, and everybody sprang to their feet.

Butcherboy and Yusef the Turk rose to confront each other anew. The giant's split cheek-bone had swollen where Yusef the Turk's first blow had struck, and his eyes glared with a red and bloody light behind the pinched flesh of the lids.

Suddenly he charged. Yusef the Turk tried to sidestep the

216

onrush, but his painful knee slowed him up, and he felt the terrible arms close round his waist, pinioning his own arms at the same time.

The crowd buzzed with excitement, and Brakes Peterson snapped at them to shut up.

As the arms closed round him, Yusef the Turk butted Butcherboy's face savagely with his head, feeling the skin of his forehead split and a trickle of blood run into his eyes. But he also heard Butcherboy's grunt of pain as his head collided with the giant's nose, drawing a stream of blood that dribbled across the twisted upper lip into the snarling mouth and over the stubbled chin.

At the same time Yusef the Turk took the weight of his body quickly onto his weak leg and jerked the other knee brutally into Butcherboy's groin. The giant cried out with the sharp pain of the driving knee-bone, but held onto the other man, settling his head into Yusef the Turk's neck, while the powerful arms drew tight, squeezing with savage strength, the muscles twitching and jumping like cats in a sack.

Yusef the Turk knew that once he bent backwards there would be no hope. He would finally drop from the gorilla-like hug with a sprained or broken back, to receive smashing kicks in the face, ribs and stomach, before the giant jumped on him with both feet and all his hulking weight.

Butcherboy put all his force into the inward-drawing hug and his biceps and forearms swelled like balloons. Yusef the Turk, for a second, resisted with all his strength and then suddenly went limp, shooting his feet between the spread legs of his opponent and using his dead weight to bring both of them crashing to the ground. As Butcherboy came down on him, taken by surprise, Yusef the Turk had the time to jerk his head aside so that the other's bleeding face thumped into the concrete floor.

As Butcherboy's arms burst apart, Yusef the Turk squirmed swiftly from under him, striking at the cut cheekbone and the neck with vicious chopping blows, scrambling to his feet. Butcherboy struggled ponderously upright, and before he could straighten, Yusef the Turk kicked him smartly in the solar plexus.

The honk as the wind was driven from Butcherboy's body was music to the ears of Yusef the Turk. He, himself, was breathing heavily now, and his back and knee pained, and he knew that he would not be able to last much longer against the stubborn strength of the big man. But he knew, too, that for seconds, with his wind gone, Butcherboy was at his mercy.

So, darting forward, he punched with left and right at the doubled-up, gasping giant, his arms jolting like piston-rods and his fists falling like hammer-blows on the bloody face. He felt the skin of his knuckles break under the force of the blows, driving the bulk ahead of him.

Butcherboy stumbled away, bellowing in a hoarse, breathless voice. He wanted to get away from the driving fists, so that he could regroup his disorganised defences. He reeled and half fell into the middle of his silent knot of henchmen and satellites, Moos, Pinks, Squinteye Samuels, the Casbah Kid, Noor, Solly, Little Johnny and the others. Against these he stumbled. Pinks and Noor put out their hands to stop him, Squinteye Samuels and Little Johnny closed to catch him, the others crowded forward in a pack, and the Casbah Kid's right hand jerked in a swift movement.

Butcherboy collapsed with a grunt, his thick legs suddenly flopping like rags, a look of amazement in the red glare of his eyes. Then the glare snapped out like a fused light and he slid to the ground in the middle of the milling throng.

He never moved or made a sound again. Somebody got a mug of water and splashed it over the bloody face, thinking that the hulk was merely unconscious. The whole cell crowded around, babbling. Somebody else turned Butcherboy over on his face. He lay big and limp and still, and a tiny fountain of blood was just slackening off into a thin trickle out of the eye of the tattooed eagle.

In another part of the crowd, the Casbah Kid's tongue flicked momentarily over his swollen lip.

At the sight of the dead body of Butcherboy, with its thin trickle of blood from the tiny hole in the back, just over the heart, the silence of shock had fallen upon the gaping crowd of prisoners. It had lasted for just a moment. Then there had been a general scramble for bedding. Mats and blankets were fought over as the men battled to spread their beds and be asleep, to disassociate themselves utterly from the incident before any further time passed.

In a few minutes they were huddled under smelly blankets,

unconcerned about the sticky heat now. Nobody would say anything, except, if asked, that he had been asleep since the last bell
had gone.

Certainly, one could think what one liked. Who had done it?
Not Yusef the Turk, true as God. Towards the end of the fight—that
had been a real wake-up scrap—he had been battering at Butcherboy's head with his fists. Not once did Butcherboy have his back to
the Turk. And yet, somebody had stuck something into him, a knit-
ting-needle or a nail or something. From behind. Well, he had been
knocked flying into that gang of hard cases who followed him, Noor,
Pinks, Moos, Little Johnny, Squinteye and others, and one of them,
who had been awaiting a chance like this, had stabbed him in the
back. But with what? Nobody knew, nobody could guess. There had
been no sign of a weapon brandished. The white men would ask
questions, make searches, but they would find nothing.

Butcherboy's former henchmen had performed certain last
rites upon his body. They had washed his face, spread his mat and
blankets, laid him out on the bed and had covered the lifeless gorilla
body. These things they had done, not out of any respect for the
dead monster, but for their own security.

One could not very well deny having seen a dead man
sprawled out on the floor for an entire night, and not call the guard.
When he came around again, he would look in and find the cell
asleep, everybody under blankets.

Yusef the Turk had limped over to the water urn and had
washed blood and sweat from his face and torso. His forehead was
cut, and one eye beginning to swell. Also, his right knee ached and
the muscles of his back were lanced with sharp, twitching pain
which came with each movement.

"What's going to happen now?" George Adams had whispered, coming up to him. "Here's your teeth."

"Nothing," Yusef the Turk said, wincing. He rinsed the dentures, inspected them briefly and slipped them into his mouth, click-
ing them to make them fit. "Nothing. Nobody is going to say a thing,
Professor. When they open up in the morning, we all go out and
leave it to the white men."

"But—" George Adams whispered, but Yusef the Turk had
cut in, speaking angrily now.

ALEX LA GUMA

"Listen, mate, this is a jail, see? This kind of thing happen now and then. They built this jail, so let them run it. The thing is, hey, that inside here people settle their own business and don't have nothing, or little, to do with the white man as possible. Now don't you go thinking this is like it is outside." He dabbed his eye with water. "Another thing, if you start to be a good boy and try to help the law, Butcherboy's pals isn't going to like it. One of them must've done it, and they won't like it talked about to the law. They's going to lay in the tracks of anybody what talks."

George Adams realized that Butcherboy's former gang, united, was as dangerous as Butcherboy had been alone, perhaps even more so. But nevertheless, he felt intimidated, and that irked him. He was feeling ill, too, and his stomach trembled like an old man's hand. He had never seen anybody murdered, and that and the fact that now he would have to spend a night in the cell, with a corpse lying nearby, horrified him.

He had swallowed the rush of saliva to his mouth, and had asked, "How you feeling, Yuss?"

Yusef the Turk sucked his skinned knuckles and scowled. "My head is not so bad. Is my back and the ———— knee."

"You got to report sick in the morning."

"I reckon so."

"What you going to tell them?"

"———— all. I's sick. I's hurt. I fell down the stairs or something. That's all, man."

"They'll ask questions all over."

"Hell, I will worry about that when the time come. ———— it."

Then he had limped back to where they had made a sleeping place for themselves, and George Adams had felt his stomach heave, and, unable to control it, had rushed over to the latrine bucket and had vomited.

Afterwards, he had lain awake for a long time, perspiring in the heat, unable to thrust from his mind the death of Butcherboy who had terrorized his fellows and then had fallen by the hand of one of them.

From The Stone Country, *by Alex La Guma, Seven Seas Books,* 1967.

PART 5

THE AFRICAN PERSONALITY

If a man sought for a companion

who acted entirely like himself,

he would live in solitude.

—IBO PROVERB

Parable of the Eagle

by JAMES E. K. AGGREY

James E. K. Aggrey was a pioneer African educator, born in 1875 in the Gold Coast, now Ghana. Educated at mission schools, he studied and taught for many years in the United States. Later as a teacher in Africa, he provided inspiration for some of the early African leaders during their formative years at Achimota.

In the days before independence, one of the problems confronting African educators and leaders was the need to encourage young Africans to believe in themselves and in their own power and intelligence. No one contributed to this growing sense of identity more forcefully than Dr. Aggrey, who used this "Parable of the Eagle" to drive home his philosophy.

A certain man went through a forest seeking any bird of interest he might find. He caught a young eagle, brought it home and put it among his fowls and ducks and turkeys, and gave it chickens' food to eat even though it was an eagle, the king of birds.

Five years later a naturalist came to see him and, after passing through his garden, said: "That bird is an eagle, not a chicken."

"Yes," said its owner, "but I have trained it to be a chicken. It is no longer an eagle, it is a chicken even though it measures fifteen feet from tip to tip of its wings."

"No," said the naturalist, "it is an eagle still; it has the heart of an eagle, and I will make it soar high up to the heavens."

"No," said the owner, "it is a chicken and it will never fly."

They agreed to test it. The naturalist picked up the eagle, held it up, and said with great intensity: "Eagle, thou art an eagle; thou dost belong to the sky and not to this earth; stretch forth thy wings and fly."

The eagle turned this way and that, and then, looking down, saw the chickens eating their food, and down he jumped.

The owner said: "I told you it was a chicken."

"No," said the naturalist, "it is an eagle. Give it another chance to-morrow."

So the next day he took it to the top of the house and said: "Eagle, thou art an eagle; stretch forth thy wings and fly." But again the eagle, seeing the chickens feeding, jumped down and fed with them.

Then the owner said: "I told you it was a chicken."

"No," asserted the naturalist, "it is an eagle, and it still has the heart of an eagle; only give it one more chance, and I will make it fly to-morrow."

The next morning he rose early and took the eagle outside the city, away from the houses, to the foot of a high mountain. The sun was just rising, gilding the top of the mountain with gold, and every crag was glistening in the joy of that beautiful morning.

He picked up the eagle and said to it: "Eagle, thou art an eagle; thou dost belong to the sky and not to this earth; stretch forth thy wings and fly!"

The eagle looked around and trembled as if new life were coming to it; but it did not fly. The naturalist then made it look straight at the sun. Suddenly it stretched out its wings and, with the screech of an eagle, it mounted higher and higher and never returned. It was an eagle, though it had been kept and tamed as a chicken!

My people of Africa, we were created in the image of God, but men have made us think we are chickens, and we still think we are; but we are eagles. Stretch forth your wings and fly! Don't be content with the food of chickens.

The African Abroad

by WILLIAM CONTON

William Conton was born near the border of Gambia and Sierra Leone in 1925 and was educated in Sierra Leone and the United Kingdom. In 1947 he was appointed Lecturer in History at Fourah Bay College, Sierra Leone. From there he went on to other educational posts in Ghana, Sierra Leone, and Liberia. He is now one of the staff directors of UNESCO in Paris. He has written one novel, *The African,* and a two-volume history of West Africa.

Kisimi Kamara, hero of *The African,* is identified as a Hausa from a fictitious country, who is awarded a scholarship to study in England. Being a thoughtful young man, his reactions to the British at home are interesting, and he sets out to get better acquainted with them on a holiday tour of the Lake District. With a rucksack on his back, packed with a few clothes and some familiar English classics, he is ready to travel.

⋏   Liverpool next day was gray, cold, wet and foggy; and the promised land looked most unpromising from the deck of the ship. Once ashore, however, the towering buildings, massed traffic, and attractive shops kept us staring and gaping while waiting for our trains to various parts of the country. The sight of white people en masse was itself something which required some getting used to; but the thing that took us really aback was our first sight of a white man sweeping a gutter.

He was a short, seedy-looking, rather dirty man, with heavy working boots and stained, well-worn clothes, but unmistakably a white man nevertheless; and actually standing right down in the gutter sweeping it, collecting the rubbish on a shovel and tipping it into a wheelbarrow. We stood in utter disbelief, at some little distance from him, expecting him at any moment either to vanish like a gremlin down the nearest drain, or else to turn dark brown.

225

I suppose if you had asked us beforehand who swept gutters in England, we should have replied, after a moment or two's reflection, that we supposed some of the English drains, at least, must have the honor of being swept by white men; for even all the stowaways and workless migrants from Africa and the West Indies could not provide enough labor for so many menial tasks. But no one had prepared us beforehand by any such question; and the sight of that man almost felled us.

"Thank God for bringing me here," breathed Appiah reverently, the first among us to recover his breath. "I always suspected there was some good reason for my coming to Britain."

And I think that summed up how most of us felt. We did not lose respect for the white man—very far from it. What we did lose, however (and long overdue was the loss), was an illusion created by the role the white man plays in Africa: that he is a kind of demigod whose hands must never get dirty, who must not be allowed to carry anything heavier than a portfolio or wield any implement heavier than a pen. Without realizing it, we had come to think of the white man only in the role of missionary, civil servant, or senior business executive, one who was always behind the desk, never in front of it. We saw him as one who always gave orders, never took them, who could have any job he liked for the asking. So to realize that that man was perfectly happy working in that gutter (snatches of his melancholy whistling reached us faintly where we stood) was a most salutary experience.

It was now possible for us to like the white man. For before you can like (as distinct from merely admiring or emulating), you must feel kinship, a shared humanity, the possibility of common experiences and destinies. As we resumed our walk past the sweeper, he looked up and grinned cheerfully at us, leaning for a moment on his brush. We waved and grinned back; and in that mute exchange of greetings there was erased in a moment the memory of the behavior of the stewards on board. The latter had acted as if the gods had decreed that the black man should minister and the white man be ministered unto, and that they were stewards and we passengers only by special dispensation. Our friend the road-sweeper, on the other hand, was so far from harboring any such notions that he had found time to give us, in his own way, a welcome to Liverpool.

We were soon to find, as countless thousands of colonial students in the United Kingdom must have found, that the Britisher at home is an altogether different creature, and a much more lovable one, than the Britisher overseas. Perhaps the same applies to most people. Abroad, too, we all to a greater or lesser extent are conscious of treading a stage; of having to live up to, or live down, a national reputation. The white man abroad has to prove that he is superior to the black man; the black man abroad has to prove that he is not inferior to the white man. The proving of both cases involves much play-acting, much assumption of false roles.

As my train to Newcastle raced through the Lancashire countryside on that wet September morning, my thoughts were on more humdrum things than finding solutions to the problems of race relations in Britain. I wondered about my luggage—would it be all right in the guard's van? Were any boxes or bottles broken, was my palm oil spilled? I wondered about the hostel I was to stay in until I could find permanent lodgings—would I find any other Africans there? Would I be able to eat the food, stand up to the weather? Suddenly I felt terribly lonely in that compartment.

In fact, I never really felt lonely again after those first few hours in the train from Liverpool. Not only were there many other Africans at King's College, The Newcastle Division of the University of Durham, of which I was now a proud undergraduate, but I found in these north-country folk a warm friendliness, and in most of my British fellow students a constant readiness to offer companionship and advice.

How adaptable is the human animal in circumstances such as these! Within a few weeks, I was moving alone through the streets of Newcastle and mixing with the students in their work and play with a freedom and an ease I never dreamed beforehand would have come to me. Even the physical adaptation to diet and climate was soon effected, and all my earlier uncertainties and anxieties were forgotten. I wrote happy letters home assuring my mother and father that they had nothing to worry about at all, and that everything had worked out to good advantage.

Some of the ways of the British students did appear to me distinctly odd, as no doubt mine did to them. I found, for example, their refusal to admit the necessity for a daily bath, even in high summer, a little disconcerting. I had been brought up to believe that cleanliness is next to godliness and also lies next to the skin. Whenever I would hear students in Britain referring to that curious institution of theirs, the "bath night," as though it were a special and not very welcome weekly recurrence, I would think of the little stream which splashed under the bridge in Lokko. It was a temperamental stream: during the dry season it would shrink to a mere trickle, and at the height of the rains it would swell to a boiling, pounding cataract which could sweep grown men away. But every day, rainy season or dry, would be the scene of busy laundry and toilet activity for a large number of people. What better and more sensible time to wash your clothes than when you yourself are having your bath? The water was soft and cool, and the rocks, hard and smooth, were perfect for beating clothes against. There was only one unwritten law about this admirable practice—no mixed bathing; and a good beating and cursing for any Peeping Tom.

I could not help noticing, too, the individualism of the Britisher, and the looseness of his family ties and obligations, as compared with ours. We were brought up to have an intense pride in our family, and an intense loyalty to it; and to feel that that pride and loyalty must extend to the most distant relative known to us. The word "family" means more to an African than it does to a European; and many of us smile quietly when we hear British people talking about family life in their country. How little of it there really is! I remember how no one either in Lokko or in Sagresa, old or young, took any important decision without first discussing the pros and cons with every available relative. A wedding, christening, funeral or initiation ceremony not attended by every member of the family who was not ill or overseas would be unthinkable. In times of adversity, there were scores and scores of relatives to console one; in times of prosperity a similar number turned up to share both your joy and your material wealth. A man who merely disliked you cursed you; a man who hated you cursed your family. It was all really an elaborate and most effective system of social security; and through it the very great extremes of wealth and poverty which have brought suffering and injustice into the social life of so many European countries (and revolution and bloodshed to some)

have thus far been avoided in Africa. We had a joke among ourselves in the hostel in Newcastle that the Englishman treats his dog
as he should his nephew, and his nephew as merely another man's
son.

I think I had as many friends as any other student in Newcastle, and could enjoy a party or a dance well enough. But when
it came to my studies (and I regarded visits to places of natural
beauty or historical interest as a vital part of my studies), I found
I could absorb the atmosphere of the place much more effectively
alone, without distraction.

So it was I set out at the beginning of my first long vacation
on a visit to the Lake District. I had joined the Youth Hostel Association and, in order to make my not over-generous allowance
stretch out as far as possible, decided to hitchhike to the Lakes
and around them, and to stay in Youth Hostels all the way.

The journey from Newcastle to Keswick I reckoned to do easily
in a day. I found that the lorry drivers were for the most part only
too ready to stop and pick me up, though many private cars slowed
down and then thought better of it on seeing the unexpected com-
plexion of the hitchhiker. No doubt I presented a rather strange
sight in my corduroy trousers and khaki shirt, and with my bulging
rucksack on a harness on my back.

My longest leg in one vehicle was thumbed from just outside
Hexham to Carlisle, in a big timber truck. The driver was alone in
his cab, and at his invitation I climbed up into the seat beside him.
I found him a genial, plump, red-faced fellow who, I immediately
decided, must be precisely the type of fellow Dickens had in mind
when he conceived the character of Mr. Pickwick. My friend was
more than a little amused at finding an African in this unusual garb.
For some time he drove slowly and examined me carefully.

"Well, well, well," he managed to say at length. "Who would
a thought of this on this fine mornin'? And where may you be
headin' for, young man?"

"Keswick, to tour the Lake District."

"You're a mighty long way from home, ain't you? And where
may your home be, anyhow?"

"Sagresa."

"And where's that?"

I smiled tolerantly. "It's the capital of Songhai."

"Oh! That there Portuguese place! And me just itching to tell you about how I feel the British Empire's a damn hypocritical setup."

"Songhai is British."

"Well, is it now!" His jovial face creased up with smiles and he chortled deep down in his throat. "Why don't they ever tell me these things?"

"Those who should tell you don't usually know themselves," I ventured. He turned and gave me a long hard look; but I think it was the naturalness of my English rather than the content of my words that had surprised him. "I am a student at King's College, so I know just how little even my fellow students really know about their Empire."

My newfound friend had quite recovered his good humor now. "There's a devil of a lot of it, you know," he said, "from what I remember of me distant and reluctant school days. So you're bound for Keswick, eh? Very sensible too. You'll have a grand time amongst them Lakes, I can promise you that. But is this how you travel around . . . er . . . Songo, did you say, hitchhiking and that, I mean?"

"No; but we have plenty of lorries—mammy-lorries we call them, as they are usually full of women going to market. They have some very amusing inscriptions painted on them too."

"Let's hear some of 'em. You never know, perhaps the week just before I'm due to retire I might have some fun brightening up this old bus just to see what 'ud happen!" And again the deep chuckle as he changed his gears down with a graceful, easy, well-practiced movement.

"'No Sweat, Sweet.' And rather ominous but well-meant sentiments such as 'In God We Trust,' 'God Is My Refuge,' 'One More River to Cross,' and so on." His resonant laugh punctuated my words.

"You get many accidents?"

"Yes, a lot, considering the fact that our traffic is not as dense as yours. But the drivers usually take good care to escape unhurt; and, if they can make it, to disappear before anyone asks them any questions."

"How's that? No police?"

"Not many up-country."

He emitted a sound which was a mixture of grunt and sigh, and which might have denoted anything from envy to incredulity. In the distance a roadside café came into view, with a cluster of heavy lorries on the open ground around it.

"You'll come in and have a bite and a cup o' tea with me chums and me, won't you, young 'un?" he asked. And then, as we came a little closer, "Oh, I see old Charlie is there—that's his truck on the far side, the big red eight-wheeler. Now he's a rare old bird, not much eddication perhaps if you compare him with you and your friends at college; but plenty o' good common sense, lots o' little bits of odd knowledge and news picked up from all over the world—he's traveled a bit in his time, has old Charlie—and can tell and take a joke with the best of them." Our gears grated slightly, the brakes hissed, and we turned in and parked neatly among the other trucks.

I felt at first a little chary about accepting my friend's invitation. One could not be sure that all lorry drivers would be as ready as he had been to welcome the intrusion of an African who was, in addition, what they would have called "one of the eddicated." But I was genuinely thirsty, and could not resist the thought of having, not so much a "cup o' tea" (I had not yet acquired that particular English habit) but a lemonade or fruit drink of some kind.

We entered a small, low-ceilinged room filled with small tables on which were plates, cups and saucers, and cutlery, but no cloths. There were a dozen or so men seated in small groups at the tables, and most of them seemed to have a greeting for my driver as we entered. He chose a table where there were two empty seats, and I could sense the curious looks turned in my direction from all parts of the room as we sat down.

"Friend of mine hitchhiking to the Lakes," said Joe (as I at once discovered he was called) by way of explanation and perhaps apology to the others at the table. "What's your name, lad? And don't be afraid of them, you know. They won't bite you. They're all very nice boys."

"Kamara," I said, feeling more than a little uncomfortable at the amount of attention I was receiving. It was the first time I had found my self among a group of Britishers most of whom were meeting a man of my race for the first time. There was a brief, awkward pause.

Then a big, broad-shouldered man with a bronzed, weather-beaten face and watery eyes, sitting opposite me, broke the ice. He leaned across the table, gripped my hand and shook it with a cordiality better befitting the reunion of long-lost friends. "You're right welcome amongst us," he said. "No better place than the Lakes for a holiday, no better way of traveling than hitchhiking, and no better company to meet on the way than the present company assembled—although I say so meself."

"Good old Charlie," said Joe. "Nothing ever robs you of words for long." So this is Charlie the traveler, I thought to myself, looking at him with fresh interest, and feeling an instinctive liking for him already. Indeed, in a very few minutes, my feeling of strangeness had worn off, as those at the other tables appeared to forget about me, and those at ours drew me into their conversation with a naturalness which I should never have believed possible. They were a forthright, unsophisticated crowd, with a wonderful fund of tales at the tips of their tongues; some witty, some sad, some lugubrious, many smutty, others merely tall, but all, even the corniest, fascinating to me.

This was just what I wanted—an opportunity to listen to good round twentieth-century English as used by those whose formal education had been limited, but whose experience of life and whose contact with other people living in those islands had been of the very widest.

Charlie had, indeed, as Joe had told me, traveled widely outside Britain, and he soon revealed to me that he had spent several days being "pressure cooked," as he chose to put it, in a troopship at anchor in Sagresa harbor during the war. But he declared himself prepared to forgive and forget that experience (it was not quite clear whether it was I or the War Office who was to be favored with his gracious pardon). He then went on to tell us how one of the Kroo canoe boys who used to dive for pennies alongside the troopships in that harbor once came up on the wrong side of the ship by mistake, and how the others took advantage of his absence by tipping his box of hard-earned coins into the water and doing a mass dive for the contents.

Everyone laughed heartily at this story, I almost as loud as any. A fat woman in a red and white check apron had placed steaming plates of boiled potatoes, cabbage and Irish stew before Joe and me (to Joe's order). I suddenly realized I was hungry as well as thirsty, and tucked in with more enthusiasm than I had ever shown before for these flavorless products of English culinary art. I wondered mildly as I did so at the understatement contained in the phrase "bite and a cup o' tea," and, had I not been prevented from doing so by both Joe and Charlie, would have risked some of my funds in ordering tea or drinks all round the table. But no; I was apparently their guest—doubly so, said Charlie, for being both in their country and their café, and was to keep my money "in case you find any Kroo canoe boys on Lake Windermere-like."

I racked my brains for a good yarn to produce for them, and finally remembered a true story which had once been the cause of much righteous indignation among Sagresan mammies. The lorry drivers appreciated it, I think; for, like Charlie's tale about the Kroo boys, it illustrated the price we paid for Western "civilization."

A woman living in Sagresa had found herself the mother of a child she did not want. As I explained to my audience, this initial situation could not have developed in African village society, where a child is soon an economic asset, not a liability, and is always regarded as a sacred and most welcome gift from the gods. However, in this case the woman in question, being partly "civilized," had struck upon an ingenious method of getting rid of the child, a method both safe and lucrative. She had gone with the infant to a market, had asked a motherly looking stall-holder to hold the baby while she went off ostensibly to look for change to buy a bale of cloth, and so had made good her escape, taking the cloth and leaving the baby. My audience seemed to find the story funny, but unlikely to be true, in spite of all my protestations.

Thus did time fly past unnoticed in that genial company; and it was only in the middle of a gruesome tale of Charlie's about the embarrassment of two thieves who had stolen a van in which he was conveying a corpse to a mortuary, that I realized that if I was to get to Keswick that day I would have to continue my journey immediately. Drivers had been going in and out of the café continuously while we were there, and the faces at our table had changed more than once. Joe and Charlie, however, were both going only as far as Carlisle that evening, and seemed to feel they had plenty of time to spare.

When I expressed some anxiety about reaching Keswick before nightfall, Joe at once suggested that I spend the night with a friend of his in Carlisle, and promised to find a driver to take me into Keswick first thing in the morning, so that my program of touring would not be upset. I was only too glad to accept this suggestion; and in a little while we took our leave of Charlie and the little café, climbed into the truck and swung out into the road once more.

From The African, *by William Conton, Heinemann Educational Books Ltd., 1970.*

Sundiata, Hero-king of Old Mali

by D. T. NIANE

D. T. Niane is a storyteller who uses all his skill to recount the heroic adventures of Sundiata, ancient conqueror and ruler of old Mali in the thirteenth century. Sundiata's exploits have been handed down from generation to generation in the oral tradition of the *griots*, the troubadours and minstrels of West Africa.

Born a cripple, Sundiata went into exile as a child to escape the schemes of a wicked and jealous stepmother. By the time he was 18, he had the stateliness of the lion and the strength of the buffalo. Judging that the time was ripe, he returned to conquer Soumaoro, the pagan sorcerer-king of the SuSu (or Sosso) who had seized power in Mali. In a great battle, he subdued the warriors, or *sofas*, but Soumaoro escaped. It seemed that no weapons could harm so powerful a sorcerer.

But Sundiata's sister, who had been married by force to the sorcerer-king, joined her brother on the road to Mali and revealed to him the secret of Soumaoro's power. At last Sundiata was ready for the final challenge, the famous battle of Krina in 1235.

人 Sundiata went and pitched camp at Dayala in the valley of the Niger. Now it was he who was blocking Soumaoro's road to the south. Up till that time, Sundiata and Soumaoro had fought each other without a declaration of war. One does not wage war without saying why it is being waged. Those fighting should make a declaration of their grievances to begin with. Just as a sorcerer ought not to attack someone without taking him to task for some evil deed, so a king should not wage war without saying why he is taking up arms.

Soumaoro advanced as far as Krina, near the village of Dayala on the Niger and decided to assert his rights before joining battle. Soumaoro knew that Sundiata also was a sorcerer, so, instead of

The Musician MSIMANGO
Reprinted from *African Arts*, Volume IV, Number 2

sending an embassy, he committed his words to one of his owls. The night bird came and perched on the roof of Djata's tent and spoke. The son of Sogolon in his turn sent his owl to Soumaoro. Here is the dialogue of the sorcerer kings:

"Stop, young man. Henceforth I am the king of Mali. If you want peace, return to where you came from," said Soumaoro.

"I am coming back, Soumaoro, to recapture my kingdom. If you want peace you will make amends to my allies and return to Sosso where you are the king."

"I am king of Mali by force of arms. My rights have been established by conquest."

"Then I will take Mali from you by force of arms and chase you from my kingdom."

"Know, then, that I am the wild yam of the rocks; nothing will make me leave Mali."

"Know, also that I have in my camp seven master smiths who will shatter the rocks. Then, yam, I will eat you."

"I am the poisonous mushroom that makes the fearless vomit."

"As for me, I am the ravenous cock, the poison does not matter to me."

"Behave yourself, little boy, or you will burn your foot, for I am the red-hot cinder."

"But me, I am the rain that extinguishes the cinder; I am the boisterous torrent that will carry you off."

"I am the mighty silk-cotton tree that looks from on high on the tops of other trees."

"And I, I am the strangling creeper that climbs to the top of the forest giant."

"Enough of this argument. You shall not have Mali."

"Know that there is not room for two kings on the same skin, Soumaoro; you will let me have your place."

"Very well, since you want war I will wage war against you, but I would have you know that I have killed nine kings whose heads adorn my room. What a pity, indeed, that your head should take its place beside those of your fellow madcaps."

"Prepare yourself, Soumaoro, for it will not be long before the calamity that is going to crash down upon you and yours comes to an end."

Thus Sundiata and Soumaoro spoke together. After the war of mouths, swords had to decide the issue.

Sundiata wanted to have done with Soumaoro before the rainy season, so he struck camp and marched on Krina where Soumaoro was encamped. The latter realized that the decisive battle had come. Sundiata deployed his men on the little hill that dominates the plain. The great battle was for the next day.

In the evening, to raise the men's spirits, Djata gave a great feast, for he was anxious that his men should wake up happy in the morning. Several oxen were slaughtered and that evening Balla Fasseké, in front of the whole army, called to mind the history of old Mali. He praised Sundiata, seated amidst his lieutenants, in this manner:

"Now I address myself to you, Maghan Sundiata, I speak to you king of Mali, to whom dethroned monarchs flock. The time foretold to you by the jinn is now coming. Sundiata, kingdoms and empires are in the likeness of man; like him they are born, they grow and disappear. Each sovereign embodies one moment of that life. Formerly, the kings of Ghana extended their kingdom over all the lands inhabited by the black man, but the circle has closed and the Cissés of Wagadou are nothing more than petty princes in a desolate land. Today, another kingdom looms up, powerful, the kingdom of Sosso. Humbled kings have borne their tribute to Sosso, Soumaoro's arrogance knows no more bounds and his cruelty is equal to his ambition. But will Soumaoro dominate the world? Are we, the *griots* of Mali, condemned to pass on to future generations the humiliations which the king of Sosso cares to inflict on our country? No, you may be glad, children of the 'Bright Country,' for the kingship of Sosso is but the growth of yesterday, whereas that of Mali dates from the time of Bilali. Each kingdom has its childhood, but Soumaoro wants to force the pace, and so Sosso will collapse under him like a horse worn out beneath its rider.

"You, Maghan, you are Mali. It has had a long and difficult childhood like you. Sixteen kings have preceded you on the throne of Niani, sixteen kings have reigned with varying fortunes, but from being village chiefs the Keitas have become tribal chiefs and then kings. Sixteen generations have consolidated their power. You are the outgrowth of Mali just as the silk-cotton tree is the growth of the earth, born of deep and mighty roots. To face the tempest the tree must have long roots and gnarled branches. Maghan Sundiata, has not the tree grown?

"I would have you know, son of Sogolon, that there is not room for two kings around the same calabash of rice. When a new cock comes to the poultry run the old cock picks a quarrel with him and the docile hens wait to see if the new arrival asserts himself or yields. You have come to Mali. Very well, then, assert yourself. Strength makes a law of its own self and power allows no division.

"*Griots* are men of the spoken word, and by the spoken word we give life to the gestures of kings. But words are nothing but words; power lies in deeds. Be a man of action; do not answer me any more with your mouth, but tomorrow, on the plain of Krina, show me what you would have me recount to coming generations. Tomorrow allow me to sing the 'Song of the Vultures' over the bodies of the thousands of Sossos whom your sword will have laid low before evening."

It was on the eve of Krina. In this way Balla Fasséké reminded Sundiata of the history of Mali so that, in the morning, he would show himself worthy of his ancestors.

At break of day, Fakoli came and woke up Sundiata to tell him that Soumaoro had begun to move his *sofas* (warriors) out of Krina. The son of Sogolon appeared dressed like a hunter king. He wore tight-fitting, ochre-colored trousers. He gave the order to draw up the *sofas* across the plain, and while his chiefs bustled about, Manding Bory and Nana Triban came into Djata's tent.

"Brother," said Manding Bory, "have you got the bow ready?"

"Yes," replied Sundiata. "Look."

He unhooked his bow from the wall, along with the deadly arrow. It was not an iron arrow at all, but was made of wood and pointed with the spur of a white cock. The cock's spur was the Tana of Soumaoro, the secret which Nana Triban had managed to draw out of the King of Sosso.

"Brother," said Nana Triban, "Soumaoro now knows that I have fled from Sosso. Try to get near him for he will avoid you the whole battle long."

The sun had risen on the other side of the river and already lit the whole plain. Sundiata's troops deployed from the edge of the river across the plain, but Soumaoro's army was so big that other *sofas* remaining in Krina had ascended the ramparts to see the battle. Soumaoro was already distinguishable in the distance by his tall headdress, and the wings of his enormous army brushed the river on one side and the hills on the other. As at Neguéboria, Sundiata did not deploy all his forces. The bowmen of Wagadou and the Djallonkés stood at the rear ready to spill out on the left towards the hills as the battle spread. Fakoli Koroma and Kamandjan were in the front line with Sundiata and his cavalry.

With his powerful voice Sundiata cried, "Forward." The order was repeated from tribe to tribe and the army started off. Soumaoro stood on the right with his cavalry.

Djata and his cavalry charged with great dash but they were stopped by the horsemen of Diaghan and a struggle to the death began. Tabon Wana and the archers of Wagadou stretched out their lines towards the hills and the battle spread over the entire plain, while an unrelenting sun climbed in the sky. The horses of Mema were extremely agile, and they reared forward with their fore hooves raised and swooped down on the horsemen of Diaghan, who rolled on the ground trampled under the horses' hooves. Presently the men of Diaghan gave ground and fell back towards the rear. The enemy center was broken.

It was then that Manding Bory galloped up to announce to Sundiata that Soumaoro, having thrown in all his reserve, had swept down on Fakoli and his smiths. Obviously Soumaoro was bent on punishing his nephew. Already overwhelmed by the numbers, Fakoli's men were beginning to give ground. The battle was not yet won.

His eyes red with anger, Sundiata pulled his cavalry over to the left in the direction of the hills where Fakoli was valiantly enduring his uncle's blows. But wherever the son of the buffalo passed, death rejoiced. Sundiata's presence restored the balance momentarily, but Soumaoro's *sofas* were too numerous all the same. Sogolon's son looked for Soumaoro and caught sight of him in the middle of the fray. Sundiata struck out right and left and the Sossos scrambled out of his way. The king of Sosso, who did not want Sundiata to get near him, retreated far behind his men, but Sundiata followed him with his eyes. He stopped and bent his bow. The arrow flew and grazed Soumaoro on the shoulder. The cock's spur no more than scratched him, but the effect was immediate and Soumaoro felt his powers leave him. His eyes met Sundiata's. Now trembling like a man in the grip of fever, the vanquished Soumaoro looked up towards the sun. A great black bird flew over above the fray and he understood. It was a bird of misfortune.

"The bird of Krina," he muttered.

The king of Sosso let out a great cry and, turning his horse's head, he took to flight. The Sossos saw the king and fled in their turn. It was a rout. Death hovered over the great plain and blood poured out of a thousand wounds. Who can tell how many Sossos perished at Krina?

The victory of Krina was dazzling. The remains of Soumaoro's army went to shut themselves up in Sosso. But the empire of Sosso was done for. From everywhere around kings sent their submission to Sundiata. The king of Guidimakhan sent a richly furnished embassy to Djata and at the same time gave his daughter in marriage to the victor. Embassies flocked to Koulikoro, but when Djata had been joined by all the army he marched on Sosso. Soumaoro's city, Sosso, the impregnable city, the city of smiths skilled in wielding the spear.

In the absence of the king and his son, Noumounkeba, a tribal chief, directed the defence of the city. He had quickly amassed all that he could find in the way of provisions from the surrounding countryside.

Sosso was a magnificent city. In the open plain her triple rampart with awe-inspiring towers reached into the sky. The city comprised a hundred and eighty-eight fortresses and the palace of Soumaoro loomed above the whole city like a gigantic tower. Sosso had but one gate; colossal and made of iron, the work of the sons of fire. Noumounkeba hoped to tie Sundiata down outside of Sosso, for he had enough provisions to hold out for a year.

The sun was beginning to set when Sogolon-Djata appeared before Sosso the Magnificent. From the top of a hill, Djata and his general staff gazed upon the fearsome city of the sorcerer-king. The army encamped in the plain opposite the great gate of the city and fires were lit in the camp. Djata resolved to take Sosso in the course of a morning. He fed his men a double ration and the tam-tams beat all night to stir up the victors of Krina.

241

At daybreak the towers of the ramparts were black with *sofas*. Others were positioned on the ramparts themselves. They were the archers. The Mandingoes were masters in the art of storming a town. In the front line Sundiata placed the *sofas* of Mali, while those who held the ladders were in the second line protected by the shields of the spearmen. The main body of the army was to attack the city gate. When all was ready, Djata gave the order to attack. The drums resounded, the horns blared and like a tide the Mandingo front line moved off, giving mighty shouts. With their shields raised above their heads the Mandingoes advanced up to the foot of the wall, then the Sossos began to rain large stones down on the assailants. From the rear, the bowmen of Wagadou shot arrows at the ramparts. The attack spread and the town was assaulted at all points. Sundiata had a murderous reserve; they were the bowmen whom the king of the Bobos had sent shortly before Krina. The archers of Bobo are the best in the world. On one knee the archers fired flaming arrows over the ramparts. Within the walls the thatched huts took fire and the smoke swirled up. The ladders stood against the curtain wall and the first Mandingo *sofas* were already at the top. Seized by panic through seeing the town on fire, the Sossos hesitated a moment. The huge tower surmounting the gate surrendered, for Fakoli's smiths had made themselves masters of it. They got into the city where the screams of women and children brought the Sossos' panic to a head. They opened the gates to the main body of the army.

Then began the massacre. Women and children in the midst of fleeing Sossos implored mercy of the victors. Djata and his cavalry were now in front of the awsome tower palace of Soumaoro. Noumounkeba, conscious that he was lost, came out to fight. With his sword held aloft he bore down on Djata, but the latter dodged him and, catching hold of the Sosso's braced arm, forced him to his knees while the sword dropped to the ground. He did not kill him but delivered him into the hands of Manding Bory.

Soumaoro's palace was now at Sundiata's mercy. While everywhere the Sossos were begging for quarter, Sundiata, preceded by Balla Fasseké, entered Soumaoro's tower. The *griot* knew every nook and cranny of the palace from his captivity and he led Sundiata to Soumaoro's magic chamber.

When Balla Fasseké opened the door to the room, it was found to have changed its appearance since Soumaoro had been touched by the fatal arrow. The inmates of the chamber had lost their power. The snake in the pitcher was in the throes of death, the owls from the perch were flapping pitifully about on the ground. Everything was dying in the sorcerer's abode. It was all up with the power of Soumaoro.

Sundiata had all Soumaoro's fetishes taken down and before the palace were gathered together all Soumaoro's wives, all princesses taken from their families by force. The prisoners, their hands tied behind their backs, were already herded together. Just as he had wished, Sundiata had taken Sosso in the course of a morning. When everything was outside of the town and all that there was to take had been taken out, Sundiata gave the order to complete its destruction. The last houses were set fire to and prisoners were employed in the razing of the walls. Thus, as Djata intended, Sosso was destroyed to its very foundations.

Yes, Sosso was razed to the ground. It has disappeared, the proud city of Soumaoro. A ghastly wilderness extends over the places where kings came and humbled themselves before the sorcerer-king. All traces of the houses have vanished and of Soumaoro's seven-story palace there remains nothing more. A field of desolation, Sosso is now a spot where guinea fowl and young partridges come to take their dust baths.

Many years have rolled by and many times the moon has traversed the heaven since these places lost their inhabitants. The bourein, the tree of desolation, spreads out its thorny undergrowth and insolently grows in Soumaoro's capital. Sosso the Proud is nothing but a memory in the mouths of griots. The hyenas come to wail there at night, the hare and the hind come and feed on the site of the palace of Soumaoro, the king who wore robes of human skin.

Sosso vanished from the earth and it was Sundiata, the son of the buffalo, who gave these places over to solitude. After the destruction of Soumaoro's capital the world knew no other master but Sundiata.

From Sundiata: An Epic of Old Mali, *by D. T. Niane, translated by G. D. Pickett, Longmans, Green and Co. Ltd., 1969.*

Master of Ceremonies

by CAMARA LAYE

Camara Laye was born in a predominantly Muslim community in Upper Guinea in 1924. He received a good secondary education and went to Paris to study engineering. He remained to become a writer. Immediately after the publication of his autobiography, *The Dark Child*, he was recognized as a man of literary talent. Published first in French (1954) and then in English (1955), *The Dark Child* is a poetic and nostalgic memory of his childhood.

His second book, *Radiance of the King* (1956), is completely different. The bizarre adventures of its hero, Clarence, a good-for-nothing white man in Africa, may be read first for the adventure alone, and then reread for underlying symbolism. Clarence, who gambles away everything but the clothes on his back, attempts to reestablish his fortunes by seeking out the king of the country.

Radiance of the King, the source of the following episode, is full of African laughter, of tricks and pranks, of quick changes of scene, as Clarence travels south to look for a job. No matter if Clarence has no skills! Can he beat a drum? No, that takes years of training. Can he serve as stud for the Naba's harem? Perhaps that is the answer.

Clarence spends many months in the Naba's employ. He moves in a dream world, mystified by his companions, uneasy at times, puzzled by the standards of the Naba's court. Clarence meets the African personality in many different forms and tries to understand it.

人   "The show is about to begin," said Samba Baloum. "The Naba wishes you to know that the spectacle is about to commence," he added unctuously.

"He just made a little sign with his beard," said Clarence.

"Precisely," said Samba Baloum. "For what he had to tell you could not be conveyed by any more expansive sign. But take a look to the right."

Clarence looked straight at the master of ceremonies. This unpleasant personage was stretched out with his face to the ground, and his hands and feet were tied to pegs. Now that he had been stripped of his *boubou*, he seemed longer and more angular than ever.

"What's happened to him?"

"Nothing—*yet*," said Samba Baloum. "But he's done for, as you can see."

"He's going to be roasted," said the boys.

"You don't mean to say he's going to be roasted alive?" asked Clarence.

"Do you take us for cannibals?" said Samba Baloum. "No, only his skin will be cooked. The skin, and of course, a little more: an inch or two of the flesh underneath the skin."

On the square, a kind of uproar was suddenly heard. A great wave of heads came swarming over to the low palace wall and at every opening in the bamboo railings eyes shining with greed peered in.

"Let us be seated," said Samba Baloum. "We shall be able to see everything from here. We can see better from here than if we were under the arcade."

The Naba wagged his beard. One of the dignitaries who was holding a stick left the group and walked over towards the master of ceremonies.

"Have you any calabashes left?" Samba Baloum asked.

"I told Akissi to bring them as soon as you arrived," said Clarence.

"Akissi!" cried Samba Baloum.

Akissi appeared with the calabashes.

"I was waiting until you had sat down," she said. "Drink as much as you like. The Naba has had a fresh lot sent."

Samba Baloum raised his calabash in the direction of the master of ceremonies.

"Your good health!" he cried.

The master of ceremonies replied with a glance full of fury.

"Don't take it to heart," said Samba Baloum. "Your health is more precious to me than you might think. It is a guarantee of your powers of endurance."

The Naba at that moment wagged his beard more energetically than he had done so until now. And the dignitary who had crouched beside the master of ceremonies, as if in order to see him better, rolled his eyes with cruel glee. At once the stick came into play; it came whistling down on the master of ceremonies' backside.

"It stings like mad," said Noaga. "It's the very stick that belonged to the master of ceremonies."

"You ought to know all about that," said Nagoa.

"But I'm not going to be the only one to know all about it!" replied Noaga. "Get that into your head, and get it firmly imprinted, just as the master of ceremonies is getting it firmly imprinted on his backside."

"It's not nice to take pleasure in another's misfortune," said Clarence.

"I don't seem to remember you sparing my feelings when you joked about my bump!" said Noaga.

"The pigeon's egg," said Nagoa.

"You'd do better to watch what's going on, instead of bringing up all that again," said Noaga.

The stick was coming down with such force and precision that the master of ceremonies could not help groaning. All along the outer wall, the people were getting noisier and noisier. They had greeted the first sharp strokes with the same indifference as the master of ceremonies. But now they were roused, though one could hardly tell whether it was intense pleasure or extreme pity that prompted their shouts. But soon it became apparent that they were prompted by pleasure alone, for short bursts of laughter kept breaking out.

"They're enjoying themselves too," said Noaga.

"There aren't many distractions in Aziana," said Samba Baloum, shrugging his shoulders slightly.

"But that does not necessarily mean the master of ceremonies agrees with you," said Clarence.

He did not feel that the pitiful spectacle, given at the expense of the master of ceremonies, and of his backside, was a fit subject for laughter, and he felt the master of ceremonies could hardly be taking much pleasure in it.

"Well, now that's where you're wrong," said Samba Baloum. "The master of ceremonies is of exactly the same mind as myself. Is it not his job to organize the public spectacles?"

"You're joking," said Clarence.

"I can assure you that that stick is no joke," replied Samba Baloum.

"That's what I was telling you."

"Well, then, we're in agreement," said Samba Baloum. He cackled faintly and raised his calabash to his lips.

"*Tan!*" exclaimed the dignitary who was wielding the stick.

"What did he say?" asked Clarence.

"He said '*ten.*' But don't worry, it's just the beginning: he can do wonders with that rod. You can look on all this as a mere hors-d'oeuvre; when the feast begins . . ."

He stopped to spit on the master of ceremonies' backside.

"What are you doing?" asked Clarence.

"It will cool him down," said Samba Baloum. "The stick warms his behind, and I cool it down."

He began cackling gently again. Behind the wall, other mouths were opened to spit at the master of ceremonies' well-basted buttocks.

"They shouldn't do that," said Clarence.

"But it cools him down, after all!" said Noaga.

And he spat in his turn.

"Well, I don't like that sort of thing," said Clarence.

Every time the rod landed on his behind, the master of ceremonies rose in the air like a fish jumping; but that was all he could do, because the four pegs prevented him from jumping any higher.

"That man is suffering," said Clarence.

"Well, you couldn't very well say he was dancing for joy," said Noaga.

"Noaga, I should never have thought it of you," said Clarence. "I tell you that this man is suffering, and that you ought to have pity on him. And you laugh, you have the nerve to laugh!"

"Was the master of ceremonies weeping his eyes out when he laid the egg?" asked Noaga bitterly.

The fact is, he was laughing, or at any rate smiling broadly. Clarence remembered quite clearly his cruelly sharpened teeth. But perhaps it was just the teeth, perhaps . . .

"*Mouan!*" exclaimed the dignitary who was laying on the rod.

"Twenty!" translated Samba Baloum. "Just a trifle!"

"When does it become something more than a trifle?" asked Clarence.

"I don't know," said Samba Baloum. "At thirty, at forty perhaps . . . The master of ceremonies is a hard nut to crack."

"You don't mean to say that he will get twice as much as he has already?" cried Clarence. "He would never stand it.'

"He can stand a great deal," said Samba Baloum. "You have no idea just how much a man *can* stand. The master of ceremonies is in excellent health. Just now, remember, we drank to his health. He is very thin, but . . ."

"But his backside's beginning to swell already," said Noaga.

"His backside has taken a lot of punishment and has swollen considerably," said Nagoa.

Under the gallery, a second dignitary got up and came over to the one who was manipulating the rod in such a sprightly fashion.

"What is he saying?" asked Clarence.

"He's telling him to lay it on a little harder over the left buttock," said Samba Baloum. "The Naba is of the opinion that the left must not be cheated in favor of the right."

"Tell the Naba that this man's had enough."

"I cannot," said Samba Baloum. "The Naba is a just man."

"All the more reason then for speaking to him. The Naba cannot be such a cruel man."

"But he is not cruel at all. He is just! He does not wish the right buttock to suffer at the expense of the left."

"It's downright cruelty," said Clarence.

"Maybe it *is* cruelty, but it is justice too."

"You call that justice?"

"I am no judge," said Samba Baloum. "I am manager of the harem. But just men call this justice. Is it my fault if just men have so much inventiveness?"

"*Tan saba!*" exclaimed the dignitary with the stick.

"Thirty!" said Samba Baloum. "Thirty already!"

"This is going to be good," said Noaga.

He spat on the backside of the master of ceremonies.

"I'm not staying here," said Clarence.

"Wait a little longer," said Samba Baloum. "The best part's still to come."

"No," said Clarence, "I'm going."

He looked at the inflamed and swollen backside of the master of ceremonies; the skin would soon be starting to split. And then . . .

"It's disgraceful!" he said, "And it's you, Baloum, you and no one else, who are the cause of it!"

"Me?" said Samba Baloum.

"Yes, you!" cried Clarence. "You and your idiotic accusations!"

But the boys were digging him in the ribs with their elbows. "Must I really hold my tongue?" Clarence wondered. "I can't stand it any longer." He could hear the shrieks uttered by the master of ceremonies, shrieks which were becoming shriller and shriller. It would certainly not be long before blood was drawn. Perhaps they stopped then? No, nothing would stop them—they were nothing but savages. . . . Clarence got up.

"You're not going away just when the nicest part is about to begin?" protested Samba Baloum.

"I'm going."

"*Do* stay! I'll request an audience with the Naba for you."

"You're a good sort, Baloum," said Clarence. "You're a bit slow, but you're a good sort. Tell the Naba this man's had enough."

He sat down again.

"Don't stir from here. I'm going to speak to the Naba straight away."

He pulled a face and struggled to his feet; then he spat copiously on the backside of the master of ceremonies.

"They have swollen to enormous proportions," he said meditatively.

"Hurry!" urged Clarence.

"Don't move from here," said Samba Baloum. "I'm going."

Taking small, tripping steps, he walked over towards the arcade and prostrated himself in front of the Naba who, with a wag of his beard, signalled to him to draw near. Samba Baloum sat down beside him. But the rod kept whistling down, each stroke ending in an agonized scream from the master of ceremonies.

"Do you think they'll take a long time to decide?" said Noaga.

"They won't do it in five minutes," said Nagoa. "You have to allow plenty of time for an exchange of flowery compliments."

"But do you think they'll take a *very* long time?" asked Noaga.

"If it lasts any longer," said Clarence, "that backside is going to split open and start bleeding. It's tight as a drum already and..."

"But of course it's going to bleed!" said Noaga.

"So you're just waiting for that?" Clarence cried. "In that case..."

Again he rose to his feet. Samba Baloum made a soothing gesture towards him with his hands, as if to say that all was going as well as could be expected and that the best thing for Clarence to do was to sit still. Then the great fat lump began whispering urgently in the Naba's ear again. Clarence sat down again. What could he do? "Savages!" he muttered to himself. But he would just have to wait; there wasn't anything else he could do. Even if Clarence went away now, the rod would go on whistling down with undiminished ferocity on those grossly swollen buttocks; on the contrary, if he remained where he was perhaps the Naba would decide to put an end to the torture.

"A little wine?" Noaga suggested.

"No," said Clarence. "I don't feel like drinking."

"Don't forget, you promised us your *boubou*," said Nagoa.

"I won't forget."

"Have some wine," said Noaga. "Then you can spit a mouthful over the backside of the master of ceremonies."

"What do you take me for?" cried Clarence.

"Have you no pity?" replied Noaga. "A good mouthful of palm wine would help to cool off the master of ceremonies' burning cheeks."

Clarence took a mouthful of wine, but swallowed it almost at once.

"No, I couldn't do it," he said.

"You are completely without pity," said Noaga. "You take a mouthful and swallow it; you swallow it, when the master of ceremonies' cheeks are burning and inflamed and swollen to bursting point. And you have the nerve to call me heartless! Just look how enormous that behind has grown!... It's easily twice its original size."

Fortunately Samba Baloum was coming back, and Clarence did not have to look again at the frightful backside of the master of ceremonies. Samba Baloum bent over the dignitary who was wielding the stick and the strokes stopped.

"The Naba, at your request, has decided to interrupt the display," Samba Boloum told Clarence. "But believe me the people of Aziana won't like it. You've offended their sense of justice."

"Hah!" Clarence scornfully replied.

They had untied the master of ceremonies and had raised him to his feet. Perhaps it would have been better if they had left him lying on the ground. The unfortunate man could hardly put one foot in front of the other and it was only with the greatest difficulty that he managed to stand upright. The dignitary had to hold him up.

"He must have received at least fifty strokes," said Noaga.

"He's more dead than alive," said Clarence indignantly.

"Nonsense!" said Nagoa. "He'll find it rather painful to sit down, at the very worst."

"Let him stand up!" said Noaga. "A master of ceremonies doesn't need to be sitting down all the time."

"What he *does* need," said Samba Baloum, "is a good cold compress on his backside."

The master of ceremonies and the dignitary had at last reached the arcade. One by one, as if regretfully, the heads had disappeared from above the outer wall.

"They're certainly far from being pleased," said Nagoa, eyeing the crowd on the square.

"They are just men," said Samba Baloum.

"That is why they are looking so ugly," said Noaga.

"Let them!" cried Clarence. " I don't care how ugly they look!"

"But they cared very much about what happened to the master of ceremonies' backside," said Samba Baloum.

"Well, you can take it from me, Samba Baloum, these "just" men's faces and the backside of the master of ceremonies look exactly alike to me. I wasn't able to bring myself to spit on the backside of the master of ceremonies, but I could certainly bring myself to spit on the faces of these "just" men!"

"Don't get worked up," said Samba Baloum. "It's not worth getting worked up about a pair of buttocks, or about any number of buttocks for that matter, even if, as in every crowd that is roused by a sense of justice, there's more than a baker's dozen. It's just not worth it!"

"Anyhow, don't forget about your *boubou!*" the boys said. Clarence pulled his *boubou* over his head.

"What are you doing?" asked Samba Baloum.

"I promised them my best Sunday *boubou,*" said Clarence.

"But you can't let the Naba see you naked! It's not done!"

"Then he'll have to give me another *boubou,*" said Clarence. "I can't bear the sight of this one any longer. These red roses on their saffron background turn my stomach."

"You've certainly had me on the hop today!" exclaimed Samba Baloum. "You can believe me or you can believe me not— I'm done up!"

He walked nonchalantly over to the gallery and began whispering in the Naba's ear again. He spoke to him for quite a long time; it seemed that the Naba was reluctant to grant his request. Finally the beard gave an affirmative wag. Samba Baloum signed to Clarence to draw near.

"The Naba wishes to know whether a green *boubou* with a pattern of pink flowers would meet your requirements," he said.

"With pink flowers?" said Clarence. "What does he take me for—a parakeet?"

"You know quite well he takes you for a fighting-cock," said Samba Baloum reprovingly. "There was no need to take all your clothes off in order to remind him of that."

"I want a green *boubou* with a pattern of white flowers," said Clarence.

"With a pattern of white flowers?" said Baloum. He seemed to be thinking it over. "I don't think that would really suit you," he said. "I don't think it would look nice."

"Who's going to wear it—you or me?" cried Clarence.

"Well, *I* shall have to look at it," said Samba Baloum in a pained voice. And he heaved a protracted sigh. "The white man desires a pattern of white flowers," he announced to the Naba.

The Naba wagged his beard, and the dignitaries arose. At a fresh sign from the Naba, they went to the main building and returned a little later with a lot of chests. They were of all ages and sizes, from the humble tin trunk of a colonial officer exiled in the bush to metal-bound teak chests, the sort that are usually full of pirate gold. The Naba handed his bunch of keys to Samba Baloum.

"Let them be opened!" he announced with great solemnity.

The first chests that Samba Baloum opened were full of rats.

"Fine lot of treasure you have there!" said Clarence.

"Don't be so sharp!" said Samba Baloum, flapping a hand at Clarence.

"You know quite well I can't go on standing naked in front of the Naba," said Clarence.

"Well, I'm glad you've realized it at last," said Samba Baloum.

He opened a chest which was full to overflowing, and there were no rats inside.

"Look right at the bottom," said one of the dignitaries. Samba Baloum plunged his hands right down to the bottom of the chest and pulled out, with a double grimace—one for the effort he was making, and another for what his hands had brought up—a green *boubou* patterned with white flowers.

"Is that what you want?" he asked Clarence, haughtily.

"That's the very thing," replied Clarence.

Whereupon the Naba rose to his feet and departed.

From The Radiance of the King, *by Camara Laye, Collier Books, New York, 1956; reprinted by The Macmillan Company, 1971.*

The Man Who Shared His Hut

by JOMO KENYATTA

Jomo Kenyatta, born in Kenya in 1889, became the first Prime Minister of independent Kenya. He is equally well known for his revealing study of the Kikuyu people, *Facing Mount Kenya,* written while he was a student of the great anthropologist Malinowski at the London School of Economics. His book is one of the earliest studies by an African of his own tribal culture.

Among good storytellers such as the Kikuyu, it is not only the old tales which are told again and again. Sometimes a new fable is added, like this one, which developed after the European colonists came to Africa.

⋏   Once upon a time an elephant made a friendship with a man. One day a heavy thunderstorm broke out, the elephant went to his friend, who had a little hut at the edge of the forest, and said to him: "My dear good man, will you please let me put my trunk inside your hut to keep it out of this torrential rain?"

The man, seeing what situation his friend was in, replied: "My dear good elephant, my hut is very small, but there is room for your trunk and myself. Please put your trunk in gently."

The elephant thanked his friend, saying: "You have done me a good deed and one day I shall return your kindness."

But what followed? As soon as the elephant put his trunk inside the hut, slowly he pushed his head inside, and finally flung the man out in the rain, and then lay down comfortably inside his friend's hut, saying: "My dear good friend, your skin is harder than mine, and as there is not enough room for both of us, you can afford to remain in the rain while I am protecting my delicate skin from the hailstorm."

The man, seeing what his friend had done to him, started to

grumble, the animals in the nearby forest heard the noise and came to see what was the matter. All stood around listening to the heated argument between the man and his friend the elephant.

In this turmoil the lion came along roaring, and said in a loud voice: "Don't you all know that I am the King of the Jungle! How dare anyone disturb the peace of my kingdom?"

On hearing this the elephant, who was one of the high ministers in the jungle kingdom, replied in a soothing voice, and said: "My Lord, there is no disturbance of the peace in your kingdom. I have only been having a little discussion with my friend here as to the possession of this little hut which your lordship sees me occupying."

The lion, who wanted to have "peace and tranquility" in his kingdom, replied in a noble voice, saying: "I command my ministers to appoint a Commission of Inquiry to go thoroughly into this matter and report accordingly." He then turned to the man and said: "You have done well by establishing friendship with my people, especially with the elephant who is one of my honorable ministers of state. Do not grumble any more, your hut is not lost to you. Wait until the sitting of my Imperial Commission, and then you will be given plenty of opportunity to state your case. I am sure that you will be pleased with the findings of the Commission."

The man was very pleased by these sweet words from the King of the Jungle, and innocently waited for his opportunity, in the belief that, naturally, the hut would be returned to him.

The elephant, obeying the command of his master, got busy with other ministers to appoint the Commission of Inquiry. The following elders of the jungle were appointed to sit in the Commission: (1) Mr. Rhinoceros; (2) Mr. Buffalo; (3) Mr. Alligator; (4) The Rt. Hon. Mr. Fox to act as chairman; and (5) Mr. Leopard to act as Secretary to the Commission.

On seeing the personnel, the man protested and asked if it was not necessary to include in this Commission a member from his side. But he was told that it was impossible, since no one from his side was well enough educated to understand the intricacy of jungle law. Further, that there was nothing to fear, for the members of the Commission were all men of repute for their impartiality in justice, and as they were gentlemen chosen by God to look after the interests

The Preacher   MSIMANGO

Reprinted from *African Arts,* Volume IV, Number 2

of races less adequately endowed with teeth and claws, he might rest assured that they would investigate the matter with the greatest care and report impartially.

The Commission sat to take the evidence. The Rt. Hon. Mr. Elephant was first called. He came along with a superior air, brushing his tusks with a sapling which Mrs. Elephant had provided, and in an authoritative voice said: "Gentlemen of the Jungle, there is no need for me to waste your valuable time in relating a story which I am sure you all know. I have always regarded it as my duty to protect the interests of my friends, and this appears to have caused the misunderstanding between myself and my friend here. He invited me to save his hut from being blown away by a hurricane. As the hurricane had gained access owing to the unoccupied space in the hut, I considered it necessary, in my friend's own interests, to turn the undeveloped space to a more economic use by sitting in it myself; a duty which any of you would undoubtedly have performed with equal readiness in similar circumstances."

After hearing the Rt. Hon. Mr. Elephant's conclusive evidence, the Commission called Mr. Hyena and other elders of the jungle, who all supported what Mr. Elephant had said. They then called the man, who began to give his own account of the dispute. But the Commission cut him short, saying: "My good man, please confine yourself to relevant issues. We have already heard the circumstances from various unbiased sources; all we wish you to tell us is whether the undeveloped space in your hut was occupied by anyone else before Mr. Elephant assumed his position?"

The man began to say: "No, but——" But at this point the Commission declared that they had heard sufficient evidence from both sides and retired to consider their decision.

After enjoying a delicious meal at the expense of the Rt. Hon. Mr. Elephant, they reached their verdict, called the man, and declared as follows: "In our opinion this dispute has arisen through a regrettable misunderstanding due to the backwardness of your ideas. We consider that Mr. Elephant has fulfilled his sacred duty of protecting your interests. As it is clearly for your good that the space should be put to its most economic use, and as you yourself have not yet reached the stage of expansion which would enable you to fill it, we consider it necessary to arrange a compromise to suit both parties. Mr. Elephant shall continue his occupation of your hut, but we give you permission to look for a site where you can build another hut more suited to your needs, and we will see that you are well protected."

The man, having no alternative, and fearing that his refusal might expose him to the teeth and claws of members of the Commission, did as they suggested. But no sooner had he built another hut than Mr. Rhinoceros charged in with his horn lowered and ordered the man to quit. A Royal Commission was again appointed to look into the matter, and the same finding was given. This procedure was repeated until Mr. Buffalo, Mr. Leopard, Mr. Hyena and the rest were all accommodated with new huts.

Then the man decided that he must adopt an effective method of protection, since Commissions of Inquiry did not seem to be of any use to him. He sat down and said: "Ng'enda thi ndeagaga motegi," which literally means "there is nothing that treads on the earth that cannot be trapped," or in other words, you can fool people for a time, but not for ever.

Early one morning, when the huts already occupied by the jungle lords were all beginning to decay and fall to pieces, he went out and built a bigger and better hut a little distance away. No sooner had Mr. Rhinoceros seen it than he came rushing in, only to find that Mr. Elephant was already inside, sound asleep. Mr. Leopard next came in at the window, Mr. Lion, Mr. Fox, and Mr. Buffalo entered the doors, while Mr. Hyena howled for a place in the shade and Mr. Alligator basked on the roof.

Presently they all began disputing about their rights of penetration, and from disputing they came to fighting, and while they were all embroiled together the man set the hut on fire and burnt it to the ground, jungle lords and all.

Then he went home, saying: "Peace is costly, but it's worth the expense," and lived happily ever after.

Call to the People

by PETER ABRAHAMS

Peter Abrahams is an articulate spokesman for the working people of South Africa. Born in Johannesburg in 1919, he grew up in the slums and ran away to sea when he was twenty.

His early novels, published in England, drew deeply on his childhood experiences. In *Mine Boy* and *Song of a City* his characters are real, and full of warmth and courage in spite of poverty and degradation. His autobiography, *Tell Freedom,* was published in 1954 and established his reputation as a major writer.

His novel *A Wreath for Udomo* is concerned with the struggle for independence and the part played by young educated Africans in London who plotted and planned to free their countries from colonial rule. Published in 1956, it was a prophetic kind of book which visualized how difficult and stormy the struggle would be. The setting of the story, Panafrica, is a mythical country.

ᚨ   Michael Udomo was returning from England. He had gone to study and had remained to edit a newspaper and talk politics, African politics. He was an angry young man, angry for freedom, angry enough to fight for it. On the boat, leaning against the rails, he brooded over the future. "Oh, Mother Africa, make me strong for the work that I must do."

On board ship he talked with the market woman, Selina, also returning from England. She shared his hopes and pledged her help. "Do not forget the women," she told him. "When you have started, come to me and I will speak for you with the women of the market. My name is Selina. Remember it. And do not forget the women."

Six months later, Udomo sought out Selina. There was a dock strike and he thought the time was ripe to use the paper he edited to rally the people for freedom. Selina sat there with a smile on her lips, nursing her baby, while Udomo explained his plan.

"When I leave you, I will go back to the paper. I will sit down at my desk and I will write a call to our people to rise against the foreigners and demand the freedom to rule themselves. I will say that the Council of Chiefs and Elders and Dr. Endura are the tools of the British. I will say that the time has come for us to fight and to go on fighting until we and our land are free of the rule of white foreigners. Then we will print the paper. It will be all over the front page. And tomorrow all the people will read it."

"And they will arrest you."

"Yes."

"What then?"

"Then you and my friend Adebhoy will rally the people. The leaders of the dock strike will join you. I have spoken to them."

"And shall we then collect money to pay your fine?"

"No!" Udomo shouted.

Selina chuckled.

"There's no need to be angry, Mr. Udomo."

"No matter what happens, you are not to pay any fine. I must stay in jail and serve my time. Your duty will be to keep up the anger of the people and to build up a party that would lead them to freedom. Don't you see, Selina, in jail I'll be the rallying point for our people. Are you with me?"

Selina rose then and went to him, holding the child carelessly. Her eyes were burning bright. She made a strange little dancing bow before him. Then she took his right hand and pressed it to her lips.

"Would you do this for your people and still ask if I am with you?"

He rose. He felt all the strength of earth rise in him, felt himself grow.

"I will die for my people!"

"They want you to live and free them, Udomo! Go and write! I have many things to do now, many people to talk with. You should have come earlier."

"The plan was only born in my mind a little while ago. I came straight to you."

"All right. There is much we must plan before they take you tomorrow. I will send a car to take you to my house when your work is done."

"It might be late, after midnight, before I am done. It is an important thing I must write."

"That is of no moment. We will be awake all this night to think and plan for tomorrow, and for all the other tomorrows. Your friend the doctor, he's a good man? A man who can plan?"

"You will see that when you meet him."

"Good. I will send the car for him. And we will talk and plan till your coming. We have not much time and there is much to do. There will be food and rest at my house when it is done. Go now, Udomo."

Selina followed Udomo out. The babel of the market hit them. Udomo had forgotten he was in the center of the market. Now it was all about him. Odd that that place should have cut off the noise so effectively. Selina gave the young man a list of names of people she wanted at her house that night. Then she turned to Udomo.

"Do you need money, Udomo?"

"No." He set off briskly, pushing his way through the crowds.

"There will be a feast for you tonight!" Selina shouted above the din.

His two assistants were droopily reading copy.

"Anybody come?" Udomo's new briskness shook them awake.

"One of the directors has been," the senior said.

"Well?"

"He went into your office and read the front-page proof. We told him you didn't like that but he said he owned the paper." The man paused expectantly. Udomo didn't explode, so he went on: "He said he'd made some changes and for you to let him know if you object to any of them before printing the paper. He said he'd wait at his office till five o'clock."

"Nearly that now," Udomo said. "You'd better run along and tell our director everything is in order. I will run it exactly as he wants. Go on, man! What are you gaping at? We mustn't disappoint our directors. They pay our wages."

261

"But, Mr. Udomo, sir!"

"And see that you are back as soon as possible. We've got great work on hand!"

The senior assistant clattered unwillingly down the stairs.

"I don't want to be disturbed by anybody—*anybody*."

He went into his office, cleared his desk with one sweep of the arm, then pulled the typewriter to him. He realized he had swept his paper on to the floor and grinned. He went on his knees and collected typing paper. He rose, slipped it into the old machine, and began to tap. The words came out hesitantly at first:

"A CALL TO THE PEOPLE! RISE AND BE FREE!

"People of Panafrica! This is a call to you to rise and free yourselves. This is a call to battle! Down at the docks today our brothers are striking. That is only a beginning. They are striking because they are tired of receiving the wages of slaves! Because . . ."

He wrote steadily for a long time. Then he closed his eyes and leaned back in his chair till the drunkenness caused by the words he had written passed. It was done now. There was no going back now. After a while he opened his eyes. He read through what he had written. He changed a line here, deleted a word there, altered a sentence. Yes. Yes, there was no other way. There was very little education among the people so he had to speak in slogans. After this it was up to the others: to Adebhoy and Selina and the dockers. But what if it didn't come off and he rotted in jail for years with no one caring? No! . . . He rose, unlocked his door and called in his assistants.

"You saw him?"

"Yes," the senior said.

"What did he say?"

"He was happy. He said you were learning sense at last. He laughed and said there had been no need for him to tell the printer not to accept any violent copy from you."

"Good. Now read this." He pushed what he had written to them.

They read, standing side-by-side, leaning over his desk. When they looked up he relaxed. Their faces told him all he wanted to know about the impact of the piece.

"My God!" the senior gasped.

"Oh man! Oh man!" the other said. He yelled suddenly: "FREEDOM!"

"Come on, we'll set that up."

"But they'll arrest you," the senior said.

"I know." Udomo grinned. He was on stage already, and he knew it. "We'll print as many copies as we have paper for. Use up all the paper. I won't need any after tonight. I think we'd better each take some copies with us. They'll want to confiscate it tomorrow."

"Yessir!" the second assistant said, eyes shining.

"Come on! We've work to do." They clattered down the rickety stairs. "Got the addresses?"

"Selina said to bring the papers to her place in a taxi."

"Good." He led the way into the printing shed. "Lock it behind you."

He beamed at the young black boy who came to him.

"I've got a big job for you, son. When you're an old man you'll tell your grandchildren about this! Hungry?"

"Yes, sah." The boy grinned.

Udomo took a pound note from the wad Selina had sent. He gave it to his second assistant.

"Get us some food. We'll need it. Lock the door behind him." He took off his jacket and rolled up his sleeves, unmindful, now, of the rents in his shirt. He gave the boy his copy. "Show us how to print and we'll do it while you set this up."

"Yes, sah," the boy said. It was a great game to him.

It was nearly two in the morning when the taxi stopped outside Selina's house on the western edge of the town. Hers was one of the few houses in the area with electric light. All the rooms were ablaze with it.

"We are here, sah," the taximan said.

The noise from the house reached Udomo and, above it, a voice:

"He has come!"

Adebhoy and Selina led the procession that came to meet him.

263

Suddenly, there were people all about him. Hands took his and shook them.

"It is done?" Selina said.

"It is done," he said. He handed the copy he held to Adebhoy. "There are ten thousand copies in the taxi, Selina."

"We will take care of that," Selina said. "Your part is done."

"You must be tired,"Adebhoy said.

"I'll have time to rest later."

"Come," Selina said. "You will first eat, Udomo. While you eat the doctor will read this to us, this call to our people. Come."

The big room was stacked with liquor. There were about twenty people. They were all sober, had drunk only moderately. This cheered Udomo. These were serious people. He found himself alone with Adebhoy for a few seconds.

"How is it?" he asked.

Adebhoy beamed happily.

"They're wonderful! They'll go all the way! They'll not let us down! That Selina, man!" He roared with happy laughter. "And we've made many plans."

Selina brought her husband and elder girl to Udomo. The man was short, fat and sleepy. He smiled amiably. The girl was a strapping twelve. Selina introduced her husband, then ordered him to go and see to the papers in the taxi and pay the taximan.

"And you are the one who reads to your mother," Udomo said to the girl.

The child hung her head shyly.

"She is the one," Selina said. "Now she has prepared your food and will see to you. Take him away and feed him well, child. He is the great blade of our land. He must be sharp. You come and read to us now, Doctor."

Udomo followed the girl into a small room that led off the big one.

"Leave the door open," he told the girl. "I want to hear."

The people ranged themselves about the big room. Adebhoy stood in the center and read what Udomo had written. As he read, his voice gained power and passion, echoed the feelings that had stirred Udomo while he had written.

Udomo stopped eating, gave all his attention to Adebhoy's

264

reading. Tomorrow thousands, maybe hundreds of thousands, would read or hear those words. They would creep through the land like fire, like the talking drums of old. Would they awake the people? Would they rouse them?

Adebhoy stopped reading. There was a long spell of silence. Then one voice, charged with passion, broke the silence.

"FREEDOM!"

Others took it up. And it was a mighty roar that shook the house.

Udomo leaned back and closed his eyes. His body tingled all over. His heart pounded. Then he sighed softly and opened his eyes. This was it, then; it was right. This *was* the moment and he had taken it well.

"But the battle is still ahead," he whispered to himself.

They all spoke now and Selina had to prevent them from rushing into the little room and falling on him.

"He's hungry and tired!" she roared. "He will eat! Then he will rest for an hour, and no one will disturb him. No one! After that he will come here and we will tell him our plans. And then he must go to wait for those who will come for him, and our work will begin. To work! He wants victory, not cheering! Heh, Doctor?"

Fine, Udomo thought, fine. Great woman, Selina. Let her manage. Adebhoy would see that she manages well. Remind Adebhoy to get a full report to the Group in London. They'd have to spread it about, organize demonstrations and questions in the Commons, get it to the Council of Nations. My God. Oh, my God. Is this how those others who made revolutions in the past felt? Those men who are history now, did they feel like this? Like being carried along on a fast-flowing river? And yet calm? And were they as sure of success, too? Must have been, otherwise they wouldn't have started. They won't let me down. They won't! Spread through the land like a fire and rouse them to action. Action, my people! You must think calmly, man. The excitement's for the others. Yours is responsibility. It could go wrong. Think about that. No. It won't go wrong! It can't. It must not! IT WILL NOT!

The town, on the surface, lay quiet under the burning sun. All the ships lay idle in the harbor. The normally busy port was silent. Even the noonday sun seemed fixed overhead, as though it, too, was on strike.

Down near the fishermen's boat, two men walked. They were deep in conversation.

"They say nothing the white man does can stop this. They say Udomo is too strong and even the prison cannot stop his spirit."

"Did you see the soldiers?"

"Ai, man! They would frighten us as you frighten children. But you will see. They will take the papers and take the papers but there will be more. They say Udomo has more of the papers than they can take. They say even now the papers are being sent all over the country so that all can see them."

"But will he make us free, this Udomo?"

"They say that if we stand with him there is nothing he cannot do. They say one day he will speak to us and we will see that."

"Have you seen the paper?"

"I had it read to me."

"What does it say?"

"You want to know?"

"I am asking."

"You can hear it for yourself. But you must swear an oath to keep it quiet."

"Even if the police came to you?"

"Even then."

"All right. But when you have heard Udomo's words you must find another person whom you trust and send him so that he, too, can hear the words. So the words will go to all the people. You know Josiah the cripple?"

"Yes."

"Go to his house."

"Will I find—"

"Go to his house and see what you will find. Say I sent you. Go now."

The one man left. The other walked among the fishermen at their nets till he came to another whom he knew well, whom he trusted.

"Well, man! What do you think of this Udomo business?"

"From what I hear he speaks for us, brother, even from prison."

266

"I have heard his words. Would you like to hear them?"

"Would I like to hear them! Why, man, I got a paper this morning, meaning to keep it until my child came from school and read it to me. But those police dogs took it from me! Took it and warned me!"

"Not so loud, brother. You can hear those words if you want to, all of them."

"How?"

"Listen—"

All over the town men and women slipped into dingy little rooms in obscure places. Someone met them at the door and made them take an oath of secrecy. Then they went into the room. There, someone read Udomo's words to them. Usually, there were only three people at a time. But as the day wore on the figure had first to be doubled, then trebled. After each reading the people were invited to join Udomo's party, the Africa Freedom Party. By the late afternoon more than ten thousand people had joined the new party. Each paid one shilling membership fee.

And all over the town the quiet reading circles took place. And the police were everywhere, going about in twos and threes, hunting out the offending issue of the *Queenstown Post*.

But there were no incidents of any kind.

Towards sundown the police got their first inkling of the readings. A zealous black inspector of police took it on his own shoulders to lead a number of raids and make a number of arrests. It threw his white superiors into a dither when they discovered this.

After the arrests two black lawyers called on Selina. One told her:

"The press regulations say nothing about people reading these papers. These people are falsely arrested. We are prepared to defend them for you, for the party."

"So you know about the party?"

"Everybody knows. We want to join."

"Come to my house tonight. We will hear what Dr. Adebhoy says. He is second to Udomo. He speaks for Udomo till Udomo can speak for himself."

The Africa Freedom Party was officially launched that night.

A hundred thousand people gathered on a strip of land on the northern outskirts of the town. In the darkness, under the new African moon, Adebhoy announced the programme of the new party. It was: Freedom.

Selina offered them Udomo as leader, chairman and president of the party for the rest of his life. Then she led them in a pledge of loyalty to Udomo and the new party. Suddenly, in all parts of the great gathering, flaming torches sprang alight. Tall young men held them high overhead.

"We, the people of Panafrica—" Selina said.

"We, the people of Panafrica—" the great throng echoed.

"Swear undying loyalty to the Africa Freedom Party—"

"Swear undying loyalty to the Africa Freedom Party—"

"And to its great and beloved leader—"

"And to its great and beloved leader—"

"UDOMO!"

"UDOMO!"

"We will follow him—"

"We will follow him—"

"To FREEDOM!"

"To FREEDOM!"

Then an old, old man stepped to the improvised loudspeaker system and prayed in a whispering voice for their ancestors to be with them in this great enterprise.

The prison stood on the hill above the Governor's Palace. Inside the prison, in a small cell, Udomo gripped the bars till his knuckles hurt. He stared out at the hundreds of flickering flames. The lawyer stood behind him.

"They are saying the oath now," the lawyer said.

"A hundred thousand, you say?" Udomo's voice choked. He didn't turn.

"More," the lawyer said. "And it's happening in other places too."

Udomo stayed there, on tiptoe, clinging to the bars, till the flames went out. Then he shut his eyes. O Mother Africa! O Mother Africa! His eyes filled with tears. The tears ran down his cheeks. He released the bars, turned and faced the lawyer.

"Go now, my friend. Tell them I wept."

"But we've got to prepare your case. It comes up tomorrow."

Udomo smiled through his tears, a smile lit with sunshine.

"Don't you understand what's happened, man! The case isn't anything now. We can see to that any time: tomorrow. Any time. Go! . . . Go to the people and tell them I wept. Say: 'Udomo stood at his prison window and held the bars and looked out. And then he saw the flames and knew they were taking the oath. And then Udomo wept.' Tell them that. Go now, man!"

The lawyer left. Udomo went and sat on his hard prison bed, smiling through his tears. There was a new brightness in his eyes. This little cell, this prison, was the gateway to freedom. I've unlocked the door, Mother Africa! I've unlocked the door!

From A Wreath for Udomo, *by Peter Abrahams, Faber and Faber Ltd., 1956.*

Inspiration and Illumination   RAKGOATHE

About the Artists

ASIHENE, EMMANUEL V., is an artist and educator, born in the eastern region of Ghana. He trained as a teacher at the Akropong Presbyterian Training College, and studied art at the University of Science and Technology in Kumasi. He is currently a graduate student in art education at Ohio State University on a fellowship from the Phelps-Stokes Fund.

GUIRMA, FREDERIC, born in Ouagadougou, the capital of Upper Volta, was educated in his native city, then in France, and at Loyola University in Los Angeles. He was the first ambassador from Upper Volta to the United States and to the United Nations. He paints murals of his native land on the walls of his home, and has written and illustrated two collections of folktales: *Princess of the Full Moon* and *Tales of Mogho.*

MSANGI, K. FRANCIS, is a lecturer in the Department of Fine Arts, University of Nairobi, Kenya. A painter and printmaker, he was educated at Makerere University College, Uganda. His work includes paintings, drawings, lithographs, and linoleum cuts. Exhibitions of his work have been held in Tanzania, Kenya, Germany, and New York City. He has received several awards, and a certificate of merit from the *Dictionary of African Biography.*

MSIMANGO, GEORGE, is a twenty-two-year-old artist from South Africa whose work is full of energy in spite of the repressive character of the country in which he lives. He is a native of Durban and is largely self-taught. The two works reproduced in this book are both large charcoal drawings with strong character interpretation.

ODITA, E. OKECHUKWU, is a printmaker, painter, and art historian. He was educated at the Nigerian College of Art, Zaria, and at the

University of Iowa. He received a Ph.D. from Indiana University and is now an associate professor at Ohio State University. He has received several art fellowships, three silver medals, and five first-class certificates from the Eastern Nigeria Festival of Arts. He has had several one-man shows in Nigeria and has been included in a five-man show of African artists in New York.

OWITI, HEZBON EDWARD, is a young artist from Kenya, now in his twenties, who was born in the province of Central Nyanza. As a child of eleven, he started making small figures of goats and cows and telling stories about them to other children. At the age of fifteen, he won the Young Artist Certificate in East Africa. He studied art at the University College in Ibadan, Nigeria, and held several one-man shows in Nigeria and Kenya. His work has been exhibited also in art centers and museums in England, the United States, and Canada.

RAKGOATHE, DAN, lives in Johannesburg, South Africa. He studied at the University of South Africa in Natal under Swedish missionaries, and was trained as an art teacher. His work has been exhibited in Africa and at the Camden Art Center in London. He was awarded several prizes at the Annual Fort Hare University Exhibition. He has produced woodcuts in a realistic vein but his personal preference is for symbolic presentation and for subjects with a mystical meaning. His portrait of the Moon-bride is based on a folk story his grandmother told him about a bride who was murdered on the eve of her marriage.

WANGBOJE, SOLOMON O. IREIN, is the founder and former director of the Ori Olokun Art Center at the University of Ife, in Nigeria, an important training center for contemporary African artists. Dr. Wangboje is a distinguished printmaker who has studied the art education program in American universities on a State Department–sponsored tour. He is the illustrator of a book of African poems, *A Crocodile Has Me by the Leg.*